I0141210

MARCHING TO A WORTHY

DRUMMER

A Christian layperson speaks out about the Holy Spirit

ARTHUR PERKINS

SIGNALMAN PUBLISHING

Marching to a Worthy Drummer:
A Christian Layperson Speaks Out About the Holy Spirit
by Arthur Perkins

Signalman Publishing
www.signalmanpublishing.com
email: info@signalmanpublishing.com
Kissimmee, Florida

© Copyright 2015 by Arthur Perkins. All rights reserved. No part of this book may be reproduced or transmitted in any form or by any means, electronic or mechanical, or incorporated into any information retrieval system, electronic or mechanical, without the written permission of the copyright owner.

Unless otherwise noted, scripture references are taken from the King James Version of the Bible.

Cover art by Karen Lucas Davis of Lucas Art and Frame,
The Gallery on the Hill,
Graham, Washington.

ISBN: 978-1-940145-43-3 (paperback)
978-1-940145-44-0 (ebook)

Signalman
Publishing

Printed in the United States of America

Also by Arthur Perkins

Buddy

Cathy

Jacob

DEDICATION

As in my Christian novels **Buddy**, **Cathy** and **Jacob**, I dedicate this work to my wife Carolyn, the joy of my life. We both dedicate this work, above all, to our God, and to our four daughters and their families.

ACKNOWLEDGEMENTS

I wish to extend a grateful, heartfelt thank-you to the following people who have been instrumental in the production of my books. First, to my God, whose loving character elicits my devotion and the thrill of learning and writing of His beautiful nature. Second, to my wonderful wife Carolyn, whose loving support in all matters of our happy marriage have given me added incentive and the freedom to pursue my writing endeavors. Third, to my brother Jon, whose support has been extremely helpful. Fourth, to my friend and publisher, John McClure of Signalman Publishing, for his enthusiasm and professionalism. I'm truly fortunate to be associated with him. I also wish to thank our pastor, F. David Lambert, ThD. While we don't always agree on every theological matter, we do agree on much, particularly on the divine inspiration and inerrancy of Scripture. I have learned much about God and the Church through his very thorough exposition of Scripture and Church doctrine.

Art Perkins
Eatonville, Washington

CONTENTS

INTRODUCTION

Love was in the air at the time of the Pentecostal birth of the Church. And hope besides, a freshness of season, a joyful anticipation. Despite the anger and persecutions of those who knew not Christ against those who did, the Church willingly, thankfully and even possessively took up the Cross, marching boldly toward a paradise restored.

A few short centuries later the Western Church, greatly enlarged and possessing the status of a state religion, had lost its newness and its joy. It was an institution now, a secular power. In the acquisition of this comfort and lofty position it now stood as a receiver of service, having forsaken the love of serving others. Far worse than that, it had lost the joy of loving God at the most basic and important level, that of natural intuition.

Some might think that this loss was an inevitable consequence of the easing of conditions for the Christians. No longer faced with persecution, they became soft of spirit and their fervor of worship decayed into indifference toward God.

Indeed, that was part of the problem. The Church always has been at her best when forced to face suffering and persecution. But looming over that external nudge toward decline was a much bigger dilemma, an internally-caused one that drove Christians away from their love of God because they could no longer see God with the intuitive clarity they possessed earlier.

This urge for reformation that stripped them of their knowledge of God was a desire to distance the Church from the sea of false notions and pagan beliefs with which she was surrounded. Sensing the great danger their Church faced from these competing ideas, many of which were lewd and corrupt, the leaders among the faithful strove to set their faith apart from the baser systems of belief in order to ensure its uniqueness and, above all, its purity. They intended to accomplish this with a thorough housecleaning and, energized with this objective, they pursued this task as if on a sacred mission.

By the time they were finished their objective was achieved beyond all rational expectations. Sexuality was completely divorced from the Christian faith as practiced by the mainstream Church. If the realization of that objective required a certain "correction" of Scripture in a few critical places, well, so be it. God certainly wouldn't frown on the desire to purify Christianity. Not only were Mary and Joseph purged of sexual experience beyond the pain of childbirth and the necessity of breast-feeding, but God Himself, being considered above the baseness of sexual experience, was neutered. The Holy Spirit was changed from a feminine Being to a weakly masculine one, and, as a consequence, the Godhead was stripped of its family context and instead came to be viewed as a fellowship of brothers.

Gone was the intuitive basis for love, as represented by the Christian's own family and spousal experience. In seeking God, the believer was forced to approach Him with *agape* love, having been made to forsake any hint of *eros* and the possessive love it engendered. From this complete lack of understanding of who God actually was, it was only a matter of time before indifference toward Him set in.

It doesn't have to remain that way. The first love of God that embraced those who experienced the Pentecost can be reclaimed by the Church. What is required as the initial step toward regaining that love is to re-acquire the understanding of God possessed by the early Christians. It is the intent of this book to help toward reclaiming that understanding.

One

My Credentials – the Good, the Bad, and the Ugly

Lorelei was as exotic as her name implied. Her beauty allowed her to breeze through our high school trigonometry class without disturbing a single neuron in her brain. When he could forego drooling over her, our math teacher would attempt somewhat half-heartedly to instruct the rest of us in the fundamentals of the course. Unfortunately, I was unteachable. At the end of the semester I had to beg him for a C– – (that's two minuses; one was insufficient to express his feelings regarding my lack of understanding).

I did graduate from high school, but not possessing the credentials for acceptance into a college of my parents' choice, I did the next best thing, which was to join the Marines. My parents wept doubly hard over that, not because I was potentially placing myself in harm's way, but because my choice emphasized my academic disgrace.

The Marine Corps, however, forced me to suck it in, to the extent that at the end of my enlistment I had acquired the necessary discipline to attempt a second try at math. I went for broke, taking a summer course in differential calculus, and can vividly remember the enormous struggle I went through to comprehend the essentials of the course. Amazingly, and I can remember that, too, like it happened yesterday, I had an unexpected breakthrough in the midst of an intense effort to understand. I not only understood, but my comprehension was of such a level as to cause me to exclaim to myself that calculus was like a beautiful picture. Not only that, but through my perception of its beauty, I developed an interest in Isaac Newton, the inventor of this branch of mathematics, discovering thereupon that this intellectual giant was an intense Christian who spent the latter forty years of his life as a priest in thanksgiving for what God had shown him. I wasn't a Christian at the time, so this facet of his personality didn't interest me.

I proceeded after that experience to continue on with integral calculus, differential equations and physics, in all of which I excelled so much that I received awards, the most memorable being that when my math instructor had to go on a trip, he assigned me to teach his calculus class. And, to the belated joy of my parents, I eventually was able to enter Cal Berkeley, wherefrom I graduated with a Bachelor of Science in Electrical Engineering. After taking a job in Baltimore, I continued on with math courses, including advanced calculus, at the University of Maryland.

The point of all this is not that everyone should join the Marine Corps, nor is it that the unteachable can be taught if he tries hard enough. The point is that in the process of discovering my mental ability in math (I bought a trig book and devoured it over the course of a weekend), I also discovered that I had both a weakness and a strength. My weakness is that I'm a very slow learner; my strength is that if and when I ever do comprehend something, I comprehend it very deeply. I have been plagued by this weakness and have excelled through this strength throughout my engineering career.

The bottom line is that if I'm ever tempted to brag, someone can always point to past demonstrations of my weakness, some events resulting from that lack of intellectual balance having been pretty spectacular. Regarding my strength, on the other hand, I shall employ examples of them below to establish my *bona fides* with regard to the subject I wish to discuss. This subject is not Lorelei, a topic that I'd enjoy dwelling on, but rather is an ambitious but very important understanding of certain aspects of our Christian faith. My particular understanding doesn't propose to separate Christians from non-Christians; it may not be that big a deal, but then again – – – . What I have found is that it has allowed me to love my God with all my heart, and for that reason I'd like to share it with you.

For the greater part of the forty-year period that I have been a Christian, I have been content to be a nominal member of the faith, attending Church when a higher-priority event didn't intervene and attempting to absorb as much of the sermons that I could without going overboard on the subject. The churches that I did attend were Protestant, first Episcopal and then Assembly of God, followed by Baptist, which I continue to attend with my wife of thirty years.

I didn't start out that way. Actually, I didn't even start out as a Christian. I was brought up as an agnostic. An event that will remain private for now occurred while I was around thirty-five years old that led me to acquire a Bible and read it from cover to cover, a process that occupied a full year. It involved a significant amount of emotional turmoil, but by the time I had finished reading it I understood far more than I had expected to and eagerly accepted Jesus Christ as my Savior and Lord. Upon that momentous decision, I received a vision that also will remain private for now, but which profoundly influenced my understanding of God.

Other events occurred that intruded upon my early enthusiasm for God and which collectively caused me to drift away from that first rush of loving, intimate connection with my Lord Jesus Christ. It would be easy to blame much of that growing indifference on mediocre and indifferent preaching, a very real problem, but the truth is that in contradiction to the teaching of the Bible, I allowed the secular world to reclaim my allegiance to it. Most happily, I have returned more recently to the more intimate connection with God that I had enjoyed at first.

Despite my personal shortcomings of character, my intellectual understanding of the Bible remained firm throughout my Christian experience. As I noted above, I have a habit of never integrating new thoughts into my internal cache of what I consider to be objective truth without thoroughly vetting it. In the process I have learned to accept and even to appreciate the personal trait that is both a handicap and an advantage, which is that I am a very slow learner but what I do learn and retain is of considerable depth. As a result, this cache of data that belongs to me probably is as self-consistent as one might expect of the human mind, or at least the mind of someone of my ilk. My knowledge of the Bible enjoys this characteristic, and out of my very thorough study of it I became convinced without reservation that Scripture is both supernaturally inspired and inerrant in the original, as claimed by Paul in 2 Timothy 3:16 and by Peter in 2 Peter 1:20 and 21. There have been many attacks on its apparent inconsistency, often by scholars possessing impressive intellectual credentials. I have found in every instance of an attack of this sort of which I am aware that, despite his air of authority, the attacker failed miserably to use the brain he was given or the mental training he obtained, his assessments being embarrassingly shallow. If one delves deeply enough into Scripture, he finds that it is very self-consistent, and in fact supernaturally so. It also supplies information that a fully human writer, uninspired by the Holy Spirit, would find impossible to obtain.

I always have been an inquisitive sort, a trait, as I've said before, that led me to a course of study in college that leaned heavily toward mathematics, physics and logic. I have applied that knowledge not only in my career but toward an in-depth understanding of the major secular paradigms of our time, which included Darwin's theory of evolution, the uniformitarian foundation of natural history, and the conflict between science and religion. Along the way, I also addressed perceived inconsistencies in Scripture, both internally to it and externally between it and the prevailing world view. One such apparent inconsistency took me ten years to resolve, but it did get resolved in the end in a delightful confirmation of the inerrancy of Scripture, and the resolution itself represented an enormously important learning experience.

The intersection of my training in mathematics, physics and logic, the prevailing secular paradigms, and my research into Scripture has given me a somewhat patchwork understanding. However, in some specific areas I have obtained a very detailed and self-consistent picture of the following specialized fields of knowledge: an overview of Scripture; theological topics relevant to my specific interests; Darwinian and neo-Darwinian evolution; intelligent design; biology, the uniformitarian worldview, the opposing catastrophic worldview, and the thought processes of the scientific mainstream, the public at large and the Christian community. I have a working knowledge of eschatology, New-Age thought, heresies, Catholicism, the free-will and dispensational controversies, the Catholic-Protestant schism, molecular biology, and the influence of earth-endangering catastrophes on the history of the human race.

The resulting specialized cache of knowledge may be unique to myself. It may or may not represent absolute truth. But for what it's worth, it has led me to certain conclusions about God that harmonize quite nicely with Scripture as well as with the natural world in which we find ourselves. The interesting thing about these conclusions is that they furnish a picture of Christianity that, while it appears to be harmonious with Scripture, not only differs radically from the various mainstream understandings of God, but explains why these understandings differ so thoroughly from each other.

It is this sharp difference between the mainstream understanding and my own on the topic that I am addressing that has caused me to dwell at length on my qualifications to discuss it, for I do not possess a formal education in theology. I have never darkened the doors of a seminary, nor have I followed a recognized curriculum in acquiring a background in Christian theology.

Is that deficiency necessarily bad? Allow me to speak in defense of the informality of the religious education that I do possess. In religious matters, knowledge and understanding come first from wisdom, and wisdom comes first from the heart. According to Psalm 1:1a and Proverb 1:7,

> *The fool hath said in his heart, There is no God... The fear of the Lord is the beginning of knowledge, but fools despise wisdom and instruction.*

Note that the fool, in denying God, speaks not from his mind but from his heart. According to Matthew 21:15 and 16, the most intellectually knowledgeable of the Jews, the religious authorities, in failing to see in Jesus their long-awaited Messiah; lashed out at him in anger for doing the work of God while ignoring them:

> *And when the chief priests and scribes saw the wonderful things that he did, and the children crying in the temple, and saying Hosanna to the Son of David! they were sore displeased, and said unto him, Hearest thou what these say? And Jesus saith unto them, Yea; have ye never read, Out of the mouth of babes and sucklings thou hast perfected praise?*

This incident is but part of a pattern that runs throughout the Gospels: Jesus' anger is directed primarily toward the religious elite who, time after time, demonstrate a head knowledge of their faith but are destitute in their hearts and consequently repetitively fail to understand the true nature of their God.

Is the situation in the seminaries of today any different from that of the Sanhedrin at the time of Jesus' sojourn on earth? Hardly. It was the seminaries that introduced the errors of the German School of Higher Criticism, which claimed on the basis of grammatical expression that the Book of Isaiah among other Scriptural documents was written, not only by several authors, but after the arrival of Jesus, negating the notion that the great Messianic Chapter 53 describing the Jesus who suffered for our salvation, was written centuries before Christ came to dwell on earth and therefore was supernaturally inspired. That worked out really well for the message of faith after multitudes of pastors departed the seminaries to preach falsehoods to their congregations, after which in boredom Ahmed the Wolf tossed a rock into a cave and uncovered the Dead Sea Scrolls which were dated to before Christ and contained the entire Book of Isaiah.

After the German School came a bleak succession of false notions to infect credulous future pastors who cared more about receiving decent grades than understanding God in their hearts. From these seminaries oozed a gangrenous intellectual pus that infected generations of would-be pastors with a distrust of Scripture and a terribly shallow insistence on perceived inconsistencies. Out of these temples of false knowledge emerged an ecumenism on steroids from which arose the abomination of thinking to merge Christianity with Islam. Also from here came the notion associated with the self-styled Emergent Church that perhaps knowledge isn't absolute after all, and just maybe we don't have the capability to understand God beyond some watered-down basics of a social gospel.

That's not to say that I wouldn't like to have an advanced degree in theology under my belt. I would, and I recognize my lack of same to be a personal and limiting deficiency. But maybe this shortcoming isn't all that bad.

I have a final comment regarding my credentials, and it's perhaps the most important by far. Since the topic is the nature of God, intellectual prowess undoubtedly takes a back seat to the guidance of the Holy Spirit who indwells all Christian believers. With respect to that indwelling, I possess abundant personal evidence of the strength of that indwelling, which at times has rescued me from certain death and guided me into displays of compassion that turned into amazing and unexpected adventures, both intensely intellectual and intensely physical, ones that I never would have dreamed of embarking on with my own limited mind. I expect that it is this same Guide who led me to pursue the present topic in depth, and who supplied much, if not all, of the information about which I write.

Two

The Issue and my Motivation to Pursue it

My earliest memory of self-awareness was of an event in which I participated while in the second grade. It left a mark. The event was a Christmas pageant in which our class had been divided into two groups, each wearing white angel costumes and sitting passively on the lawn on either side of the front entrance. As the older children began to perform in front of the entrance, I developed the phobia that somehow I had gotten in the wrong group. While an objective viewer would have the impression that changing the head count of one quietly-sitting, passive group at the expense of the other wasn't going to ruin the pageant, my own mental faculties weren't developed to the point that such a perception would enter my tiny brain. I kept my peace in fear for a while, but eventually I could stand it no longer. Terror-stricken, I interrupted the show by dashing through the middle of the performers to what I thought was the correct side, in the process tripping one girl and causing her to cry. As I looked at the expressions of astonishment that surrounded me, I was forced to re-examine the thought that I had been on the wrong side. Slowly, I realized that this new side might well be the wrong one. But it was way too late to set things straight. In my fear, I had indeed ruined the pageant. My career as a showman was over.

Later that day as we were driving home from the debacle, my mother turned around in the front seat and looked at me strangely. "Arthur," she pronounced solemnly, shaking her head, "you march to a different drummer."

The pronouncement was not meant to encourage, as was confirmed a year later when another mother pronounced the same words to a different boy who stood in the street in front of a crowd of cars whose drivers were waiting to pick up their children, dropped his pants, and peed in their sight.

Other things happened as the years went by that reinforced that heavy-hearted pronouncement upon me. There was the Great Watermelon Incident that occurred on a very hot day when everyone was anticipating relief in the form of juicy, cold slices of watermelon fresh from the refrigerated shelf of the local store. When it arrived home I insisted on carrying it up the stairs into the house. Mother shook her head, indicating that I was too small to be entrusted to the task. Despite my father's menacing glare, I lifted it up from the trunk of the car, hoisted it to my waist, and marched with it up the stairs. I actually reached the top step before it popped out and bounced back down the stairs, shedding pieces as it traveled, its progress accompanied by the changing of the sound of its repetitive impacts from *thunks* to *squishes*. I won't go into what happened afterwards. It's just too painful to recall.

Returning home from high school once when the transmission got stuck I was forced to drive my car several miles in reverse, displaying the same directional challenge in my movements as following a different drummer. Fortunately, I was outdone by a high school classmate, who was so desperate to relive the life of actor Jimmy Dean that he re-created a dramatic scene from the movie

Giant by pouring a can of oil over his head in front of the lunchtime crowd. He owned a '50 Merc, just like his idol Jimmy Dean, and tooled around the school re-creating a scene from *Rebel Without a Cause*, his head almost out of sight below the windshield, a cigarette dangling from his sneering mouth and his wrist atop the steering wheel in a pose of bored indifference. Only he kept on re-creating this particular scene, up to that fateful Saturday night when, tooling past the immensely popular local drive-in restaurant, he cut a corner too close and mounted a fire hydrant that, while elevating the car to a position of non-operability, cracked open to emit a huge geyser of water. There he sat, trapped in his car. The noise of the water and the sirens did manage to drown out the surrounding laughter, but that didn't help him, because he could clearly see in all the faces that what they were indulging in was side-splitting hilarity.

For a period of time I was straightened out by the Marine Corps, who rather forcefully insisted on everyone marching to the same drummer, in the same direction and at the same pace. Rather early on in boot camp, we received an inkling of this insistence by a "chat" that our senior drill instructor (I have a hard time not capitalizing his title, for during that period of our lives he was equivalent to God) had with us feckless recruits. "You sorry bunch of pussies," he said, "I have a message for you and you'd best listen up. The message is this: my father died on Tarawa. You will pay dearly for that." We did. That sight of his angry face as he spoke those words are burned into my psyche. But many years later, as I read an account of that battle of Tarawa, I understood something of the nobility of those Marines who managed to stay on their feet and fight in the midst of rampant slaughter with its threat of almost certain death and overcome their fear to eventually take the tiny little island. I thus give this message to my D.I.: Semper Fi, man.

Now, as I attempt to explain my position with regard to the feminine nature of the Holy Spirit, I am forced to appreciate that the position I have taken is that of a different drummer. I can only say that even if I tend to see things differently than others, and even if the directions my marches take me are not usually highly regarded, they are not necessarily wrong or bad. This particular march regarding the Holy Spirit may well be the right one, for a change. But I realize that it's up to me either to demonstrate the validity of my position on this topic in the face of my rather poor track record with regard to my direction of march, or alternatively, in the light of my failure to demonstrate the validity of that position, to accept that this is just another case of "marching to a different drummer". But because my own understanding of the nature of the Holy Spirit has given me such an intensely beautiful picture of the Godhead and one which is so worthy of fervent love, it is extremely important to me that I enter the fray. That love created out of this understanding is the essence of my primary motivation to pursue the justification of my particular vision, as it profoundly reaches my heart.

Briefly, I consider the Holy Spirit to be the second Member of the Trinity, fully God, and functionally fully feminine. Moreover, I understand Her to possess all the basic attributes normally associated with femininity. If a Christian brother or sister would insist on the Holy Spirit being the third Member of the Trinity, I won't argue the point. Her feminine gender, on the other hand, is not a negotiable item with me.

The female attributes of the Holy Spirit, as I view them, do not necessarily correspond to those possessed by Her human counterparts. However, I do view Her to possess the ability as Divine Means to unite with the Father, or the Divine Will as His Complementary Other in a partnership corresponding to Family in a perfect sense. I also view this unity to result in a procreative function, endowing the Holy Spirit with the attributes of intimate Consort to the Father, Divine Mother to the Son, and, eventually, Divine Mother-In-Law to the Church. In that context, I view the result of Divine Means' procreative function to be the Divine Word, or the Divine Implementation of Creation, Jesus Christ as fully God and the third (or second, whatever you wish) Member of the Holy Trinity.

Moreover, I view the Holy Trinity as having existed throughout and beyond eternity either within or outside the Personage of the Divine Will. Eternity in this context began with time at the beginning of Creation. At some point beyond time as we know it, the human race being dimensionally limited, the Divine Father chose in love to separate Himself into two Beings, Father and Holy Spirit, thereby voluntarily in love choosing to reduce his status as All-in-All to one Member of a Partnership. That which the Father lost in the process was reclaimed in love according to the words given to Adam by the Holy Spirit in Genesis 2:23 and 24, and applied to the union between the Divine Will and the Holy Spirit:

> *And Adam said, This is now bone of my bones, and flesh of my flesh; she shall be called Woman, because she was taken out of man. Therefore shall a man leave his father and mother, and shall cleave unto his wife; and they shall be one flesh.*

I believe that Scripture corroborates this origin of the Holy Spirit, as well as the origin of Jesus, as the result of the Divine union between Will and Means, specifically following the pattern presented in Genesis 1:1-5, 14-19, John 1:1-5 and Revelation 3:14:

> *In the beginning God created the heaven and the earth. And the earth was without form, and void; and darkness was upon the face of the deep, and the Spirit of God moved upon the face of the waters. And God said, Let there be light: and there was light. And God saw the light, that it was good: and God divided the light from the darkness. And God called the light Day, and the darkness he called Night. And the evening and the morning were the first day.*
>
> *And God said, Let there be lights in the firmament of the heaven to divide the day from the night; and let them be for signs, and for seasons, and for days, and years. And let them be for lights in the firmament of the heaven to give light upon the earth: and it was so. And God made two great lights, the greater light to rule the day, and the lesser light to rule the night: he made the stars also. And God set them in the firmament of the heaven to give light upon the earth, and to rule over the day and the night, and to divide the light from the darkness: and God saw that it was good. And the evening and the morning were the fourth day.*

In the beginning was the Word, and the Word was with God, and the Word was God. The same was in the beginning with God. All things were made by him; and without him was not anything made that was made. In him was life; and the life was the light of men. And the light shineth in darkness; and the darkness comprehended it not.

And unto the angel of the church of the Laodiceans write: These things saith the Amen, the faithful and true witness, the beginning of the creation of God.

In the context of the origin of the Holy Spirit and Jesus Christ out of the Divine Will, I interpret the Scriptural portrayal of the Godhead as three Divine Members in their unity as a Divine Family to form the basis of Judeo-Christian monotheism. I therefore consider the design of the individual human, male and female as presented in Genesis 2:26 and 27, to profoundly represent, in a lesser dimensional order, the image of God, first as representing, depending on gender, either the Father or the Holy Spirit, second as united in love, and third as procreators of offspring and consequent generators of families.

And God said, Let us make man in our image, after our likeness; and let them have dominion over the fish of the sea, and over the fowl of the air, and over the cattle, and over all the earth, and over every creeping thing that creepeth upon the earth. So God created man in his own image, in the image of God created he him; male and female created he them.

The problem with this viewpoint is that it is at odds with the understanding of the mainstream Western Christian Church and of the authorities who consider themselves to be in a position to challenge thoughts that they consider to be heretical.

This antagonism toward a female Holy Spirit expands the issue from being a perception of a female Holy Spirit to that of being a perception of the same in contradiction to mainstream Western Christian Theology.

My motivation at the beginning was innocent enough. I merely wanted to be obedient to God, which, to me, meant being obedient to His commandment in Deuteronomy 6:4 and 5:

> *Hear, O Israel: The Lord our God is one Lord: and thou shalt love the Lord thy God with all thine heart, and with all thy soul, and with all thy might.*

What that meant to me was that my love for God must be fervent. The call to that love is amplified by Jesus Christ's repetition of that commandment of Moses in Matthew 22:37 and 38, along with His commentary that this commandment was the greatest of them all:

> *Jesus said unto him, Thou shalt love the Lord, thy God, with all thy heart, and with all thy soul, and with all thy mind. This is the first and great commandment.*

The problem with my ability to be obedient to this commandment was that nowhere either in Scripture or in Church was I able to obtain sufficient insight into God as to justify this kind of love. In the first place, I couldn't even understand the notion of monotheism in the face of a supposedly Trinitarian Godhead. How could three be considered as one? Even Islam struggles with that, to the extent that this religion is so strictly monotheistic as to deny the Christian Trinity as being fully God. Within Christianity, the 'Jesus Only' Church does the same, as did some early heresies within the Christian Church, including Arianism.

I didn't want to be a heretic—I wanted to be anything but. However, I also knew that I must learn to love God with passion, which was my prime motivation for pursuing an understanding of God beyond what I was able to obtain either in Church or in the Church's interpretation of Scripture.

Eventually, after reading Scripture with an open mind, I came to appreciate that the only way that the Trinity could be reconciled with monotheism was in the context of a Divine Family. Having acquired that answer, I was excited to find that it came with a blessing —an instant appreciation of the Godhead that induced the desired passion, natural, intuitive and unforced, into my love for God. I first described this understanding in a short piece that is attached herein as *Appendix 1: Implications of God's Transcendent Nature on the*

Orthodox Christian Understanding of God. I next described the process in greater detail in Part 1 of my Christian nonfiction work *Family of God.* At the end of Chapter 1 of that book I summarized the problem, as I have noted it above; at the beginning of Chapter 2 of Part 1 I presented the answer, describing the wonder of this comprehension:

"Surely by raising this issue [of monotheism in a Trinitarian setting] we have placed ourselves in the midst of a basic conflict, one that was not resolved when Jesus came to the earth in the flesh, nor has it been settled in the two millennia since that event. Perhaps, given the assault on family values experienced by our generation, the timing is appropriate for God to favor this same generation with an understanding, rich in information as to His own nature, which will lead to a resolution of this conflict. It is with this hope that we continue our review, searching Scripture for something we may have missed before."

"As would be expected, God furnished man with His own straightforward answer to the paradox of His triune nature. It is profound in its simplicity and astonishingly beautiful in form. In the second chapter of Genesis, Adam speaks thus:

And Adam said, This is now bone of my bones, and flesh of my flesh: she shall be called Woman, because she was taken out of man. Therefore shall a man leave his father and his mother, and shall cleave unto his wife: and they shall be one flesh.

"The essence of this passage was repeated by Jesus and later by Paul. In the contexts in which it was presented, it is obviously of importance to God. Could there be a significant relation between the unity of flesh in marriage and the unity of spirit, as was often claimed by Jesus, between the Father and Him, and in fact, among the three Members of the Holy Trinity?"

This is an enormously important insight, and, in forming a logical basis for considering God to be one and three at the same time, it furnishes a strong secondary motivation to pursue the justification of my particular vision, as it profoundly reaches my intellect. In summary then, I have been urged on by two strong motivators: first,

the intrinsic love that appeals to my heart and second, the logic of it
that appeals to my intellect.

In my several books including the Christian nonfiction work
Family of God and the novels *Buddy*, *Cathy*, and *Jacob* I have,
out of an urgency of heart, put forward the notion that the Holy
Spirit possesses a functionally feminine gender. This isn't just a pet
idea of mine, one that I toss out for trivial reasons. I believe with
all my heart, for the reasons given in the development above, that
Christianity as it is practiced today in an overwhelming number of
Churches has been terribly wounded, and that from nearly the very
outset of the Church's existence, to the extent that Her members hold
fast to a false and destructive viewpoint that renders them unable to
love their God with the intimate fervor that Jesus commanded in
Matthew 22, nor even to understand the Word of God in the depth
it deserves. I feel that this attitude, derived from a misconception
of God's nature, grieves the Holy Spirit to the extent that She is
now actively pushing certain individuals to attempt to correct that
situation. If I've been getting a shove from Her in that direction,
well, that's a pretty big motivator, and I'm not complaining a bit.

Three

GOD'S CREDENTIALS

I rush to qualify the title of this chapter, knowing with no doubt whatsoever that God, like the *bandido* in the Bogart movie *Treasure of Sierra Madre*, "don' gots to show us no stinkin' bodges." By the word "credentials," I hint at the apparent discrepancy, at least in the minds of some scoffers, between God's loving goodness and the bad things that happen in the world. This argument is often used to justify a rejection of Scripture as the inerrant Word of God. As a consequence, the scoffers feel free to accept what, if anything, they wish to take away from Scripture and to reject all else. Herein, I endeavor to demonstrate that God indeed displays love in everything that might happen to a believer, and that Scripture can be trusted as well. That beautiful hope-filled passage in Romans 8:28 immediately comes to mind:

> *And we know that all things work together for good to them that love God, to them who are the called according to his purpose.*

I've driven a rather large variety of vehicles, at least in the planes and automobiles department. Come to think about it, it would be kind of fun to drive a train, like the ad of the winner in the Washington State Lotto who used his vast income to buy his own diesel locomotive for the trip out to his mailbox and back. Unfortunately, I personally haven't won the lotto, so that experience is off the table for now. I've wrecked a few vehicles, too, but all-in-all, I've had some good rides. Of course, in that experience I'm certainly not alone.

One time during a getaway weekend on the Washington coast not long after we married, we rented little motor scooters to drive along the broad sandy beach. Carolyn enjoyed the experience until the front wheel hit a rut and she did a faceplant in the sand. I truly wanted to be of more help to her, but she looked so cute with all that sand on her face broken up by two channels of tears down her cheeks that all I wanted to do was hug her.

Carolyn and two of our daughters are the snowmobile experts in our family. It was their primary sport before I came into their lives. They'd go off to wilderness areas near Mount Adams in the Champion motor home and spend days out in the snow. After our marriage I borrowed a snowmobile and went with them for a day in the area around Easton, just east of Snoqualmie Pass. I enjoyed it, but somehow I felt like I was intruding into Carolyn's past. Then again, the situation was like that with our rafting: while we enjoyed the experience we had so much else on our plates that there simply wasn't time to do it all. Nevertheless, the same two daughters have continued the activity to this day as their main family sport.

Carolyn has a favorite whistle-blowing tale about snowmobile rides. Her uncle Dick and aunt Olga also had snowmobiles, and for several years they'd go along on snowmobiling trips with Carolyn's family in their own motor home. Everybody noticed Olga's unusual caution with her machine. She never seemed to get to the point where she was comfortable with the sport. Nobody, not even uncle Dick, talked to her about it because they simply assumed that it was in her nature to be cautious and they were thankful that she was brave enough to continue with the activity despite her obvious fear of it. One day near the end of their run they found themselves on a fairly steep hill with the motor homes parked below. They went down the hill and stopped, looking up at poor Olga, all alone at the top and attempting to muster the courage to take the plunge. Finally she did it, and the speed with which she tore down the hill had everyone gasping. Her charge was arrested by a bush. As she lay there in the snow with a broken leg, everyone ran up to comfort her. Running a hand through his thinning hair, Dick asked with deep concern, "Why on earth didn't you use your brakes?"

"Brakes?" she questioned back in bewilderment. "What brakes?"

I've ridden jetskis twice. Like with the snowmobile and rafting experiences it was great fun and if we didn't have other activities going on we'd probably have pursued it more. My brother had a jetski experience once that ended somewhat badly. While picnicking on a lake with a number of friends and wives, he borrowed a friend's jetski and tore off across the water. Full of himself as he returned, he thought he'd buzz the wives who were sitting at a picnic table very close to shore. He cut it a little too close and ran into sand. His trajectory was terminated by the picnic table, from which the wives had fled screaming.

I told the story in *Buddy* about another person's ride that I consider to be among the most epic that I've ever witnessed. I'll repeat it below:

"Tell me, Earl," Janet said, a smile forming on her mouth. You probably like thrills of any flavor. Are you planning on taking Joyce to the fair this year? Maybe try the Slingshot? If you do, I want the video." She looked at Joyce and laughed, knowing that the only way she would take the ride would be if she was unconscious. Earl needed to know her limitations.

"I have ridden on roller coasters, but I don't like them," Earl answered shortly. "There are at least two reasons why. The first is that on a roller coaster I'm a passenger. Being a passenger doesn't agree with my stomach. The second reason is more urgent than the first: roller coasters are sinister. I say that because I know. I've seen things."

"That sounds kind of dark," Janet said, hoping that it was, and that it involved a good story. She wasn't disappointed.

"Once, against my better judgment," Earl volunteered, "I joined a 'public service' mens' group, a branch of one of those well-known national organizations. If there was anything that just wasn't 'me', that was it."

"Oh, I don't know," Joyce spoke up in his behalf. "You have a compassionate heart, and those groups seem to do a lot of good."

"Maybe some of them do, but this didn't. From the head man on down, it was all about power, control and manipulation. But the new president was by far the worst. He was just about the most arrogant, obnoxious windbag I'd ever had the misfortune of being acquainted with. As a matter of fact, I almost immediately quit after his election. But the club was in the midst of its semi-annual fundraiser and my conscience forced me to stick around long enough to help out with the event."

Janet was confused. "What's he got to do with sinister rides?"

"Believe me, I'm getting there. The fundraising event happened to a fair, the kind of thing that's held in the parking lot of a mall. One of the biggest attractions was a 50-foot Ferris Wheel. This guy, the president, came to the event wearing one of his typical flashy suits. It was so garish it was radioactive. Plaid vest and da-glo yellow pants, I remember it well. A boardwalk huckster would have turned his nose up at the sight."

They both laughed and looked at him expectantly, sensing that they would be well-entertained by what would come next.

"Anyway, one of the members asked him, as the senior official present, to make the symbolic first ride on the wheel. The president accepted the offer as his due. Had he been a bit more astute, he might have noticed that the guy who made the offer had a big grin on his face.

"That's when the fun began. He climbed in at the bottom, a fat cigar dangling out of his mouth, and, with a flourish, allowed himself to be strapped in. I guess that I wasn't the only individual who harbored ill feelings toward him, because another of our members, behind his back of course, slipped a twenty onto the palm of the ride operator with the instruction that our president was to be the only passenger. He put another twenty on top of that with the additional instruction, accompanied with a knowing wink, to "give him a good ride".

The girls began to snicker as he continued. "There were four major components to the system: the passenger, the operator, the wheel, and the engine. The operator was dressed somewhat less formally than the passenger. He was wearing dirty old Levis that didn't completely cover his butt. His face hadn't been shaved for several days and his shifty eyes were red, probably from too much Muscatel the night before. Like the passenger, the operator was smoking, but the contents originated in Colombia rather than Cuba. He didn't even smile when he received the forty. He simply gave a one-eyed Jack Elam trademark acknowledgement and fired up the machine.

"The wheel looked like any parking-lot Ferris Wheel, tall and spindly. It looked as if it needed to be handled with care. The engine was the only bulky component of the entire setup. It was a six cylinder Diesel, probably a Cummins —the kind that goes snorting around in Dodge Rams. The operator yanked open the throttle and it shouted out an angry bellow as a jet of hot gas blew out the exhaust stack. It shook when he popped the clutch. The acceleration was impressive, whisking the passenger up into the wild blue as if he was riding a catapult. We could see his face every time that he'd come back around, and with every cycle it underwent an astonishing transformation. The first time around he still had the cigar in his mouth, but his eyes were registering surprise. He lost the cigar near the top of the next cycle, and when he came back around the surprise had turned into horror. The wailing began after that, and remained for the next several passes. We could tell where he was by the Doppler shift of his screams. That's when I noticed that the legs of the wheel were shaking so bad that they were beginning to walk along the asphalt."

By this time the girls were shaking too. Joyce had to put her wine glass down before she'd spill it all over the carpet.

"At that point some of us began to feel that enough was enough, but the guy with the twenties signaled to wait just a little bit more. The operator didn't respond either way. I think he was ogling some girl in the parking lot while mellowing out on his toke. Soon after that the screams ended and the head was lolling as it passed by. We signaled our demand to stop it before the whole thing came crashing down and someone nudged the operator. He gave a surprised jolt as if the nudge woke him up and reluctantly wound down the speed. The passenger remained quiescent in his seat, his yellow pants now fouled with purple puke. Eventually he collected himself, exited the machine with as much dignity as he could muster, and staggered home. After witnessing that scene I rode an arcade attraction just once more in my life, and I did so very reluctantly and only because it was for an extraordinary cause."

The ultimate ride isn't really a ride at all, but rather a lifestyle. Specifically, it's life as experienced by the fully-committed Christian. To the outsider it may seem to be impossibly bleak and colorless, but it's anything but that. (I know full well what it means to be an outsider, having been one for half of my life.)

But, you might ask, if the ride is so good, why do bad things happen to good people, especially those who are thought of as good Christians? That was the question a family member shot in my direction a short time ago. Most of my family thinks that I went off the deep end on the religion thing a distressingly long time ago. They think of me in terms of victimhood, the culprit being the scrambled neurons in my brain. Correspondingly, as I well knew, the question wasn't so much a question as a challenge.

What the asker didn't know was that it says more about the asker than it does the askee. What the question really says is that since bad things obviously do happen to good people and because our 'God' is supposed to be a good God, there is a disconnect between this 'God' and His behavior. This 'God', then, if He truly existed, would amount to a paradox. Ergo, He cannot exist.

Nonexistence, of course, would represent the ultimate bad rap, equivalent to the complete lack of credentials. At this point, I could point to the amazing track record of Scriptural prophecy and its intersection with history as it has played out, and to Scripture's amazing internal consistency in the most minute details, and, regarding the world around us, modern advances in biological knowledge that refute Darwinism. For those readers who may be interested in learning of the supernatural credentials of Scripture, I have included Appendix 4: The Inerrancy of Scripture.

Instead, given the behavioral nature of the argument against God's existence as presented above, I wish to address God's actual credentials regarding what Scripture in 1 John 4:7-10 declares about the basic nature of God: that He represents the essence of love:

Beloved, let us love one another; for love is of God, and everyone that loveth is born of God, and knoweth God. He that loveth not knoweth not God; for God is love. In this was manifested the love of God toward us, that God sent his only begotten Son into the world, that we might live through him. Herein is love, not that we loved God, but that he loved us, and sent his Son to be the propitiation for our sins.

It is in this attribute of love that God's credentials are most relevant to the nature of the Holy Spirit.

I responded to the doubter's assertion of the disconnect between God's alleged goodness and the reality of evil by giving him what to me was an obvious answer. "Read my book *Family of God*," I told him. "Especially the chapter with the title *The Utility of Evil*."

I was surprised to hear back from him. I was more surprised with his subdued attitude. "What you were saying," he offered, "was that a person has to experience the effect of evil to appreciate the goodness of God and what Jesus suffered on the cross." I replied in the affirmative, hoping that he would understand that the concept he handed back to me was just a part of the whole picture, although he appeared to be satisfied with the gist of the chapter.

I should have been more direct with him and let him know that the ability to appreciate God's self-sacrificial goodness was just a portion of the story. A bigger part of it is that we don't live for ourselves. We were created by God and we do indeed live for Him rather than for ourselves. This isn't as onerous as it sounds, because it is love-centered: God wants to have a loving relationship with each of us. Almost as important as this is that God wishes to develop us from the self-centered persons most of us are into a nobility fitting for our future relationship with Him as His Bride. That means that our present physical existence is simply a kind of boot camp for our future spiritual existence. For those readers who may be interested in learning of the supernatural credentials of Scripture and the bankruptcy of evolution, I have included in this book *Appendix 4: The Inerrancy of Scripture* and *Appendix 5: The Incompatibility of Macroevolution with both Judeo-Christian Scripture and Physical Reality.*

Paul said it well when he noted in 1 Corinthians 15:19 that Christians are the most miserable of all people if indeed this physical existence is all that we have to look forward to. Most of us remain so confined within our narrow concept of reality that we have no understanding whatsoever of how limited our physical universe is. We're not only lacking a dimension or two of the greater spiritual realm inhabited by God, but are forced to live within the physical laws appropriate to that constraint. It appears, from reading between the lines of Scripture, that quantum mechanics on a macro scale plays a big role in the interface between the spiritual universe and our physical realm.

I know now that I can't leave the person who thrust the question upon me with just the notions that are in my book *Family of God.* I'll have to give this person another dose of information beyond those considerations, because he phrased his question differently than I addressed in the chapter *The Utility of Evil.* He didn't ask why bad things happen to people. He asked why bad things happen to *good* people. For that particular question he needs a good dose of the basic Gospel, for as every Christian knows, there is not one of us that is truly good. According to God's standards of righteousness, all our 'good' works, as Paul often echoed the prophet Isaiah, are like filthy rags (Is 64:6). Compared to His selfless nobility, we're all mired in the slime of self-interest, which is exactly why we can't storm the gates of heaven on our own merit. For our reconciliation with a holy God, we desperately need God's substitutionary atonement on the cross for our evil natures, as enacted by Jesus Christ: it is to the cross that we must look for that, not to ourselves.

This is the core problem with countless unfortunate, lost, people: not troubling themselves to read the Bible, they have bought into the devil's own lie about the meaning of Christianity. Considering themselves to be basically 'good', they claim to be Christian. It is hard to picture any attitude that can be more fundamentally in opposition to Christianity. In the first place, with that attitude they don't need Jesus at all. Completely disregarding Jesus' own words that nobody comes to the Father except through Him, they arrogantly think that they just need their own good works, making a mockery of the cross. In the second place, they are so comfortable with the prevailing attitude toward self and self-gratification that they fail to appreciate just how bad off we all are. None of us is good. Persons having the mindset that they are 'good' think that they can even perform 'good' acts with nothing but 'good' consequences, when history is full of the collateral damage caused by 'good' acts that have met with unintended but disastrous consequences.

In sharp contrast, the real Christian is humble enough to admit to his own shortcomings, thereby enabling him to gladly accept Jesus' very difficult work on his behalf on the cross.

Throughout his letters canonized in Scripture, Paul noted often that his fellow Christians shouldn't expect their faith to result in the lavishing of physical blessings upon them. It is in the spiritual world instead upon which they should set their sights and to which they should look with hope. Nowhere does he present this focus on another world more clearly than in 1 Corinthians 15:12-19:

> *Now if Christ be preached that he rose from the dead, how say some among you that there is no resurrection of the dead? But if there be no resurrection of the dead, then is Christ not risen; And if Christ be not risen, then is our preaching vain, and your faith is also vain. Yea, and we are found false witnesses of God, because we have testified of God that he raised up Christ, whom he raised not up, if so be that the dead rise not. For if the dead rise not, then is not Christ raised; And if Christ be not raised, your faith is vain, ye are yet in your sins. Then they also who are fallen asleep in Christ are perished. If in this life only we have hope in Christ, we are of all men most miserable.*

Jesus and His apostles explained numerous times just what Christians should expect during their time here on earth. Among these comments is Paul's summary given in Philippians 1:29:

> *For unto you it is given in the behalf of Christ, not only to believe on him but also to suffer for his sake, having the same conflict which ye saw in me, and now hear to be in me.*

Golly, that doesn't sound like fun. Oddly, though, there is actual joy in living the Christian life despite the apparent negatives. First is the Christian's peace with God and the certain knowledge of His love. An intimate part of this peace is the great advantage possessed by the Christian in having the indwelling of the Holy Spirit, something that is completely unexplainable to the unbeliever, who has little idea of what he is missing. Then, too, there is the peace and satisfaction of selfless living. Mature Christians understand the difference between this life and the next quite well, having perceived the necessity of life's trials in producing men and women of selfless nobility who are fit to inhabit the spiritual kingdom of God. As I noted above, the situation is really very similar to that of the military services in their utilizing the rigors of boot camp to produce men and women fit to fight our country's battles.

Some other religions also look to the next life for rewards to be conferred upon them for sacrifices made in this. But there is an extreme difference of motivation and expectation between the Christian and the participant of a different religion. For the Christian the reward is the development of a character suitable for the glorification of God in love; for the other individual the motivation is not noble at all but self-serving, the expectation of the Islamic male "martyr", for example, being a perpetual gratification of sexual lust via the services of virgins reserved for his pleasure. This "martyr", to be sure, must die to get his goodies, but the violence of the expected death is so sudden as to guarantee the minimization of any pain and the reward is equally forthcoming, the expectation being that it shall occur immediately after the terminal event. The same comforts do not extend to the most unfortunate Islamic female.

Unlike the Muslim "martyr" whose focus remains on the physical plane even with regard to his afterlife, the Christian enjoys the advantage of spiritual knowledge and support even in this life, for Jesus has promised (John 3) a spiritual rebirth to every person who in humility accepts His work on the cross performed on the believer's behalf. As a result, every believer is "born again" and experiences the loving guidance of the indwelling Holy Spirit as promised by Jesus Himself. Therefore, he is blessed with the intimate presence of God in his life.

Further, unlike those involved in the world's religions, those who consider themselves to belong to the Church don't see themselves as being members of a religion; rather, while they see religions as representing man's attempt to storm the gates of heaven on his own merits, they perceive their own experiences to be direct relationships with God, needing no rote ceremony for membership in good standing. Uniquely, Christianity imposes no requirement other than faith for entrance into heaven, for Jesus paid the price alone and fully for the shortcomings of every person on earth. The Christian alone recognizes the necessity for this, perceiving that we humans, being so far beneath God that any "goodness" we might possess, or any efforts we might personally make toward imposing ourselves upon the gates of heaven, are insignificant next to the expectations of a noble and holy God.

Yet more, Christianity alone possesses in its Scripture a written message from God Himself to mankind, in which the essence of our relationship with God is given to us through the inspiration upon man by the Holy Spirit. Not only that, but the unique predictive accuracy and consistency (to those who actually understand its contents) of this Scripture firmly squares it with absolute truth: to Christians, it is the real deal.

Finally, the message that God gave us defines our God as possessing the authority of our Creator, Who is the embodiment of Love and Wisdom, a most fortunate claim that sets Him apart from the many gods that man has created for himself in opposition to the One God of Scripture. The reality of this claim is certainly demonstrated by the supernatural consistency and prophetic accuracy of Scripture; it is also demonstrated by the lives of historical figures who acted out the revealed will of God.

Here's where the nature of the Holy Spirit comes into play, by indwelling the believer to comfort him as would a mother to reconcile the loving nature of God with the suffering that the believer must face to strip him of his selfishness and thus render him capable of the love necessary for him to enjoy full communication and companionship with God.

I can attest to the comfort offered by the Holy Spirit in the face of external discomfort with the authority of personal experience. In the particular example I present below, the primary discomfort was the overcoming of fear. The discomfort was so strong that I can't conceive of myself doing on my own what God had me do for the sake of another individual.

Here I wish to boast on the Lord. If He has used me, it gladdens me that He saw fit to do so, for the chance to participate in God's work is infinitely better than personal accomplishment. Were it not for Paul's statement in 1 Corinthians 1:26-31, I'd be tempted to brag a bit about some of my experiences, but this particular passage goes a long way toward putting me in my place:

For ye see your calling, brethren, how that not many wise men after the flesh, not many mighty, not many noble, are called; but God hath chosen the foolish things of the world to confound the wise; and God hath chosen the weak things of the world to confound the things which are mighty; and base things of the world, and things which are despised, hath God chosen, yea, and things which are not, to bring to nought things that are, that no flesh should glory in his presence. But of him are ye in Christ Jesus, who of God is made unto us wisdom, and righteousness, and sanctification, and redemption; that, according as it is written, He that glorieth, let him glory in the Lord.

That passage simply reinforces what I already know about myself. I noted in Chapter 1 that I'm a slow learner. What I neglected to add was that my slowness extends to my body. At my advanced age it doesn't matter anyway, but I know that I'd never have been a race car driver, nor a sports athlete, nor anything that requires a quick eye and speed of response. The hearing issue that prevented me from remaining a commercial pilot has been a blessing to all the lives that I'd have endangered in the process of taking to the sky with them as paying passengers. That God used me in the way that He did in the following account greatly appeals to my sense of humor, and I'll bet His too, because it is entirely consistent with the passage from 1 Corinthians that I quoted above.

Once my frequent flying companion Harold helped me accomplish a task of such personal importance that I won't forget it as long as I live. For a couple of years before I had taken up my brother's challenge to go hang gliding, I had been volunteering on a weekly basis at a local home for severely handicapped persons. Among these residents was Danny, a young man in his twenties afflicted with cerebral palsy, a terrible disability that so thoroughly restricted his movements that his limbs would fight violently with each other whenever he attempted to move, leaving him entangled and grimacing in frustrated effort. Yet in the face of this he persisted in maintaining a basically cheerful nature, a trait that should put to shame those of us who spend time focusing on our own relatively trivial problems. I know that his attitude has affected me this way, and probably did much to develop my character, such as it is, beyond what it might otherwise be.

As my association with this terribly encumbered individual developed, I began to notice that his intelligence most likely surpassed my own, which just made the fact of his affliction even worse: he represented a mind imprisoned in an almost nonfunctional body. Despite the severity of his affliction he showed an interest in adventure, exemplified by an incident that took place during an outing where I pushed his wheelchair around a few residential blocks near the nursing home. Coming upon a slight dip in the sidewalk, I released my hold on the handles of the chair and told him, jokingly, to "go for it." Fighting unwilling muscles, Danny screwed up his face in a grin and lifted an arm in a semblance of a pump, attempting to make a thumbs up sign.

It was inevitable with that kind of attitude that eventually the thought of taking Danny hang gliding would enter my mind. In time, this notion became a burning desire. Being but a novice at the time, I realized that I didn't have the experience to accomplish this on my own. I approached several pilots who were far younger and had more air time than I did but was turned down flat. I wouldn't say that they were all afraid to do it, although I'd bet that it was at least a factor with some; it was more of an affront: they couldn't comprehend why a severely handicapped person should be on the big hill. Realizing that if anyone was going to do the job it would have to be me, for the next several months I worked hard at acquiring the necessary experience. Toward the end of that time, I had Danny weighed at 94 pounds and took to the big hill wearing a backpack into which I inserted a progressively increasing number of lead SCUBA weights. I had gotten up to about 60 pounds when I really began to worry about overstressing my glider. About that time also my flying friends, including Harold, were venturing farther afield with their gliders in search of better lift conditions. Not willing to be left behind on the big hill, I went along with them, essentially putting the project with Danny on semipermanent hold.

One morning a few months later something happened right out of the blue that changed my life the instant that I woke up. When I did awake it was to a strange peace and the certain knowledge—it wasn't just a feeling, but a deeply rooted understanding—that on that day I would take Danny up to the big hill and we would jump off together. I had no idea how that might be done, but I was sure that it would, despite the fact that I had never flown in a glider with another person, even as a passenger, and had no idea what to expect. As a Christian I understood this knowledge and especially the peace regarding it to be a gift from the Holy Spirit. Every year that passes I am more certain of this fact. And very, very grateful.

The first thing I did after getting dressed was to call Harold, asking him to come with me and help to figure out how we were going to get Danny into the air. Then I went to the nursing home, told the staff what I intended to do, and picked up Danny. (Wow! Things sure were different back then. I can't imagine being able to get away with something like that in today's over-regulated society. But then again, perhaps the Holy Spirit had something major to do with the nurses' compliance with my intentions.) We met up with Harold on the big hill, where he was already attempting to figure out how the launch was going to take place. He had a rope slung over his shoulder when Danny and I arrived and was eyeing a big stump. He wrapped the end of the rope around the stump as I came up to him, and walked over to the edge. "I think this is gonna work," he said as he wrapped the other end around his waist, cinching it tightly. "Go ahead and set up," he continued as he tested it. He had just enough slack to get him over the edge at a 45 degree angle.

Harold was one strong guy. He was brave and compassionate as well, being exactly the person I needed for help. As I walked the glider to where I'd run off the edge, Harold cradled Danny in his harness. We hooked him into the keel, along with me, while he continued to hold Danny in his arms. When I signaled my intent to go, he ran with me to the edge and, just as he felt the tug of the rope around his waist, flung him away in front of the glider.

I felt a twist of Danny's harness on the keel and, having not quite achieved flying speed, we momentarily dove in dubious control. But we had a thousand feet to sort things out, and eventually gained a semblance of normal flight. Danny's excitement was extreme, his jaw dropping as he attempted to grin, and it gave me a wonderful feeling that this strange thing we were doing was being smiled upon by God. This feeling of euphoria continued after we landed, when Danny gave me a look of pure joy.

After our first landing Danny was totally pumped. He flung his arms akimbo and strained to speak. I understood him as clearly as if his speech was perfect. Harold and I were both pumped too. It probably was the most significant moment of my life. No bones were broken, Danny and I were alive, Harold hadn't fallen off the cliff and we had acquired the experience of a successful venture. We could, in fact, do it again, and now without the fear of the unknown.

It's best to wait until the adrenalin leaves the system before attempting something that demands logic. We didn't and it was almost our undoing. Grinning stupidly at each other, Harold and I both said "Let's do it again!"

We returned to the top of the big hill and set up the glider once more. Harold wrapped the rope around his waist, tugged on it, and took Danny and his harness in his arms. I signaled and began to run, and Harold followed and flung Danny off.

Oh-oh. It being later in the day, the wind had changed. I had checked it before launching, and knew about it but it's hard to argue with invincibility. On the other hand, it's also hard to ignore the laws of physics, as I now found out. It's about the first thing that hang gliding instructors tell their students, usually expressing the importance of it by shouting: "Don't launch downwind! It won't work!"

Indeed. Human power is notoriously weak. The hang glider pilot needs all the help he can get to attain flying speed. Anything less results in a stall, which means that gravity rules over everything else.

So here we were, heading downward in a stall. Theoretically, we had a thousand feet to sort things out and recover. The cliff, however, had a prominent ledge a couple of hundred feet down. Trees resided on the ledge. Big trees, over a hundred feet tall. By the time Danny and I had attained flying speed, we found ourselves below the treetops and heading rapidly toward them. Most fortunately, the wing itself remained above the tops and our combined mass was sufficient to plow through them. We were through the gauntlet, and after that the flight was uneventful. But we didn't fly any more that day.

The next flight didn't work out too well either. The flight itself was fine, but my landing lacked perfection. I was too low in the flare-out, just about kissing the grass. Danny's chin was lower yet. When he gets excited he drops his jaw. When we land he remains prone, thus making his jaw the lowest part of his body and, in actuality, the entire hang glider system. This would have been acceptable if the field contained nothing but grass. But it didn't. Cows grazed there. They ate the grass. They did other things on it, too, so it was inevitable that Danny's jaw would scoop up a cow pie.

It wasn't as funny as it sounds. He was choking and I was terrified that he wouldn't be able to breathe. As soon as I could I scrambled to clear his airway by poking my finger into his throat and pulling out the poop. His gasps reassured me that he was able to breathe, and I continued to kneel there, thanking God for His mercy in the face of my stupidity.

When we returned to the nursing home I felt compelled to tell the nurses about what had happened, because I wasn't sure that he wouldn't need a shot of something to immunize him against infection. The fact that Danny was there and he was alive and apparently in good spirits lightened up the situation considerably. They asked if there were flies on the poop. When I replied in the negative, they said that there was no real problem. Then they began to laugh. They were still laughing as I left the building.

We had four more flights together after that, three of which were made without untoward incidents. But the next flight was a real doozy.

To this point we had one very successful flight together, followed by two more somewhat marginal ones. The next flight was marginal too. In fact, it was the scariest of the lot. As before, Harold ran next to me with Danny, flinging him into the air as I reached the edge of the big hill. This time there was an added spin to the thrust, causing Danny's right arm to loop around the left flying wire that ran between the left tip of my crosstube and the left tip of my basetube.

If Danny's arm had been capable of flexing at the elbow, this wouldn't have mattered. The arm simply would have slipped back down, allowing Danny's harness to come back alongside mine when I went prone and put my hands on the basetube for control.

But Danny's arm was quite rigid at both elbow and shoulder, causing him to remain where he was, on the left side of the glider rather far away from the basetube.

If hang gliders had control surfaces common to airplanes like rudders and ailerons, that might not have been so terribly important. But hang gliders are controlled in flight by weight-shift, making control surfaces unnecessary under most conditions. Therefore, most hang gliders don't have control surfaces.

As didn't we. There we were then, flying marginally above stall speed with the glider sensing Danny's position as a rather stern command for a sharp left turn. A sharp left turn at that point would have brought us back toward our launch point. The problem with that, of course, is that now we were well below the launch point. As we began to turn, the cliff face came back into sight. It wasn't a pretty picture. Although he was fully aware of the situation, Danny's handicap prevented him from moving his arm. His frustration was extreme, matching the intensity of my terror. All I wanted then was my mama. I think that Danny wanted the same.

I had no choice. Tugging on the right flying wire, I pulled myself (scrabbled would be more accurate) out to the right to compensate for Danny's position. We straightened out and I was then able to turn us away from the cliff and back into unobstructed airspace. But in that position my control was marginal, especially with respect to pitch. We were flying, but barely. Setting up for a landing and then executing it without compromising our health would be extremely difficult under those conditions.

When we had enough room to recover from a complete loss of control, I took a few deep breaths to calm myself and let go from my precarious but relatively stable perch, swinging over toward Danny. As the glider, under our combined weight on the left side, began a turn again to the left, this time more abruptly than the last, I reached out and attempted to unhook the arm. Failing to do it, I scrambled back to the right just as the glider began its entry into a spiral from which it may not have recovered.

Noting with dismay that we were closer to the ground and were approaching the point where we'd have insufficient altitude to recover from that kind of attitude, I took a few more deep breaths, prayed for God's help and repeated the maneuver. Spurred on by desperation, I did so more boldly than during my previous attempt. This time we were successful. We returned to stable flight greatly relieved and breathing heartfelt thanks to God for getting us out of that situation. The landing turned out to be good.

Danny and I, with Harold's continued help, had three more flights after that. They all were relatively uneventful. In fact, I had become so comfortable flying with another that I had begun flying with my wife as well. Then a number of significant events occurred in my life, all of which were unrelated to Danny, but which conspired against any further launches with him.

It was an experience that I'll never forget, not for the scares, but for the joy of the doing. I don't think Danny will forget it either. I suppose that I could feel guilty about having exposed Danny to such danger, but, given that he survived intact, his life ended up being far more meaningful than it otherwise would have been. I'm sure that Danny would agree to that also. Besides, God was in charge all the time.

As if that adventure with Danny wasn't proof enough of the power of the indwelling Holy Spirit, there was also the business of Her softly but insistently prodding me over a ten-year period of an on-again, off-again algebraic analysis of Jesus' feeding of the multitudes, along with the like events of Elisha and Peter, to arrive at an understanding of what Jesus' feeding events actually symbolized. This quest, driven by the Holy Spirit, led me into Scripture at a depth that I had no idea existed. It resulted in a profound understanding of the true meaning of His feeding events, complete with His signature. I share that information in my book *Family of God* and the novel *Cathy* and in Appendix 2 in this book. As I noted in an addendum to *Family of God*, the algebraic analysis presented in an appendix was necessary to lead me into an initial understanding, but once that understanding was attained, the entire process can be readily visualized by inspection without resorting to math, as detailed in Appendix 2, entitled *Jesus' Feeding of the Multitudes*. This ease of visualization extends to the numbers involved, including the means by which 5000 can be fed with 5 loaves and leave 12 baskets' remainder, and 4000 can be fed with 7 loaves and leave 7 baskets' remainder. In my novel *Cathy*, I describe the feeding process in narrative form. As far as I'm concerned, that understanding, like the flights with Danny, is a proof of God's existence in the form of a gift, one that I'll treasure forever.

After having experienced the direct presence of God in my life, whenever I'm in the vicinity of a doubter or scoffer, I'm tempted to scoff at the offender. But if I have the presence of mind to remember that I, too, was once a doubter, I offer a more gentle, albeit firm, response. Whatever my actual words turn out to be, however, I remember those experiences told above as representing the ultimate proof of God's existence and goodness—His credentials, if you will.

Four

The Western Christian Church's Viewpoint of the Nature of the Holy Spirit

An essential item on our dogtags was our religious affiliation. In our boot camp entrance paperwork we were instructed to fill in the appropriate blank, which would then go onto the dogtags. As I had no religious affiliation at the time, I didn't know what to put down. When I asked, a corporal supervising our assembly set me straight. "You're either Catholic or Protestant, screw," he explained. "What's a Protestant?" I pressed. "A Protestant is someone who's not a Catholic, dumbass," he sneered. (His epithet actually was more colorful than that, equating me to a part of my anatomy that never sees the light of day.) I knew I wasn't a Catholic, so I put down "Protestant", and "Protestant" is what my dogtags read, although I didn't know what a Protestant was.

I had no religious affiliation for the simple reason that I wasn't religious. My parents weren't religious and, in fact, often scoffed at those who were. But I did have some minimal exposure to the concept of God, as a few years previous my brother and I, along with a friend, decided to embark on a life of crime. We had acquired a taste for beer, but, not being old enough to buy it legitimately, we decided to steal it. When the inevitable happened, I was dragged out of the police station by very angry parents, who tossed me into a Methodist Church forthwith for sorely-needed instruction in morals.

That didn't work out too well, because the Church itself offered no insight regarding God. On the third Sunday, after the pastor expressed his opinion from the pulpit that "nobody really expects Jesus to return again", I went home and confronted my parents with the certain knowledge that God didn't exist, even in the eyes of the pastor. "If there really is no God," I told them, what good is moral instruction that comes from a lie?"

They were forced to agree, after which I didn't darken the doors of a Church again until I was in my late thirties. Perhaps it was a good thing that when I did go back to Church after realizing that God did indeed exist and accepted Jesus Christ as my Savior and Lord, I possessed some maturity of thought, including a certain cynicism regarding the plethora of differing doctrines associated with the various Christian denominations. It was this understanding of Church fallibility that led me to sample a number of different Churches before settling into a favorite. But even after finding a Church that we called home, I was well aware of the confusing number of issues over which the various denominations disagreed: infant baptism, free will, the identity of the elect of God, the stance regarding modern Israel, Mary's immaculate conception, Mary's perpetual virginity, Mary's status in heaven, the role of the Holy Spirit in the modern Church, dispensationalism, etc. The list went on and on.

I soon discovered that among all the contentious issues there was one that nobody wanted to address: the nature of the Holy Spirit. Holy Father and Holy Son were well-defined, but the Holy Spirit was not, and it became apparent that this absence of comprehension was common to virtually all the Churches whose doctrines I was familiar with. I eventually came to my own understanding of the Protestant viewpoint regarding the nature of the Holy Spirit: there wasn't a viable position. The typical position was that the Holy Spirit, like Father and Son, was truly and fully God, existed with Father and Son throughout eternity, and, like Father and Son, was to be worshiped and adored as a Member of the Trinitarian Godhead. There were accompanying relational words like "proceeding from", but which were intuitively empty of substance. Beyond this common vague description, there was an essentially universal acknowledgement of confusion and incomplete understanding. I was to find out later that the Catholic Church suffered under the same vagueness of understanding, although she responded to that confusion in a strikingly different manner. The following is my take on the nature of that confusion and some preliminary thoughts as to how it came about. I go into greater detail on the "how" in Chapters 10 and 11.

From the very birth of Christianity at the first Pentecost following Jesus' resurrection, there was a sweeping away from the Christian faith of the decadent and often lewd practices associated with the worship of the pagan gods. Gone was the old leaven, and, like a breath of fresh air, the Holy Spirit came to indwell, ennoble and thoroughly clean human temples. With the new faith came an urgent call to demonstrate its difference from the crassness and moral filth of the surrounding secular society.

The Church eventually trespassed beyond the bounds of loving worship, propriety and common sense in her effort to cleanse herself, even to the extent of corrupting Scripture. But that took more time, on the order of several hundred years.

The Church's initial success in this endeavor generated a loathing for Christians among their secular associates that contributed greatly to the persecutions that followed, particularly as the rulers found it convenient to exploit this antipathy of secular society toward Christians for their own benefit. But the persecutions only stiffened the Christian resolve to stand apart from the surrounding society.

It was in this setting that the Christian faith developed the canon of the New Testament and established its structure and dogma as it confronted a number of serious heresies that threatened to undermine the character and teachings of Jesus and His Apostles. The canon of Scripture, always directed by the Holy Spirit, remained untouched by the human condition. But the Church and the formulation of her dogma were heavily influenced by the deep antagonism in the minds of the Christian leadership between the new nobility of spirit and the old darkness of self-absorption and lust.

Foremost in the minds of many of the new Christians were the lewd and disgusting bacchanalias associated with the devotions to the Greek and Roman gods, who themselves were prone to bouts of lust and sexual perversions. In sharp contrast to the gross depravity of these gods, Jesus stood apart, radiant in shining moral splendor. At a time of rampant sexual excess, Jesus' Words sparkled like swords of righteousness and were taken deeply to heart. Among these were His own pronouncements of the place of sexuality within the Christian economy, which were immortalized in Scripture. His Words that are handed down to us in Matthew 19 must have been very important to the new Christians:

> *The Pharisees also came unto him, tempting him, and saying unto him, Is it lawful for a man to put away his wife for every cause? And he answered and said unto them, Have ye not read that he who made them at the beginning, made them male and female; and said, For this cause shall a man leave father and mother, and shall cleave to his wife, and they twain shall be one flesh? Wherefore, they are no more twain, but one flesh. What, therefore, God hath joined together, let not man put asunder. They say unto him, Why did Moses then command to give a writing of divorcement, and to put her away? He saith unto them, Moses, because of the hardness of your hearts, permitted you to put away your wives, but from the beginning it was not so. And I say unto you, Whosoever shall put away his wife, except it be for fornication, and shall*

marry another, committeth adultery; and whosoever marrieth her who is put away doth commit adultery.

His disciples say unto him, If the case of the man be so with his wife, it is not good to marry. But he said unto them, All men cannot receive this saying, except they to whom it is given. For there are some eunuchs, who were so born from their mother's womb; and there are some eunuchs, who were made eunuchs by men; and there are eunuchs, who have made themselves eunuchs for the kingdom of heaven's sake. He that is able to receive it, let him receive it.

The new Christians, in overlooking much of what Jesus actually was teaching, placed a heavy emphasis on the latter part of this saying by Jesus, the part that dealt with eunuchs. It may have called to mind a piece of Old Testament Scripture, verse five of David's fifty-first Psalm, attaching to it a meaning that went beyond the words:

Behold, I was shaped in iniquity, and in sin did my mother conceive me.

This passage was written after Nathan confronted David with a scathing rebuke over David's murderous lust for Uriah's wife Bathsheba, and was an expression of guilt, which very much included his own, over the baseness of motivation behind some sexual unions.

Paul, too, in support of the Christian desire for moral cleanliness and writing to a Church that was in danger of returning to the materialism of society at large, added his obviously conflicted opinion of the meaning of sexual purity and the role of women within the Christian economy, but questioning himself as he did so as to whether he was writing on behalf of the Holy Spirit, or whether his was doing so entirely on his own. In 1 Corinthians 7:1 and 2, 25-40, he said this:

Now concerning the things about which ye wrote unto me, it is good for a man not to touch a woman. Nevertheless, to avoid fornication, let every man have his own wife, and let every woman have her own husband. . . .

Now concerning virgins, I have no commandment of the Lord; yet I give my judgment, as one that hath obtained mercy of the Lord to be faithful. I suppose, therefore, that this is good for the present distress, I say, that it is good for a man so to be. Art thou bound unto a wife? Seek not to be loosed. Art thou loosed from a wife? Seek not a wife. But and if thou marry, thou hast not sinned; and if a virgin marry, she hath not sinned. Nevertheless, such shall have trouble in the flesh; but I spare you. But this I say, brethren, The time is short; it remaineth that both they that have wives be as though they had none; and they that weep, as though they wept not; and they that rejoice, as though they rejoiced not; and they that buy, as though they possessed not; and they that use this world, as not abusing it; for the fashion of this world passeth away. But I would not have you without care. He that is unmarried careth for the things that belong to the Lord, how he may please the Lord; but he that is married careth for the things that are of the world, how he may please his wife. There is a difference also between a wife and a virgin. The unmarried woman careth for the things of the Lord, that she may be holy both in body and in spirit; but she that is married careth for the things of the world, how she may please her husband. And this I speak for your own profit; not that I may cast a snare upon you, but for that which is comely, and that ye may attend upon the Lord without distraction. But if any man think that he behaveth himself uncomely toward his virgin, if she pass the flower of her age, and need so require, let him do what he will, he sinneth not; let them marry. Nevertheless, he that standeth steadfast in his heart, having no necessity, but hath power over his own will, and hath so decreed in his heart that he will keep his virgin, doeth well. So, then, he that giveth her in marriage doeth well; but he that giveth her not in marriage doeth better. The wife is bound by the law as long as her husband liveth; but if her husband be dead, she is at liberty to be married to when she will, only in the Lord. But she is happier if she so abide, after my judgment; and I think also that I have the Spirit of God.

Although Paul repeatedly noted that the union between man and wife is not sinful, it was his admonition that life as a eunuch was better, in that it permitted undiluted focus to the Lord. It was that sentiment which stood out in the early Christian mind as the golden standard of behavior.

That standard was expressed, for example, by Justin the Martyr in his first apology for (defense of) Christianity, as compiled in the book *Early Christian Fathers,* edited by Cyril C. Richardson. This commentary was written around the middle of the second century A.D., about a half century after the Apostle John wrote the Book of Revelation. In it, Justin echoed the sentiment of Paul regarding sexual circumspection:

> About continence [Jesus] said this: "Whoever looks on a woman to lust after her has already committed adultery in his heart before God." And: "If your right eye offends you, cut it out; it is better for you to enter into the kingdom of Heaven with one eye than with two to be sent into eternal fire." And: "Whoever marries a woman who has been put away from another man commits adultery." And: "There are some who were made eunuchs by men, and some who were born eunuchs, and some who have made themselves eunuchs for the Kingdom of Heaven's sake; only not all [are able to] receive this."

> And so those who make second marriages according to human law are sinners in the sight of our Teacher, and those who look on a woman to lust after her. For he condemns not only the man who commits the act of adultery, but the man who desires to commit adultery, since not only our actions but our thoughts are manifest to God. Many men and women now in their sixties and seventies who have been disciples of Christ from childhood have preserved their purity; and I am proud that I could point to such people in every nation... But to begin with, we do not marry except in order to bring up children,

or else, renouncing marriage, we live in perfect continence. To show you that promiscuous intercourse is not among our mysteries—just recently one of us submitted a petition to the Prefect Felix in Alexandria, asking that a physician be allowed to make him a eunuch, for the physicians there said they were not allowed to do this without the permission of the Prefect. When Felix would by no means agree to endorse [the petition], the young man remained single, satisfied with [the approval of] his own conscience and that of his fellow believers.

In writing about the sexual purity of Christians, Justin intended to contrast this behavior with that associated with the false gods and the rampant and often cruel immorality that not only was involved in the worship of them, but which had infected secular life as well:

Far be it from every sound mind to entertain such a concept of deities as that Zeus, whom they call the ruler and begetter of all, should have been a parricide (killer of a relative) and the son of a parricide, and that moved by desire of evil and shameful pleasures he descended on Ganymede and the many women whom he seduced, and that his sons after him were guilty of similar actions. But, as we said before, it was the wicked demons who did these things. We have been taught that only those who live close to God in holiness and virtue attain to immortality, and we believe that those who live unjustly and do not reform will be punished in eternal fire.

Secondly, out of every race of men we who once worshiped Dionysus the son of Semele and Apollo the son of Leto, who in their passion for men did things which it is disgraceful even to speak of, or who worshiped Persephone and Aphrodite, who were driven made by [love of] Adonis and whose mysteries you celebrate, or Asclepius or some other of those who are called gods, now through Jesus Christ despise them, even at the cost of death, and have dedicated ourselves to the unbegotten and impassible God. We do not believe that he ever descended in mad passion on Antiope or others, nor on Ganymede, nor was he, receiving help through Thetis, delivered by that hundred-handed monster, nor was he, because of this anxious that Thetis' son Achilles should destroy so many Greeks for the sake of his concubine Briseis. We pity those who believe [such stories], for which we know that the demons are responsible."

That we may avoid all injustice and impiety, we have been taught that to expose the newly born is the work of wicked men —first of all because we observe that almost all [foundlings], boys as well as girls, are brought up for prostitution. As the ancients are said to have raised herds of oxen or goats or sheep or horses in their pastures, so now [you raise children] just for shameful purposes, and so in every nation a crowd of females and hermaphrodites and doers of unspeakable deeds are exposed as public prostitutes. You even collect pay and levies and taxes from these, whom you ought to exterminate from your civilized world. And anyone who makes use of them may in addition to [the guilt of] godless, impious, and intemperate intercourse, by chance be consorting with his own child or relative or brother. Some even prostitute their own children or wives, and others are admittedly mutilated for purposes of sodomy, and treat this as part of the mysteries of the mother of the gods—while beside each of those whom think of as gods a serpent is depicted as a great symbol and mystery. You charge against us the actions that you commit openly and treat with honor, as if the divine light were overthrown and withdrawn—which of course does no harm to us, who refuse to do any of these things, but rather injures those who do them and then bring false witness [against us].

Two and a half centuries later, Augustine experienced much the same revulsion as Justin did over the moral tawdriness of the Roman society in which he lived. Having become a Christian thirty two years after his birth in 354 A.D., Augustine had spent much of his dissolute pre-Christian years in the enjoyment of the depravity of the society in which he lived. The shame and regret of these

early years served to drive Augustine into a passionate rejection of
loose morality and unbridled lust. The strength of his feelings in
that regard are demonstrated throughout his book *City of God*, an
example of which is given in Chapters 4 and 5 of Book II:

> When I was a young man I used to go to sacrilegious shows
> and entertainments. I watched the antics of madmen; I listened
> to singing boys; I thoroughly enjoyed the most degrading
> spectacles put on in honour of gods and goddesses—in honour
> of the Heavenly Virgin, of Berecynthia, mother of all. On the
> yearly festival of Berecynthia's purification the lowest kind of
> actors sang, in front of her litter, songs unfit for the ears of even
> the mother of one of those mountebanks, to say nothing of the
> mother of any decent citizen, or of a senator; while as for the
> Mother of the Gods—! For there is something in the natural
> respect we have towards our parents that the extreme of infamy
> cannot wholly destroy; and certainly those very mountebanks
> would be ashamed to give a rehearsal performance in their
> homes, before their mothers, of those disgusting verbal and
> acted obscenities. Yet they performed them in the presence
> of the Mother of the Gods before an immense audience of
> spectators of both sexes. If those spectators were enticed by
> curiosity to gather in profusion, they ought at least to have
> dispersed in confusion at the insults to their modesty.
>
> If these were sacred rites, what is meant by sacrilege? If
> this is purification, what is meant by pollution? And the
> name of the ceremony is "the *fercula*" which might suggest
> the giving of a dinner-party where the unclean demons could
> enjoy a feast to their liking. Who could fail to realize what
> kind of spirits they are which could enjoy such obscenities?
> Only a man who refused to recognize even the existence of
> any unclean spirits who deceive men under the title of gods,
> or one whose life was such that he hoped for the favour and
> feared the anger of such gods, rather than that of the true God.
>
> *5. The obscenities performed in the worship of the "Mother
> of the Gods"*

The last people I should choose to decide on this matter are those who are more eager to revel in the obscene practices of this depraved cult than to resist them. I should prefer the decision of Scipio Nasica, the very man whom the Senate chose as their best man, whose hands received this devil's image and brought it to Rome. Let him tell us whether he would wish his mother to have deserved so well of her country that she should be accorded divine honours. For it is well known that the Greeks and the Romans, and other peoples, have decreed such honours to those whose public services they valued highly, and that such people were believed to have been made immortal and to have been received among the number of the gods. No doubt he would desire such felicity for his mother, if it were possible. But let me go on to ask him whether he would like such disgusting rites as those to be included among the divine honours paid to her? Would he not cry out that he would prefer his mother to be dead, and beyond all experience, than that she should live as a goddess, to take pleasure in hearing such celebrations? It is unthinkable that a senator of Rome, of such high principles that he forbade the erection of a theatre in a city of heroes, should want his mother to be honoured as a goddess by such propitiatory rites as would have scandalized her as a Roman matron. He would surely have thought it quite impossible for a respectable woman to have her modesty so corrupted by the assumption of divinity that her worshipers should call upon her with ritual invocations of this sort. These invocations contained expressions of such a kind that had they been hurled at any antagonist in a quarrel, during her life on earth, then if she had not stopped her ears and withdrawn from the company, her friends, her husband and her children would have blushed for her. In fact, the "Mother of the Gods" was such a character as even the worst of men would be ashamed to have for his mother. And when she came to take possession of the minds of the Romans she looked for the best man of the country, not so as to support him by counsel and help, but to cheat and deceive him, like the woman of whom the Bible says, "she ensnares the precious souls of men." Her purpose was that a mind of great endowments should be puffed up by this supposedly divine testimony and should think itself truly exceptional, and therefore should cease to follow the true religion and piety—without which every national ability, however remarkable, disappears in the ruin which follows on pride. And thus that goddess should seek the support of the best men only by trickery, seeing that she requires in her worship the kind of behaviour which decent men shrink from even in their convivial moments.

Augustine was enormously influential to the Christian Church at a time when Church doctrine was still being formulated and heresies were still emerging, to be debated upon and rejected. In his wake, the Church charted a course that polarized itself away from any hint of the depravities associated with the corrupt gods and goddesses of the world about her. This extremity of purification, for which purity was equated with chasitity, cleansed the Judeo-Christian God of any taint of sexuality.

A thousand years later, this insistence upon purity had not only remained, but had crystallized into a rigid perfectionism, enshrined by the medieval cleric Jerome Zanchius, a rigid adherent of the heavenly perfection envisioned by Aristotle and Ptolemy. I describe this attitude in the words of Earl's wife Joyce in my novel *Buddy*:

"The sixteenth century was especially bad," she continued. "The reactionary atmosphere at that time virtually ensured that perfectionists would enter the religious scene. Their theological precepts constituted a complementary philosophical companion to Ptolemy's geocentric cosmology of perfection. God, they claimed, being the Creator of that perfection, was Himself of a like nature. Listen to these characteristics, Earl. To them, God was the Embodiment of simplicity, perfection, unchangeability and independency of being. These qualities, in turn, implied to them that God was above some of the defining characteristics of lesser beings such as the human race. Passion is included among these 'lesser' characteristics constituting the human nature that don't belong to God."

Zanchius, in his rather pretentious work *Absolute Predestination Stated and Defined*, included some Scripturally unjustified statements regarding the nature of God, of which the following excerpts are representative:

VI.—I shall conclude this introduction with briefly considering, in the sixth and last place, THE MERCY OF GOD.

POSITION 1.—The Deity is, throughout the Scriptures, represented as infinitely gracious and merciful (Exod. 34.6; Nehem. 9.17; Psalm 103.8; 1 Peter 1.3).

When we call the Divine mercy infinite, we do not mean that it is, in a way of grace, extended to all men without exception (and supposing it was, even then it would be very improperly denominated infinite on that account, since the objects of it, though all men taken together, would not amount to a multitude strictly and properly infinite), but that His mercy towards His own elect, as it knew no beginning, so is it infinite in duration, and shall know neither period nor intermission.

POSITION 2.—Mercy is not in the Deity, as it is in us, a passion or affection, everything of that kind being incompatible with the purity, perfection, independency and unchangeableness of His nature; but when this attribute is predicated of Him, it only notes His free and eternal will or purpose of making some of the fallen race happy by delivering them from the guilt and dominion of sin, and communicating Himself to them in a way consistent with His own inviolable justice, truth and holiness. This seems to be the proper definition of mercy as it relates to the spiritual and eternal good of those who are its objects.

Zanchius continues as follows in his Chapter 1, entitled in grandiose manner "Wherein the Terms Commonly Made Use of in Treating of this Subject are Defined and Explained.":

HAVING considered the attributes of God as laid down in Scripture, and so far cleared our way to the doctrine of predestination, I shall, before I enter further on the subject, explain the principal terms generally made use of when treating of it, and settle their true meaning. In discoursing on the Divine decrees, mention is frequently made of God's love and hatred, of election and reprobation, and of the Divine purpose, foreknowledge and predestination, each of which we shall distinctly and briefly consider.

"I.—When love is predicated of God, we do not mean that He is possessed of it as a passion or affection. In us it is such, but if, considered in that sense, it should be ascribed to the Deity, it would be utterly subversive of the simplicity, perfection and independency of His being. Love, therefore, when attributed to Him, signifies—

(1) His eternal benevolence, *i.e.,* His everlasting will, purpose and determination to deliver, bless and save His people. Of this, no good works wrought by them are in any sense the cause. Neither are even the merits of Christ Himself to be considered as any way moving or exciting this good will of God to His elect, since the gift of Christ, to be their Mediator and Redeemer, is itself an effect of this free and eternal favour borne to them by God the Father (John 3.16). His love towards them arises merely from "the good pleasure of His own will," without the least regard to anything *ad extra* or out of Himself.

(2) The term implies complacency, delight and approbation. With this love God cannot love even His elect as considered in themselves, because in that view they are guilty, polluted sinners, but they were, from all eternity, objects of it, as they stood united to Christ and partakers of His righteousness.

(3) Love implies actual beneficence, which, properly speaking, is nothing else than the effect or accomplishment of the other two: those are the cause of this. This actual beneficence respects all blessings, whether of a temporal,

spiritual or eternal nature. Temporal good things are indeed indiscriminately bestowed in a greater or less degree on all, whether elect or reprobate, but they are given in a covenant way and as blessings to the elect only, to whom also the other benefits respecting grace and glory are peculiar. And this love of beneficence, no less than that of benevolence and complacency, is absolutely free, and irrespective of any worthiness in man.

II.—When hatred is ascribed to God, it implies (1) a negation of benevolence, or a resolution not to have mercy on such and such men, nor to endue them with any of those graces which stand connected with eternal life. So, "Esau have I hated" (Rom. 9.), *i.e.,* "I did, from all eternity, determine within Myself not to have mercy on him." The sole cause of which awful negation is not merely the unworthiness of the persons hated, but the sovereignty and freedom of the Divine will. (2) It denotes displeasure and dislike, for sinners who are not interested in Christ cannot but be infinitely displeasing to and loathsome in the sight of eternal purity. (3) It signifies a positive will to punish and destroy the reprobate for their sins, of which will, the infliction of misery upon them hereafter, is but the necessary effect and actual execution.

I respond to this odd theology as follows, which I present in my novel *Buddy* in terms of Joyce's continuing commentary to her husband Earl:

"Ouch. God above passion? That's not what I get out of the Bible. Think about it. The consequence of a passionless God is a Deity possessing neither romance nor intimacy within or outside the Godhead. That would make the Godhead void of any gender-driven feelings, which is essentially equivalent to a genderless God. But if gender is not involved in the Godhead, God being above that kind of thing, we would end up with a passionless God incapable of experiencing for Himself that which He fashioned in His creation and asks of us to respond toward Him. That would give us an experiential edge on God as well as to suggest hypocrisy in His nature.

"I'm with you," Joyce replied. "Beyond that problem, the perfectionists' definition of God not only suppresses love, His most important attribute, but inhibits those to whom Scripture was written from loving Him back. This is a serious issue because it runs counter to His Great Commandment to love Him with all our hearts, and our souls and our minds.

"Their God was instead, in His perfection, of a remote grandeur. This notion gave rise to a God whose primary attribute is his majestic greatness. By defining God with majesty in mind, love became a secondary attribute, despite John's emphatic identification of God as the very embodiment of love. They went too far. The perfection embodied in their eulogies renders them sterile.

"The perfectionists' Pasteurization of God has led them to a view of God as residing in absolute flawlessness, so void of blemish that, like the smooth and featureless moon of their era, their statements of position approach the theological equivalent of Aristotle's perfect cosmos, which was embellished upon by Ptolemy and published in his *Almagest* in 150 A.D. They had nothing whatsoever to do with Scripture. In their application of Ptolemaic principles of perfection in the cosmos to their theology, the perfectionists' God, then, is a perfectly round, gigantic, cold and opaque marble."

In brief, Zanchius defines a God whose primary attribute is his majestic greatness. Had his mind access to expressions denoting higher level superlatives, he certainly would have included them. In defining God in this way, he automatically makes love a secondary attribute, despite John's emphatic identification of God as the very embodiment of love. Zanchius' passionless God, in fact, is alien to the God of Scripture. This is to be expected, as he assigns attributes to God without any reference whatsoever to Scripture itself.

Zanchius' God, then, being positionally remote from and by nature very different from the mankind of His creation, is alien to it as well.

In opposition to Zanchius, Scripture paints a far more beautiful picture of God, depicting His majestic glory as His willingness to give up the majesty of greatness and power in favor of a love of great fullness and depth. The Gospels appear to support this view, depicting Jesus Christ (as God) as a Being full of the attributes of love as we know it, including passion. Examples that come to mind include His weeping over Jerusalem and Lazarus and His ordeal in the garden of Gethsemane. It is difficult to picture the risen Jesus talking to His followers on the road to Emmaus in the context of Zanchius' notion of God's remote perfection.

Zanchius' definition of God not only suppresses His most important attribute, but inhibits those to whom Scripture was written from loving Him back. This is a serious issue as noted by Joyce in the novel *Buddy* because it runs counter to His Great Commandment to love Him with all our hearts, and our souls and our minds.

Leaving Zanchius behind for now, we return to a historical perspective of the Church in general, resuming at the Middle Ages. By this time the Western Christian Church had thoroughly purged its God of all sexual connotations. It understood the association of gender with the Holy Spirit in one of two ways, both of which had strong followings that currently still exist: some Churches insisted upon a gender-neutral God, including the neutrality of the Holy Spirit, while others asserted the asexual masculinity of all three Members of the Godhead, again including the Holy Spirit in that categorization. The difficulties attending either of these viewpoints are many and varied. These problems will be addressed later in this chapter and in Chapter 5.

From that time, through the turbulent years of the Reformation, and beyond into modern times, the basic removal from the human experience of this extreme cleansing of God increasingly became untenable. Would-be worshipers drifted far away from the love of God demanded by Scripture but denied by the Church. Theologians questioned the notion of a God without passion, which seemed to (and did) contradict the teaching of Scripture.

The Catholic Church responded in a unique way. Having removed the female gender from the Holy Spirit, the Catholic Church, to her credit, understood that an unnatural gap was created in her perception of the Godhead. She filled the perceived and all-too-real void of a genderless or all-male God with Mary, the mother of Jesus, whom she elevated to a superhuman status that fell just short of deity. Henceforth it would be Mary upon whom the Catholic Church would place her love and devotion, restoring a semblance of the fervor of worship commanded by both Moses and Jesus. To most Catholic laypersons, Mary's position of subordination to diety is so miniscule as to be nonexistent, wherein the veneration of her is indistinguishable from worship.

The Catholic text *Mary in the Church Today*, a compilation by Father Bill McCarthy of papal pronouncements and other official Catholic teachings regarding Mary, mother of Jesus, is an excellent source book for the understanding of the Catholic position regarding Mary. The teachings, from which the following entries are gleaned, speak for themselves.

> "For," the text [Lumen Gentium, 62] goes on, "taken up to heaven, [Mary] did not lay aside this saving role, but by her manifold acts of intercession continues to win for us gifts of eternal salvation." With this character of "intercession," first manifested in Cana in Galilee, Mary's mediation continues in the history of the Church and the world. We read that Mary "by her maternal charity, cares for the brethren of her Son who still journey on earth surrounded by dangers and difficulties, until they are led to their happy homeland." In this way Mary's motherhood continues unceasingly in the Church as the mediation which intercedes, and the Church expresses her faith in this truth by invoking Mary "under the title of Advocate, Auxiliatrix, and Mediatrix."
>
> Through her mediation, subordinate to that of the Redeemer, Mary contributes in a special way to the union of the pilgrim Church on earth with the eschatological and heavenly reality of the Communion of Saints, since she has already been "assumed into heaven." The truth of the assumption defined

by Pius XII, is reaffirmed by the Second Vatican Council, which thus expresses the Church's faith: "Preserved free from all guilt of original sin, the Immaculate Virgin was taken up body and soul into heavenly glory upon the completion of her earthly sojourn. She was exalted by the Lord as Queen of the Universe, in order that she might be the more thoroughly conformed to her Son, the Lord of lords (cf. Rv 19:16) and the conqueror of sin and death." In this teaching Pius XII was in continuity with Tradition, which has found many different expressions in the history of the Church, both in the East and in the West.

—exerpted from *Redemtoris Mater,* Articles 40 and 41

In the light of Mary, the Church sees in the face of women the reflection of a beauty which mirrors the loftiest sentiments of which the human heart is capable: the self-offering totality of love; the strength that is capable of bearing the greatest sorrows; limitless fidelity and tireless devotion to work; the ability to combine penetrating intuition with words of support and encouragement.

—excerpted from *Redemptoris Mater,* Article 46

Subsequently, in 1962, on the feast of the Purification of Mary, Pope John set the opening of the Council for 11 October, explaining that he had chosen this date in memory of the great Council of Ephesus, which precisely on that date had proclaimed Mary "Theotokos," Mother of God . . .

2. At the second session of the Council it was that the treatment of the Blessed Virgin Mary be put into the Constitution of the Church. This initiative, although expressly recommended by the Theological Commission, prompted a variety of opinions.

Some, who considered this proposal inadequate for

emphasizing the very special mission of Jesus' Mother in the Church, maintained that only a separate document could express Mary's dignity, pre-eminence, exceptional holiness and unique role in the Redemption accomplished by the Son. Furthermore, regarding Mary as above the Church in a certain way, they were afraid that the decision to put the Marian teaching in the treatment of the Church would not sufficiently emphasize Mary's privileges and would reduce her role to the level of other members of the Church. . .

—excerpted from the ninth of Pope John Paul II's series of catecheses on the Blessed Virgin

In the same context, the Council also calls God "most wise," suggesting a particular attention to the close link between Mary and the divine wisdom, which in its mysterious plan willed the Virgin's motherhood.

3. The Council's text also reminds us of the unique bond uniting Mary with the Holy Spirit, using the words of the Nicene-Constantinopolitan Creed which we recite in the Eucharistic liturgy: "For us men and for our salvation he came down from heaven: by the power of the Holy Spirit he was born of the Virgin Mary, and became man."

In expressing the unchanging faith of the Church, the Council reminds us that the marvelous incarnation of the Son took place in the Virgin Mary's womb without man's cooperation, by the power of the Holy Spirit.

The Introduction to the eighth chapter of *Lumen Gentium* thus shows in a Trinitarian perspective an essential dimension of Marian doctrine. Everything in fact comes from the will of the Father, who has sent his Son into the world, revealing him to men and establishing him as Head of the Church and the center of history. This is a plan that was fulfilled by the Incarnation, the work of the Holy Spirit, but with the essential cooperation of a woman, the Virgin Mary, who thus became an integral part in the economy of communicating the Trinity to mankind.

4. Mary's threefold relationship with the divine Persons is confirmed in precise words and with a description of the characteristic relationship which links the Mother of the Lord to the Church: "She is endowed with the high office and dignity of the Mother of the Son of God, and therefore she is also the beloved daughter of the Father and the temple of the Holy Spirit." (*Lumen Gentium,* n. 53).

Mary's fundamental dignity is that of being 'Mother of the Son', which is expressed in Christian doctrine and devotion with the title "Mother of God."

This is a surprising term, which shows the humility of God's only-begotten Son in his Incarnation and, in connection with it, the most high privilege granted a creature who was called to give him birth in the flesh.

Mother of the Son, Mary is the "beloved daughter of the Father" in a unique way. She has been granted an utterly special likeness between her motherhood and the divine fatherhood. And again, every Christian is a "temple of the Holy Spirit" according to the Apostle Paul's expression (1 Cor 6:19). But this assertion takes on an extraordinary meaning in Mary: in her the relationship with the Holy Spirit is enriched in a spousal dimension, I recalled this in the Encyclical *Redemptoris Mater*: "The Holy Spirit had already come down upon her, and she became his faithful spouse at the Annunciation, welcoming the Word of the true God..." (n. 26).

—excerpted from the eleventh of Pope John Paul II's series of catecheses on the Blessed Virgin

The freedom "from every stain of original sin" entails as a positive consequence the total freedom from all sin as well as the proclamation of Mary's perfect holiness, a doctrine to which the dogmatic definition makes a fundamental contribution. In fact, the negative formulation of the Marian privilege, which resulted from the earlier controversies about original sin that arose in the West, must always be complemented by the positive expression of Mary's holiness more explicitly stressed in the Eastern tradition.

Pius XII's definition refers only to the freedom from original sin and does not explicitly include the freedom from original concupiscence [generally, the desires of the flesh in the Catholic vernacular]. Nevertheless, Mary's complete preservation from every stain of sin also has as a consequence her freedom from concupiscence, a disordered tendency which, according to the Council of Trent, comes from sin and inclines to sin (DS 1515).

—excerpted from the twenty third of Pope John Paul II's series of catecheses on the Blessed Virgin

In recounting the birth of Jesus, Luke and Matthew also speak of the role of the Holy Spirit. The latter is not the father of the Child. Jesus is the son of the Eternal Father alone (cf. Lk 1:32-35), who through the Spirit is at work in the world and begets the Word in his human nature. Indeed, at the Annunciation the angel calls the Spirit "the power of the Most High" (Lk 1:35), in harmony with the Old Testament, which presents him as the divine energy at work in human life, making it capable of marvelous deeds. Manifesting itself to the supreme degree in the mystery of the Incarnation, this power, which in the Trinitarian life of God is Love, has the task of giving humanity the Incarnate Word.

—excerpted from the twenty eighth of Pope John Paul II's series of catecheses on the Blessed Virgin

1. The intention to remain a virgin, apparent in Mary's words at the moment of the Annunciation, has traditionally been considered the beginning and the inspiration of Christian

virginity for the Church.

St. Augustine does not see in this resolution the fulfillment of a divine precept, but a vow freely taken. In this way it was possible to present Mary as an example to "holy virgins" throughout the Church's history. Mary "dedicated her virginity to God when she did not yet know whom she would conceive, so that the imitation of heavenly life in the earthly, mortal body would come about through a vow, not a precept, through a choice of love and not through the need to serve;" (De Sancta Virg. IV. PL 40 398).

The angel does not ask Mary to remain a virgin, it is Mary who freely reveals her intention of virginity. The choice of love that leads her to consecrate herself totally to the Lord by a life of virginity is found in this commitment.

In stressing the spontaneity of Mary's decision, we must not forget that God's initiative is at the root of every vocation. By choosing the life of virginity, the young girl of Nazareth was responding to an interior call, that is, to an inspiration of the Holy Spirit that enlightened her about the meaning and value of the virginal gift of [sic, substitute 'chasitity'] heresy. No one can accept this gift without feeling called or without receiving from the Holy Spirit the necessary light and strength.

—excerpted from the twenty ninth of Pope John Paul II's series of catecheses on the Blessed Virgin

2. It may be presumed that at the time of their betrothal there was an understanding between Joseph and Mary about the plan to live as a virgin. Moreover, the Holy Spirit, who had inspired Mary to choose virginity in view of the mystery of the Incarnation and who wanted the latter to come about in a family setting suited to the Child's growth, was quite able to instill in Joseph the ideal of virginity as well.

—excerpted from the thirtieth of Pope John Paul II's series of catecheses on the Blessed Virgin

2. The Council stresses the profound dimension of the Blessed Virgin's presence on Calvary, recalling that she "faithfully persevered in her union with her Son unto the Cross" (*Lumen Gentium,* n. 58), and points out that this union "in the work of salvation is made manifest from the time of Christ's virginal conception up to his death" (ibid., a. 57).

Mary Joins Her Suffering To Jesus' Priestly Sacrifice.

With our gaze illumined by the radiance of the resurrection, we pause to reflect on the Mother's involvement in her Son's redeeming Passion, which was completed by her sharing in his suffering. Let us return, again, but now in the perspective of the resurrection, to the foot of the Cross where the Mother endured "with her only-begotten Son the intensity of his suffering, associated herself with his sacrifice in her mother's heart, and lovingly consented to the immolation of this victim which was born of her" (ibid., n. 58).

With these words, the Council reminds us of 'Mary's compassion'; in her heart reverberates all that Jesus suffers in body and soul, emphasizing her willingness to share in her Son's redeeming sacrifice and to join her own maternal suffering to his priestly offering.

The Council text also stresses that her consent to Jesus' immolation is not passive acceptance but a genuine act of love, by which she offers her Son as a 'victim' of expiation for the sins of all humanity.

—excerpted from Pope John Paul II's address to the General Audience on April 2, 1997

This view of Mary, as described by the highest Catholic authority and seconded by the entire Church, presents Mary with the warmth of humanity. But she, like the Godhead Itself, has been stripped clean of all sexual experience except for the pain of childbirth. In thinking about that rampant sexual housecleaning, it seems strange indeed that Peter, the iconic and revered founder of the Catholic Church, was himself married, according to Matthew 8:14 and 15, while his successors and the entire body of clergy eventually were and continue to be prohibited from doing so:

> *And when Jesus was come into Peter's house, he saw that his wife's mother laid, and sick of a fever. And he touched her hand, and the fever left her; and she arose, and ministered unto them.*

We all know how that worked out in practice: instead of taking wives and thereby participating in a relationship established and condoned by God, the clergy instead took the wives of other men, prostitutes and, ultimately, altar boys.

For the most part the Protestant Church, in contrast with her Catholic sister, simply accepts the lack of the feminine and ignores the issue altogether, treating it as beyond the pale of appropriate intellectual investigation. Despite this general official refusal of the Protestant Churches to address the void caused by the removal of functional gender from God, a number of interested theologians have attempted to explain the nature of the Holy Spirit in a way that, while conforming to Church doctrine, presents the Holy Spirit in a logical and, as they struggle to achieve, a warm manner.

Yet both Catholic and Protestant Churches have in common a view of the Trinity in which sexuality is at most a superficial feature even for birth and in which vital aspects of femininity are denied altogether. This view leads most investigators into the nature of the Trinity into an admission that the topic is very complex, to the extent that in the end they admit further that. like attempting to understand the duality of light or the logic behind quantum mechanics, they can't comprehend it completely. This limitation has and continues to have a profound influence on the entire nature of Christianity. Didn't any of these investigators grasp a hint in the wake of this inability to comprehend such an important topic that perhaps the standard view of the Trinity might need some revision?

Both the Father as the divine Will and the Son as Jesus Christ, the divine Word, are well-defined in Scripture as to their general natures and their functional roles. Of the three Members of the Trinity, the Holy Spirit is by far the most enigmatic. It is the lack of understanding, or perhaps simply the misunderstanding, of the nature of this divine Member from which the confusion and apparent complexity of the Trinity has arisen. A substantial part of this confusion is the obviously apparent but discomforting feature of the Holy Spirit's character as embracing specifically feminine elements in contradiction to the general view of the Trinity as being either gender-neutral or masculine. Because the Holy Spirit is the ultimate source of the Church's difficulty regarding the nature of the Trinity, the present work will focus primarily on this Entity.

Many expositors of the Holy Spirit see in Genesis 1 the active participation of the Holy Spirit in the act of creation. This is the position taken by respected scholar of Scripture Benjamin B. Warfield, who describes this functional attribute of the Holy Spirit in Chapter Seventeen of his book *The Holy Spirit*:

> His offices in Nature – The "Spirit" or personal "Breath" is the Executive of the Godhead, as the "Son" or "Word" is the Revealer. The Spirit of God moved upon the face of chaos and developed cosmos (Gen. 1:2). Henceforth he is always represented as the author of order and beauty in the natural as of holiness in the moral world. He garnished the astronomical heavens (Job 26:13). He is the organizer and source of life to all provinces of vegetable and animal nature (Job 33:4; Ps. 104:29, 30; Isa. 32:14, 15), and of enlightenment to human intelligence in all arts and sciences (Job 32:8; 35:11; Ex 31:2-4).

Dr. H. A. Ironside, in a little tome first printed in 1941 entitled *The Holy Trinity,* also interprets Genesis 1:2 as asserting that the Holy Spirit, in concert with the Father, was actively involved in creation. Interestingly, in referencing Isaiah 66 as an Old Testament reference to the Trinity he quotes from verse 13:

> *As one whom his mother comforteth so will I comfort you.*

Although Ironside invariably interprets the Holy Spirit in terms of the masculine pronoun 'he', he also confesses a lack of full understanding of the nature of the Trinity. Yet the passage quoted above, by associating the word 'mother' with 'comfort', furnishes a key argument for the feminine function of the Holy Spirit. For Jesus, in John 14:16 and 17, directly links the Holy Spirit with the name (implying role) Comforter:

> *And I will pray the Father, and he shall give you another Comforter, that he may abide with you for ever; Even the Spirit of truth; whom the world cannot receive, because it seeth him not, neither knoweth him: but ye know him; for he dwelleth with you, and shall be in you.*

Could it be that the masculine pronouns in this passage, as well as elsewhere in Scripture, refer to the substance of the Holy Spirit rather than functional nature? Or is it even more likely that the original "she" was deliberately changed to "he" in opposition to the maintenance of Scriptural integrity, as indicated by John 14:26 in the original Siniatic Palimpsest? This issue will be revisited in Chapter 7, wherein both possibilities are discussed in greater detail.

Dedicated theologian Dr. Bruce A. Ware makes similar statements as Warfield regarding the executive (implementation of will) role of the Holy Spirit in his work *Father, Son, & Holy Spirit.* In fact, this executive role of the Holy Spirit is a general theme among theologians. In his own work, Ware encapsulates the roles of Father, Son and Holy Spirit as follows: Father – Grand Architect; Son – Submission to the Father in doing (displaying) His Will; Holy Spirit – Carrying out the work of the Father.

Alister McGrath, who wrote the work *Understanding the Trinity*, provides a representative viewpoint of this genre, yet also furnishes some remarkably fresh insights. He stands on what I humbly perceive as firm soil in his eloquent and moving descriptions of God and the incarnate Jesus in chapters 1 through 6. In reading it for a second time quite recently I realized afresh how his treatment of the Trinity had influenced my own work *Family of God.* It was Dr. McGrath, in fact, whom I mentioned on pages 24 through 26:

> Some theologians, having briefly noted the one intuitively satisfactory functional description of the Trinity, reject this particular answer quite abruptly, justifying their rejection on the basis of insufficient logic. They proceed from there to hammer out tortuously-derived and ultimately insufficient, emotionally empty alternatives. One such expositor, who otherwise paints with highly readable and insightful words a delightful description of God, mentions the Trinity with profound understanding and then quickly discards it as a misapplication of a familiar model in an attempt to apply too much of what is, after all, just a simplistic and imperfect model to the reality of God Himself. In his haste to reject that application, however, he violates the same logical guidelines which he carefully presented in the immediately preceding pages of his discussion.

> This same theologian, in viewing the Trinity in the uncontroversial terms of man's encounters with God, explains it as different facets of His nature through which God has chosen to reveal Himself to man. God, he asserts, is altogether too vast for man, with his limitations in time and space, to acquire a complete picture of His entire nature. We can sample portions of this Divine Entity, however, and by thinking through the implications of the composite picture that He has given us through Scripture, we perceive His Trinitarian nature and the necessity for it. This experiential description is, I think, a valid one and has the advantage of being safely neutral with respect to gender. It is certainly the most intuitively satisfying characterization of the Trinity that I have seen to date. Yet such an exclusively man-centered description yields a disappointing poverty of information about God Himself, leaving the reader to ask why, if God does indeed have a Trinitarian nature, He is so reluctant to share a picture of that characteristic with us in terms of His intrinsic functional attributes. It would seem, after all, that

a God-centered intuitive understanding would naturally lead to a greater appreciation of Him, and consequently a greater love toward Him on the part of His subjects. One might easily suspect, as a matter of fact, that those individuals in the past who were named in the Book of Hebrews, did indeed have personal insights into the nature of God beyond those which the usual churchgoer might have access to via his pastor or his reading of Scripture.

The description of the Trinity that Dr. McGrath presented with profound understanding and subsequently discarded in haste begins on page 57 of *Understanding the Trinity*. An important continuation is presented twelve pages later, where the author appears to wish to tone down his rejection of the earlier model by presenting some qualifying remarks which suggest that perhaps he himself had some persistently lingering thoughts about the nature of the Holy Spirit that he didn't wish to assert directly:

> It was therefore assumed that light also needed to travel through something [as was the case for sound, upon which light was modeled], and the word 'aether' was coined to describe the medium through which light waves traveled. If you read old radio magazines, or listen to old radio programmes, you'll sometimes find people referring to "waves traveling through the aether." But by the end of the century it had become clear that light did not seem to need any medium to travel through. What had happened was simply that the logical necessity of one aspect of the model (sound) had initially been assumed to apply to what was being modeled (light), and this assumption was gradually recognized to be incorrect as the experimental evidence built up.
>
> And so it is with models of God. For example, we often use "father" as a very helpful model of God, emphasizing the way in which we are dependent upon God for our existence. But for every human child there is a human mother as well as a human father. This would seem to imply that there is a heavenly mother in addition to a heavenly father. But this

assumption rests upon the improper transfer of the logical necessity of an aspect of the model (father) to what is being modeled (God), in just the same way as the necessity of one aspect (the need for a medium of propagation) of the model (sound) was transferred to what was being modeled (light)...

...Although the strongly patriarchal structure of society of the time inevitably meant that emphasis was placed upon God as father (e.g., Jeremiah 3:19; Matthew 6:9), there are several passages which encourage us to think of God as our mother (e.g., Deuteronomy 32:18). We shall be considering these two images together, and ask what they tell us about God.

The first, and most obvious, point is that God is understood as the one who called us into being, who created us. Just as our human parents brought us into being, so God must be recognized as the author and source of our existence. Thus at one point in her history, Israel is chided because she 'forgot the God who gave [her] birth' (Deuteronomy 32:18; cf. Isaiah 44:2, 24; 49:15).

The second point which the model of God as parent makes is the natural love of God for his people. God doesn't love us because of our achievements, but simply because we are his children. "The Lord did not set his affection on you and choose you because you were more numerous than other peoples, for you were the fewest of all peoples. But it was because the Lord loved you" (Deuteronomy 7:7-8). Just as a mother can never forget or turn against her child, so God will not forget or gturn against his people (Isaiah 49:15). There is a natural bond of affection and sympathy between God and his children, simply because he has brought them into being. Thus God loved us long before we loved him (1 John 4:10, 19). Psalm 51:1 refers to God's "great compassion," and it is interesting to note that the Hebrew word for "compassion" (*rachmin*) is derived from the word for "womb" (*rechmen*). God's compassion towards his people is that of a mother towards her child (cf. Isaiah 66:12-13). Compassion stems from the womb.

A delightful feature of Dr. McGrath's discourses, remarkable for its rarity, is a description of God's loving relationship to mankind in romantic terms, a facet of God with which I wholeheartedly agree. Another feature of his presentation which I admire is his lengthy discussion of the necessities of Jesus' essence as both man and God, and of His resurrection. Yet another interesting item that he presents in his chapter entitled *A Personal God* is his strong intimation of free will with respect to salvation in the face of his self-proclaimed deep interest in Martin Luther. Here he makes statements such as "In no way does God force us to respond positively to him." He goes on to liken the notion of God's exclusive influence over our salvation as akin to rape rather than love. This item is worthy of further exploration.

Unfortunately, Dr. McGrath appears to be on less stable ground in his discussion of the Trinity. In his presentation of this dogma he avoids delving too deeply into God's intrinsic nature or attributes by substituting in its place a lengthy experientially-based account of Him in terms of His interaction with mankind. He is careful near the outset of his discourse, however, to distance himself from any notion that the Trinity includes a female Persona. He does so in his chapter entitled *Thinking About God* by noting that intellectual models are subject to misapplication through the improper assumption that every attribute of a model must apply to its counterpart in reality. As already noted, he cites as an example the wave characteristic of sound as a model for light, as was quoted directly from his work above.

But is the assumption of a Divine Mother in the economy of God necessarily a misapplication of the human parent model? It could be, but that's a long way from must be. Nowhere does Dr. McGrath justify the necessity that he associates with that application. Instead, he elevates a mere illustrative example to the status of a law, which easily could be construed as either less than honest or less than brilliant. (Actually, I recognize my lack of qualification to cast such judgment on a man who possesses doctorates in both theology and science; indeed, I suspect quite strongly that he is neither dishonest or less than brilliant. Rather, I think that his presentation here is an overzealous attempt to distance himself from an extremely controversial topic.)

Moreover, and again as we have already noted, a short twelve pages further along, Dr. McGrath equivocates a bit regarding the possibility of motherhood in God's economy, citing a number of Scriptural passages that describe God in a role more appropriate to motherhood than to fatherhood.

Almost at the end of his book it can be seen how Dr. McGrath rescues himself from this apparent inconsistency: as discussed in more detail below, he does not posit a distinct member of the Godhead who possesses the attributes of femininity; instead, he attributes this characteristic to the same Person as the Father. But rather than solving the problem of the feminine side of God, he comes dangerously close both to ultra-monotheism and modalism. Beyond that, he defines a God with gender characteristics indeed, but in the same Person. According to 1 Corinthians 6:9, 10, this suggests a model for a human malady known as hermaphroditism, which is contrary to Scripture, even to the extent of being labeled as unrighteous:

> *Know ye not that the unrighteous shall not inherit the kingdom of God? Be not deceived: neither fornicators, nor idolaters, nor adulterers, nor effeminate, nor abusers of themselves with mankind, nor thieves, nor covetous, nor drunkards, nor revilers, nor extortioners, shall inherit the kingdom of God.*

I find it hard to believe, given its treatment in Scripture, that in His own organization God would wish even to hint at sexual perversion, or even sexual difficulty.

The essence of McGrath's description of Jesus may be encapsulated in this passage, found in his chapter entitled *God as Three and God as One*: "The difficulties really begin with the recognition of the fundamental Christian insight that Jesus is God incarnate: that in the face of Jesus Christ we see none other than the living God himself. Although the New Testament is not really anything like a textbook of systematic theology, there is nothing stated in the great creeds of the church which is not already explicitly or implicitly stated within its pages. Jesus is understood to act *as God and for God:* whoever sees him, sees God; when he speaks, he speaks with the authority of God; when he makes promises, he makes them on behalf of God; when he judges us, he judges as God; when we worship, we worship the risen Christ as God; and so forth." Dr. McGrath goes on to characterize Jesus in his incarnate form as not actually comprising the fullness of God, but merely as a representative sample of God suitable for furnishing humanity with some comprehension, consistent with their limitations, of the far more complete spiritual God who resides in heaven. He claims in a similar vein that the Holy Spirit, like Jesus, is another manifestation of God, in this case one that indwells the believer, that furnishes another way by which redeemed mankind can encounter, or experience, God.

Dr. McGrath ends with this commentary:

> We can now see why Christians talk about God being a "three-in-one." One difficulty remains, however, which must be considered. How can God be three persons and one person at the same time? This brings us to an important point which is often not fully understood. The following is a simplified account of the idea of "person" which may be helpful, although the reader must appreciate that simplifications are potentially dangerous. The word "person" has changed its meaning since the third century when it began to be used in connection with the "threefoldness of God." When we talk about God as a person, we naturally think of God as being *one* person. But theologians such as Tertullian, writing in the third century, used the word "person" with a different meaning. The word "person" originally derives from the Latin word *persona*, meaning an actor's face-mask – and, by extension, the role which he takes in a play.

> By stating that there were three persons but only one God, Tertullian was asserting that all three major roles in the great drama of human redemption are played by the one and the same God. The three great roles in this drama are all played by the same actor: God. Each of these roles may reveal God

in a somewhat different way, but it is the same God in every case. So when we talk about God as one person, we mean one person *in the modern sense of the word*, and when we talk about God as three persons, we mean three persons *in the ancient sense of the word*. It is God, and God alone, who masterminded and executes the great plan of salvation, culminating in Jesus Christ. It is he who is present and active at every stage of its long history. Confusing these two senses of the word "person" inevitably leads to the idea the God is actually a committee, which, as we saw earlier, is a thoroughly unhelpful and confusing way of thinking about God.

One certainly could not accuse Dr. McGrath of being a tritheist. On the other hand, despite his denial on the back cover of the book that he entertains the heretical notion of modalism, he's on shaky ground there, being right on the edge or over it according to his own words.

Dr. McGrath is somewhat unique among other well-established theologians in that his scientific training has furnished him with an ability to be objective in his presentation and make use of useful intellectual tools such as models to make his points. Further, he at least addresses some notions that others avoid like the plague, as if they themselves might be infected by ideas they may have been taught were close to blasphemous. He has in common with the others, however, several notions regarding the Holy Spirit that are generally accepted within faithful Christendom: while all Members of the Trinity possess the same substance and are fully and equally God, they differ with respect to functional role; the role for the Holy Spirit conforms most closely to that associated with executive companion and motherhood; the Holy Spirit is a background Entity, more self-effacing than Father and Son; the Trinity (as confessed by the Church) is a mystery beyond man's comprehension. The 'others' who share these particular view with Drs. McGrath and Ware include Dr. Peter Masters (*The Faith*) and James R. White (*The Forgotten Trinity*).

I agree quite thoroughly with all of these points except the last, regarding the mystery which appears to be beyond comprehension, with which I disagree quite thoroughly. To me, the incomprehensibility in understanding the Trinity is another typical case of man's brain outsmarting his heart. What should be an extremely simple and intuitive understanding, man has turned into a riddle, in the process wrapping himself tightly around the intellectual axle.

A case could be made that in the many attempts made by scholars of Scripture to describe the Holy Spirit, they end up implying an association of the Holy Spirit with Wisdom. Wisdom, of course, is given a lengthy treatment in Proverbs, with a female gender association.

As I have noted, I appreciated Dr. McGrath's extensive use of models. I believe that they are so effective, as a matter of fact, that I'd like to offer one of my own: that of a war ship. In this model the commanding officer, or CO, would be the functional counterpart of the Father. Under rigid shipboard discipline there is only one leader of the entire vessel, and that is the CO. He must make the tough decisions and live with the consequences; correspondingly, it is his will, and his alone, that must be instantly obeyed by the rest of the crew. The counterpart of Jesus in this model is the action that results from the CO's orders. The next in the chain of command is the executive officer, or XO. The XO has the responsibility of executing, or carrying out, the CO's commands; like the XO's counterpart the Holy Spirit, it is the XO who makes the will of the CO actually happen. While the XO is subordinate to the CO, he is in an understudy mode, being in constant readiness to assume command should some misfortune befall the CO. Therefore, the XO is capable of being CO, but willingly assumes a subordinate position for the sake of the ship's welfare. One can readily perceive that the CO and XO are an interdependent pair, each having different but complementary functions. It is in these complementary functions that the CO serves in a male role and the XO in a female role. One might well argue that on a warship, both CO and XO are eminently masculine. Both, to be sure, are cut from the same masculine cloth, just as (I perceive) the Holy Spirit is male with respect to substance, proceeding from the Father. On the functional side of things, however, one must be careful to note that the XO doesn't initiate the basic commands, but rather responds to them in a subordinate manner by carrying them out in fulfillment of the CO's will. This responsive characteristic, I would assert, is eminently feminine. Note in this context the synergy in the complementary interaction, which indeed is suggestive of a male-female relationship. The only thing that could bring it closer and more effective would be the level of communication intrinsic to a love-based relationship, i.e. the marital union, which for that reason, in my mind, remains a more representative model of the relationship between Father and Holy Spirit than the shipboard chain of command.

Maybe it's not the case with God, but in the (human) marriage union, there is some functional ambiguity. I would love to visualize a well-groomed lawn, thus commanding my wife to mow it promptly, watching benignly from my deck chair as she executes my edict forthwith. I don't do that, however, comprehending somehow that it's not going to work out as I would wish. The end result would be that I would mow the lawn anyhow and work under the additional burden of having to peer out of black and swollen eye sockets. At any rate, I'd much prefer doing a little grunt work while enjoying a loving relationship with my life partner that points to the way we were made by God.

Five

THE PROBLEMS ASSOCIATED WITH AN INSISTENCE UPON A GENDER-NEUTRAL OR MASCULINE HOLY SPIRIT

I love my brother Jon. After all, we are twins. But sometimes I get the suspicion that his placenta was bigger than mine and he hogged the incoming nutrients. What's worse, when I confront him with that, he readily agrees as he pats me on the head condescendingly. He also smiles about it, which I find infuriating. I'm not sure that this phobia of mine is a contributing factor, but we also are fiercely competitive.

When Jon became a licensed pilot, I followed suit. When I took up SCUBA diving, so did Jon. Same with the Marines.

When I took up hang gliding, Jon bought an ultralight, an Eipper Quicksilver MX-2 two-seater. It was a beautiful craft. My admiration for it won him over and he allowed me to take lessons in flying it. We both were among the last to receive the Aircraft Owners and Pilots Association pilot's licenses for Ultralight Craft before AOPA got out of the business due to a rash of accidents and lawsuits.

Once in a while my brother and I would fly together, but we were somewhat on the heavy side, which tended to limit the performance of the craft and we were happier flying solo. The time eventually came when we decided to fly together again, at a point where we had gained so much weight that the unfortunate vehicle was barely able to take off.

The problem with that was that the runway was short, narrow and primitive, which didn't allow any margin for deviating from the runway heading. Compounding that limitation was a huge tree that stood precisely at the end of the runway. Further restricting our options was the performance of the engine, which, despite its mighty labors, was insufficient to the task of clearing the tree.

The biggest problem of all was that we were slow to appreciate the situation that we had gotten into until we were committed to taking off. Our response was a reprise of the Stan and Ollie comedy act, wherein I shouted to Jon, "Look what you got us into now!" His reply was a hurled oath, which included a command to shut up, and which elicited a like response from me. We traded insults in that manner, bickering all the way to the expected point of impact, whereupon an updraft raised us just above the treetop.

That incident didn't involve any confusion whatsoever; we both knew with certainly that our doom was approaching. What we were doing was simply assigning blame for the debacle.

But there are indeed times while aviating that one can get confused, especially if that one happens to be me. A good example, one that I recall with dread, is making a timed instrument approach under the hood to a new and strange airfield, in turbulence, with numerous background distractions. Given my limitations in that regard, I consider myself to be quite fortunate to have acquired an instrument rating. But at least I had the sense enough never to subject a passenger to the kind of situation where confusion of that brand could pop up.

But I had a flight instructor once who did encounter kind of a worst-case situation. And he wasn't flying under the hood, because he was flying in actual instrument conditions, complete with lightning, thunder, extreme turbulence, and no visibility out the windscreen.

And with a passenger. An airsick woman, who hurled her ample dinner past his shoulder onto the instrument panel, obliterating his only sources of information. He flew perfectly blind until he was able to wipe the goo off the instruments, a process that included the use of his undershirt while he was still wearing it, and while straining with all his might to prevent his own stomach from adding to the mess he was trying to clean up.

Judging from his eyeballs and the suppressed retching as he told the story to me, he'll be telling it until his dying day.

Confusion is not good. It bodes ill, the threat of something very wrong. It can be dangerous. In another sense, it can be harmful to the soul.

The overview presented in the previous chapter on the Church's understanding of the Godhead indicates a rather continuously-held view from just a few hundred years past the beginning of Christianity to the present in which gender was associated with the Holy Spirit in one of two ways, both of which had strong followings that currently still exist among the various sects and factions within the boundaries of recognized Christian belief: some Churches insisted upon a gender-neutral God, including the neutrality of the Holy Spirit, while others asserted the masculinity, albeit asexual, of all three Members of the Godhead, again including the Holy Spirit in that categorization. The difficulties attending either of these viewpoints, as we noted earlier, are both numerous and significant.

The first problem, and this applies to both the gender-neutral and all-male viewpoints, is one of confusion. Two teachers of the Bible of my personal acquaintance, one of whom is a close friend and an excellent pastor in other respects, have at separate times while adhering to the gender-neutral view, personally confessed to me their inability to fully understand the nature of the Holy Spirit. One of the teachers possesses a doctorate in Theology; the other was a respected long-time Bible Study lecturer. The tenor of this incomplete understanding demonstrated an awareness of a confusing inconsistency within the little understanding that they did possess. Their personal resolution of this problem was an admission that mankind was not given to fully understand God, and must wait until it sees God face-to-face in order to obtain a more complete and accurate picture of Him than it now possesses. The logical inconsistency lurking in the background of both of their minds was associated with the necessity, given the gender-neutral or all-male viewpoints of the Godhead, of its differentiation into separate Entities without a clearly-defined functional distinction among them. The most confusing aspect of this obscurity is the strength of the Godhead's unity in the face of the vagueness of its Members' respective roles.

The second problem, which again applies to both the gender-neutral and the fully masculine viewpoints, is the inability, given the lack of clearly-defined differentiation among the Members of the Godhead, to reconcile their unity of being with the necessity of a Trinitarian nature. This problem differs from the first in that while the first is merely confusing as to the importance and application of love in what appears to be a collegiate unity, this latter issue represents a sharp logical inconsistency.

One readily can grasp, given the nature of this apparent inconsistency, how the heresy of Modalism emerged. Modalism views the Godhead as consisting of one God, as opposed to the three distinct Entities of mainstream Christianity. This singular Individual, in the Modalist view, presents the three distinct attributes of Will, Power and Glory usually attributed to Father, Holy Spirit and Son as the situation and audience require.

The third problem is related to the first, extending the issue beyond mere intellectual confusion to the more significant one of loving God. Adding to the confusing sense of incompleteness, the intra-Godhead love, being limited by this view to that of *agape*, does not connote the sense of common ownership of each other that a more romantically-driven relationship would elicit. It is most difficult to love with fervor and passion a Godhead whose unity is seen to be based on commonality of thought and purpose, as in a corporate boardroom, than one whose unity is inextricably associated with a fervent, even possessive love akin to romance within its own Members. Yet, in contradiction to this difficulty, Scripture commands us, as directly stated in Deuteronomy 6:4 and 5 and Matthew 22:37 and 38, to love God with fervor.

The fourth problem is the disassociation in those viewpoints from the family connection that exists within the higher forms of animal life in Creation, and with the Scriptural admonitions and laws associated with family and heterosexuality.

The fifth problem is the weakness of gender distinction among all three Members of the Godhead, which contradicts the Scriptural portrayal of strong masculinity of both The Father and Jesus, as well as the proscriptions in both the Old and New Testaments against weak masculinity and sexual impotence. Among these are the following clearly-stated passages in both the Old and New Testaments:

> *He who is wounded in the stones, or hath his privy member cut off, shall not enter into the congregation of the Lord.*
> —Deuteronomy 23:1

> *Know ye not that the unrighteous shall not inherit the kingdom of God? Be not deceived: neither fornicators, nor idolators, nor adulterers, nor effeminate, nor abusers of themselves with mankind, nor thieves, nor covetous, nor drunkards, nor revilers, nor extortioners, shall inherit the kingdom of God.*
> —1 Corinthians 6:9 and 10

One of the more intelligent discussions of the Godhead that remains within the Church-imposed boundary of asexuality has been supplied by Catholic Father John Macquarrie in his book *Mary for all Christians*. In his chapter entitled "God and the Feminine", he acknowledges the incompleteness of male alone or female alone without its complement. While touching on the all-important notion of complementary otherness, he goes on to other topics rather quickly, largely overlooking the most important aspect of otherness, which is its necessity in supporting the noble selflessness intrinsic to God as emphasized throughout the Bible.

Father Macquarrie also openly states, reminiscent of medieval theologian Jerome Zanchius, that God transcends sex. How does he apply that concept that God is above matters of gender to his perception of the incompleteness of a single-gender Godhead? He does so in distressingly extra-Biblical fashion. Being well-read in psychology, Macquarrie turns to C. J. Jung and his concept of shared gender. In that context, Macquarrie asserts, all the Members of the Trinity share both male and female characteristics.

Many Catholic theologians, perceiving despite the Church's grand elevation of Mary that there were some elements of the feminine within the all-male Godhead, grasped onto the Jungian notion that each of the divine Entities possessed both male and female attributes. Here again is a view that suggests gender weakness in contradiction to Scripture. In addition to promoting a divine narcissism in distinct opposition to the general tenor of Scripture, this notion is logically untenable in the face of the pronounced masculinity of both the Father and Jesus Christ and the proscription against male neutrality in Leviticus 21:20 and against male femininity in 1 Corinthians 6:9. That leaves the Holy Spirit alone as the possible embodiment of the female gender.

As if the direct problems associated with the gender-neutral or all-male viewpoints of the Godhead aren't bad enough of themselves, they sometimes create collateral difficulties. Among some Christian communities the ever-present threat that these viewpoints will inhibit ardor in worship has led to further misunderstandings that are intended to correct their deficiencies and restore the fervor suggested by Scripture. One such compensating offshoot practice is the Catholic veneration of Mary as the primary female persona of our religion. Despite protestations to the contrary from Catholic authorities from the Pope down to the pastoral level, this veneration, as was noted in Chapter 4, approaches actual worship to such a degree that it represents a *de facto* integration of Mary into the Godhead. Indeed, Mary is endowed in the Catholic Church with a number of attributes that rightly belong within the Godhead, specifically the Holy Spirit.

Before proceeding further on the topic of the Catholic veneration of Mary, I wish to state at the outset that I consider the mistaken Catholic attribution to Mary of what rightfully belongs to the Holy Spirit to be far superior to the standard Protestant practice of overlooking these attributes altogether. I suspect, moreover, that God Himself might not look all that unfavorably toward this perceived mistake of the Catholic Church, to the point that perhaps the Holy Spirit Herself has a name in heaven, that name being Sophia Mary, of which the earthly Mary was a type in the same sense that Joseph and Isaac and a host of other precursors to Jesus represented Him.

As was noted in Chapter 4, the highest Church authorities themselves name Mary as Co-Redemptrix, Queen of Heaven and Mother of God, insist upon her sinless birth, and claim that she was assumed body, soul and spirit, into heaven. Yet, even Mary, although she was fully female, was stripped of her sexuality. The Catholic Church's assessment of moral purity as including sexual abstinence is amply demonstrated by her insistence on Mary's perpetual virginity, meaning that her husband Joseph was himself subjected to sexual abstinence for the entire period of his marriage to Mary.

The Catholic teachings on Mary beg for a number of comments. First, in opposition to the Catholic view on Mary's virginity, Scripture itself, in Matthew 13:55 and 56, notes that Mary had children other than Jesus:

> *Is not this the carpenter's son? Is not his mother called Mary?*
> *And his brethren, James, and Joseph, and Simon, and Judas?*
> *And his sisters, are they not all with us? From where, then,*
> *hath this man all these things?*

The Catholic position that these "children" were actually cousins rather than siblings of Jesus is logically weak, given that Scripture suggests in Matthew 1:24 and 25 that Mary's virginity was only temporary:

> *Then Joseph, being raised from sleep, did as the angel of the Lord had bidden him, and took unto him his wife, and knew her not till she had brought forth her first-born son, and he called his name Jesus.*

The Catholic Church's claims regarding Mary's virginity involve a chain of attributions to both Mary and the Holy Spirit that manifestly lack Scriptural justification. Indeed, with regard to this topic the Catholic Church displays a shockingly arrogant freedom of interpretation, all to justify a view that itself is at odds with Scripture.

A second comment elicited from the Catholic understanding of Mary relates to the mechanics of Jesus' birth. The primary information given in Scripture relating to the process is in Luke 1:30-35:

> *And the angel said unto her, Fear not, Mary; for thou hast found favor with God. And, behold, thou shalt conceive in thy womb, and bring forth a son, and shalt call his name Jesus. He shall be great, and shall be called the Son of the Highest; and the Lord God shall give unto him the throne of his father, David. And he shall reign over the house of Jacob forever; and of his kingdom there shall be no end.*

> *Then said Mary unto the angel, How shall this be, seeing I know not a man? And the angel answered, and said unto her, The Holy Spirit shall come upon thee, and the power of the Highest shall overshadow thee; therefore also that holy thing which shall be born of thee shall be called the Son of God.*

The Catholic Church views both the Father and the Holy Spirit as male. Therefore she perceives Mary as the only female associated with the birth of Jesus. Understanding Jesus to be the Son of the Father (the divine Will), the Church insists that the Holy Spirit is not the father of Jesus, and yet, noting that Luke involves the Holy Spirit in Jesus' birth, the Church in some undefined and logically contradictory way also considers the Holy Spirit to be the divine

Spouse of Mary in the creation of Jesus in the Flesh while claiming that the Father rather than the Holy Spirit was the father of Jesus.

In view of the functional femininity of the Holy Spirit there is nothing whatsoever contradictory or difficult to understand about Jesus' birth. Considering the union of Father and Holy Spirit as between the Will and the Means, it is readily understood that the Holy Spirit, responding to the Will of the Highest (the divine Father) fashions the seed of Jesus, perhaps in a rearrangement of the software code represented by Mary's DNA, which is then combined with Mary's egg in her womb. The resulting Implementation represents another representation of the Divine Word, namely Jesus in the flesh. This scenario, which is intuitively accessible, also enjoys the support of a passage in Genesis that is contradictory under the Catholic scenario. According to Genesis 3:14 and 15,

> *And the Lord God said unto the serpent, Because thou hast done this, thou art cursed above all cattle, and above every beast of the field; upon thy belly shalt thou go, and dust shalt thou eat all the days of thy life. And I will put enmity between thee and the woman, and between thy seed and her seed; he shall bruise thy head, and thou shalt bruise his heel.*

It is generally understood that the man (seed) in this passage is Jesus Christ. However, despite the fact that in general the seed is the male contribution to life whereas the female contribution is the egg, the seed in the Catholic scenario appears to belong to Mary. Given a female Holy Spirit, the male seed, representing the will of the Highest but fashioned by the Holy Spirit, is indeed, in a perfectly natural sense, the seed of the Woman, the woman in this case being the Holy Spirit.

The Protestant Church, to its own credit, generally acknowledges that Mary had children in the natural way after the birth of Jesus. However, as noted before, its indifferent stance regarding the issue which generally ignores the lack of femininity within the Godhead in the face of the strong Scriptural suggestion to the contrary is even more bizarre than that of her Catholic sister.

My third comment regarding the Catholic understanding of Mary pursues in more detail my praise to that understanding despite my opinion of it as a false viewpoint. Although the primary attribution should be made to the Holy Spirit, Mary may well be a part of it. This comment relates to the Catholic vision of Mary as representing the utmost in selfless nobility, a view with which I wholeheartedly concur. This vision is beautifully encapsulated in two Catholic commentaries on Mary, the first from Dominican Father Gerald Vann in a book entitled *Mary's Answer for our Troubled Times*, in which he addressed the hatred and suffering in the world during the Second World War. Like the title suggests, he wrote about Mary's own suffering while Jesus was on the cross, a theme which the Catholic Church frequently visits. While Father Vann's scenario may not be historically accurate, it certainly captures the essence of Scripture's portrayal of Mary in a magnificent way. It represents a stunning and deeply moving demonstration of nobility on Mary's part, which is entirely consistent with Scripture's portrayal of a major function of femininity, which is to evoke nobility from her masculine complement.

Father Vann talked of Mary's concentration of gaze and rapt, exclusive focus on Jesus as He endured His suffering. He contrasted the mutual sorrow-laden silence between her and Jesus with the noisier, more self-serving lamentations of the other women, developing a picture of Mary of stoic determination. She had a task, Vann claimed. This task involved the double sorrow of the mother as she watched the torments of the Son, and of the girl who flinched at the sight of naked evil and cruelty destroying innocence and beauty and love. She remained silent, because it was not for her to find an emotional outlet for her grief, for she is here because of Him, to fulfill her vocation as mother by helping Him to fulfill His as Savior. "In her," Vann claims, "there are two conflicting agonies: the longing to save Him from His agony and the effort to help Him to finish His work. It is the second that she must do, giving Him to the world on the Cross as she has given Him to the world in the stable."

Another beautiful representation of Mary in Catholic lore is a historic incident that took place just outside Mexico City in the year 1531. In that tale, as related by Father John Macquarrie in his book *Mary for all Christians,* an apparition of Mary appeared to a peasant, one Juan Diego. At the time, Juan's uncle was very ill, to the point of near-death. He spent a day trying to relieve his uncle's sufferings and left him only on Tuesday, to get a priest. An apparition of Mary barred his way. She told him,

> My little son, do not be distressed and afraid. Am I not here who am your Mother? Are you not under my shadow and protection? Your uncle will not die at this time. This very moment his health is restored. There is no reason now for the errand you set out on, and you can peacefully attend to mine. Go up to the top of the hill: cut the flowers that are growing there and bring them to me.

As Juan's uncle was awaiting the priest, his room was filled with light. A luminous figure of a young woman appeared. He was indeed cured, but that's not the essence of this story. The main event occurs with Juan, who obeys the order to go to the flowers on the hill.

Juan Diego didn't expect to see flowers on the hill because it was the middle of winter. But he did indeed find flowers there. They were Castilian roses. He cut them as Mary had instructed and carried them back to her in his crudely-woven cape. She spent some time arranging the flowers, and then tied the corners of the cape behind his neck to prevent the roses from falling out. She told him to let only the bishop see the sign that she had given him.

When he reached the bishop's palace several servants made sport of him, pushing him around and trying to snatch the flowers from his cape. But the flowers dissolved when they reached for them. Amazed, they let him go. When he reached the bishop, Juan Diego untied the corners of the cape and as the ends dropped the flowers fell out in a jumbled heap. The disappointed peasant became confused as to the purpose of his visit. But then he was astonished to see that the bishop had come over to him and was kneeling at his feet. Soon everyone else in the room had come near and they all were kneeling with the bishop.

Juan Diego's cape now hangs over the altar in the basilica of Our

Lady of Guadalupe in Mexico City. Over eight million persons were baptized there in the six years that followed this event. Many millions more of people since that time have knelt before the two-piece cape, coarsely-woven of maguey fibers, for imprinted on it is an intricately detailed, beautiful figure of Mary. In her graceful posture she appears kind and lovable. She is surrounded by golden rays. Fifteen hundred persons a day still visit the shrine. The image is available on the Internet by Googling on "Juan Diego".

Some items of interesting information have come to my attention regarding Our Lady of Guadalupe, as the Catholic Church has named this apparition. Although I have yet to verify this information, I'll pass it along. First, She apparently never identified Herself to Juan Diego as Mary, but rather as Juan Diego's Mother. Second, Her image, as can be seen by Googling Juan Diego, matches that of the Aztec goddess. Third, according to a Mexican theologian as referenced in http://www.laermita.org/spanish/articulos/senoraguad. htm, the indigenous converts to Christianity, in opposition to the Catholic insistence on perceiving the apparition as Mary, refused to worship Her as such and insisted themselves upon worshiping Her as God.

Of all the difficulties associated with failing to identify the Holy Spirit as female, the worst is yet to be noted: the falling away of the Church into acceptance of the forbidden practice of homosexuality while failing to respond firmly against the threat of Islam. Here the issue is not intellectual but one of survival.

At present, despite the obvious fact that Scripture itself in Leviticus 18 and 20 and in Romans 1 describes homosexuality as an abomination, many mainstream Churches are accepting active homosexuals in their congregations, not only as laypersons, which would be acceptable to many Christians, but as Church authorities. And, if they take rather loose views of the authority of Scripture, why shouldn't they? The Godhead Itself, as they perceive it, is quite weakly connected to sexuality. If God, then, resides some distance away from matters sexual, why should He care?

On the other hand, if human sexuality is somewhat representative, shadowy as it may be, of that aspect of the Godhead, wherein the Godhead itself represents a Divine Family consisting of Father, Mother and Son, then it can be readily perceived that homosexuality in the human domain rather openly violates the human representation of the Godhead. This view cannot but elicit a firmer, logically-based stance against that practice among members of the Church, perhaps even help to lift her up from her present survival-endangering apathy. (I should point out here that God frowns upon other sexual sins, including those committed by heterosexuals, such as infidelity to a marriage partner, and for precisely the same reason that they also represent violations of type.)

In fact, the growing issue of homosexuality within the Church is but a small part of the much larger problem of the variety of sexual perversions taking place within a significant portion of the Christian community, even among those who profess to be conservative in their outlook. It's not a minor problem. It's so enormous, in fact, that it overshadows the issue with gays, rendering hypocritical many of those within the Christian leadership who are outspoken with regard to homosexuality. The real issue is this: given the denial of strong femininity within the Godhead, sexuality isn't considered to be relevant to God, and the correlation of sexual deviation of any flavor with violation of type just isn't on the table. Under the current understanding of the Godhead, the problem isn't limited to the denial of a role model for women, who constitute fully half the world's population. Serious as that particular issue is, the menfolk suffer too, for the present vision of God embraced by the Church denies them an appreciation of the importance of the feminine to God or even its relevance, placing both women and sexuality in the category of elements foreign to God.

The bottom line is that in the minimization of sexuality regarding our creation in the image of God, an extensive list of possible deviations from the standard of a monogamous male-female relationship is fair game—even for Christians.

Maybe even especially for Christians. Quite recently in a *Prophecy News Watch* enews article, it was estimated that almost eighty percent of Christian men regularly indulge in the viewing of pornography. It's not difficult to imagine where that behavior leads. The number of actual pornography addicts is about half of those. That's a very distressingly large portion of the Church. In effect, the cleansing of God of sexuality has not led to the cleansing of Christians from sexual deviation. To the contrary, it has had precisely the opposite effect. Not only have women been degraded in this monstrous misrepresentation of the Godhead, but Christian men have allowed themselves to be degraded as well. It doesn't end there—degradation, whether or not it is perceived as relevant to God, leads directly to alienation from God.

Of perhaps equal danger to the Christian Church is the attempt to assimilate the Muslim faith into Christianity in the name of ecumenicism. This can't be done without destroying the Trinitarian essence of Christianity, as the Bible and the Quran are in sharp disagreement over some very basic issues. Among the foremost of these incompatibilities is the Muslim monotheism, in which their god Allah is perceived as the Father alone, unencumbered with Jesus and the Holy Spirit as companions in Godhood. To them, Jesus is not God, but merely a prophet. Nor, to them, is the Holy Spirit a Person who shares Godhood with the Father.

In contrast to this view, Christians perceive God as one within a Trinitarian Godhead. It is here that the mainstream Christian Church is weak and open to perversion by other, more man-centered and materialistic religions like Islam, for Christians themselves have such a vague understanding of the Holy Spirit that even they fail to comprehend how God can manage strict unity in the face of threeness. They simply accept that it is what it is, but when threatened with intellectual attacks on this apparent inconsistency they have absolutely no answer.

On the other hand, as with the homosexuality issue, the Christian individual who perceives the Holy Spirit as feminine has no difficulty whatsoever in addressing the issue with Islam. He merely extends that perception of the Holy Spirit's femininity to one in which the Godhead is a Divine Family. In that context, of course, the oneness of God is in the Family, its Trinity of Members being subordinate to that Entity. Given that view, the Christian can readily and quite logically reject the Islamic perception of God.

Six

THE BENEFITS ASSOCIATED WITH AN UNDERSTANDING OF THE HOLY SPIRIT AS A FULLY-GENDERED FEMALE

Clarity of thought, unlike its opposite, confusion, is generally benign. Good things happen when straight thinking is engaged. Problems are solved. Things get done. Happiness prevails.

Back in the somewhat distant past, cars were a lot simpler, so they were understandable. I remember driving our car up a mountain highway when the engine suddenly died. I lifted the hood, did some basic trouble-shooting and identified the problem as a faulty fuel pump. With a basic wrench I undid two bolts and lifted off the fuel pump. Then I unfastened the top with a screwdriver, whereupon the problem immediately became apparent as a torn diaphragm. Hitching a ride to the nearest town (another thing that was a lot more commonplace back when), I bought a new diaphragm from the local auto supply store and, after hitch-hiking back to my car, was back on the road in another ten minutes. Several years later, but when vehicles were still on the simple side and when attempting to return home after fishing with my new family in a mountain lake, the car failed to start. Basic troubleshooting procedures identified the problem as a bad starter solenoid. Being near a rural junkyard that I knew well from previous outings, having flown into it in the evenings when thermal activity had died down and the only flights to be had were sled rides, I hiked over to it, and within a quarter hour had a solenoid in my hand. Again, we were on the road in less than an hour.

Cars are so complicated these days that when opening the hood, I can't even find a fuel pump. I can't even find the spark plugs in the maze of pipes and tubing. There's just no way that I could even begin to sort out a problem with my engine. Even if I could manage to identify what component had failed, I'd never be able to find it. And even if I did find what may have been the cause of the problem, I'd probably need to have an electron microscope to inspect the offending circuitry, along with, of course, PhDs in a number of scientific fields to interpret the microscopic rat's nest in the field of view. And then, even if, by some miracle, I was correctly able to diagnose the problem, it's highly doubtful that an appropriate fix would be available at the local auto parts store. Give me simple and readily understandable any day over complicated and confusing.

Scripture portrays both the Father and Jesus as eminently masculine, so masculine they must remain. Scripture, however, is far more ambivalent as to the gender of the Holy Spirit. If indeed the Holy Spirit is functionally feminine, this situation immediately introduces romance into the intra-Godhead relationship. Romance, in turn, elicits an appreciation of fervent, passionate love, as directly expressed in the Song of Solomon, as well as the notions of mutual ownership, complementary otherness in harmonious partnership, the transcendence of family over individuality, and strength of gender. All these notions are fully compatible with the following attributes of God as described in Scripture:

Fervor of love, both within the Godhead and by the observer toward the Godhead.

Heterosexuality: in this context, homosexuality is seen as a violation of type, since strong and full gender pertains to the Godhead Itself (keeping in mind the numerous other sexual transgressions other than monogamous male-female marital unions that also represent violations of type).

A full reconciliation of unity and Trinity: unity is perceived in the family nature of the Godhead, whereas individuality is seen within the Members of the Holy Family.

Selfless nobility: selfless devotion to the complementary Other leads to the elimination of self-absorption and narcissism.

Gender differentiation supports an understanding of the Godhead and the Holy Spirit that is both intuitive and logical.

In brief, a gender-differentiated view of the Holy Spirit is intuitively easy to grasp and is quite beautiful and harmonious with the Scriptural portrayal of God as well, while in its self-consistency it permits the viewer to hold fast to his perception of Scripture as inerrant in the original and inspired by the Holy Spirit. A viewpoint of the Godhead as a divine Family causes the confusion to evaporate rather abruptly, answering all the intellectual difficulties instantly at the levels of both the mind and the heart. Not only does it address the confusion head-on, but with it the Godhead Itself becomes open-ended with the awesome prospect of expanding to admit the Church, as the Bride of Christ, as an additional Member.

The notion of the spiritual Church becoming a Member of the Godhead raises some interesting possibilities about the nature of heaven. At the very least, heaven in this context becomes an exciting, dynamic entity wherein we, as members of the Church, are busily involved at Jesus' side in whatever loving business He may be engaged in, which may well involve creative activity.

In the context of this gender differentiation, wherein the Church stands alongside Jesus as His Partner, Paul's letter to the Ephesians displays a concept of the Church's marriage to Christ that is breathtakingly beautiful in the richness of its imagery of a spiritual marriage which represents the best, and more, that an earthly marriage can offer. Described here is not a partial marriage that is never consummated, but rather a marriage in which the partners belong to and complement each other in perfect harmony. Here also is a partnership in love that is anything but barren: our expectation is that it will give birth to something yet to be understood, but to which the Church in the spiritual realm can endow her love in union and joint ownership with her divine Husband. Moreover, it is a marriage that presents Father and Holy Spirit to us as adoptive In-Law Parents wherein the Trinity is anything but static, itself morphing into a Quaternary union. It is a view of God where it is easy and natural to love with ardor in a spontaneous manner and one in which Jesus Christ belongs to us in a way that would be inconceivable under the traditional view.

Paul E. Billheimer captured the essence of this relationship between Jesus and His Church in his book *Destined for the Throne*, which lived up to its cover billing as "A Remarkable New Perspective on the Eternal Destiny of the Bride of Christ", and which Billy Graham claimed to have been inspired in his forward to it. Excerpts from the Introduction and Chapter 1 are given below:

> The following chapters present what some consider a totally new and unique cosmology. The author's primary thesis is that the *one* purpose of the universe from all eternity is the production and preparation of an Eternal Companion for the Son, called the Bride, the Lamb's Wife. Since she is to share the throne of the universe with her Divine Lover and Lord as a judicial equal, she must be trained, educated, and prepared for her queenly role.
>
> From this it is implicit that romance is at the heart of the universe and is key to all existence. From all eternity God purposed that at some time in the future His Son should have

an Eternal Companion, described by John the Revelator as 'the bride, the Lamb's wife' (Rev. 21:9) John further revealed that this Eternal Companion in God's eternal purpose is to share the Bridegroom's throne following the Marriage Supper of the Lamb (Rev. 3:21). Here we see the ultimate purpose, the climactic goal of history.

As in the case of Adam, God saw that it was not good for His Son to be alone. From the very beginning it was God's plan and purpose that out of the riven side of His Son should come an Eternal Companion to sit by His side upon the throne of the universe as a bona fide partner, a judicial equal, to share with Him His sovereign power and authority over His eternal kingdom. 'Fear not, little flock, for it is your Father's good pleasure to give you the kingdom' (Luke 12:32). 'To him that overcometh will I grant to sit with me in my throne, even as I also overcame and am set down with my Father in his throne' (Rev. 3:21).

To be given a kingdom is more than to internalize kingdom principles and ethics. That is only one phase of it. To be given a kingdom is to be made a king, to be invested with authority over a kingdom. That this is God's glorious purpose for the Church is authenticated and confirmed by Paul in 1 Corinthians 6:2-3: 'Do ye not know that the saints shall judge the world? . . . Know ye not that we shall judge angels?' This is an *earnest* of what Jesus meant when He said, "The glory that thou gavest me I have given them." (John 17:22)

This royalty and rulership is no hollow, empty, figurative, symbolical, or emblematic thing. It is not a figment of the imagination. The Church, the Bride, the Eternal Companion is to sit *with* Him on His throne. If His throne represents reality, then here is no fantasy. Neither joint heir can do anything alone (Rom. 8:17).

We may not know why it pleases the Father to give the kingdom to the little flock. We may not know why Christ chooses to share His throne and His glory with the redeemed.

We only know that He *has chosen* to do so and that it gives Him pleasure.

Billheimer stopped short of asserting that the Church, in her spiritual form, may be integrated into the Godhead, nor did he directly imply that a feminine element exists within the Trinity. For example in his Chapter 2, page 37, he commented: "As sons of God [speaking of the individuals within the Church], begotten by Him, incorporating into their fundamental being and nature the very 'genes' of God, they rank above all other created beings and are elevated to the most sublime height possible short of becoming members of the Trinity itself."

But Billheimer came very close to those two intimately related associations. Two pages earlier, on page 35, he stated "Thus, through the new birth – and I speak reverently – we become 'next of kin' to the Trinity, a kind of 'extension' of the Godhead." Even more telling, in a footnote at the end of that chapter, he claimed "There is a clear and convincing implication in Genesis 1:27 that sex, in its spiritual dimension, constitutes an element of the image of God."

Regarding Billheimer's comment on not knowing "why it pleases the Father to give the kingdom to the little flock," I do believe that Scripture supplies the answer to that question as to why Christ chooses to share: because, in harmony with the selflessness intrinsic to the Him, the Father Himself chose to share, as I noted in my novel *Buddy*:

That night She was there, looking at him fondly when he awoke. "It's time we got into some serious theology," She remarked as he rubbed the sleep out of his eyes.

"Serious theology? What do you think you've been giving me?"

"Just the basics of Jesus in the Old Testament. Beyond that, you'll have to know how He came to be. You could get it yourself out of the Bible, but you don't have time for that. After all, the vast majority of Christians never do get it. Sadly, that's the situation out there, so that's one thing I'm going to take care of with you right now. Earl, you've been blessed. You have a special mission in this life, something to add a splash of color to God's grand tapestry. For that, you'll need to be familiar with Jesus' family roots. Then you'll really understand who you'll be in love with." She reached out to brush a wisp of hair from his forehead, but dallied with a lock, twirling it lovingly in her fingers.

"Earl," She continued presently, "Jesus and I were always part of the Father, but at the very beginning there was no separation. We existed together as One, and that One was the Father, the Divine Will. Being alone and in full command of Himself, He had the choice to remain in that state and retain within Himself absolute power and authority over everything that He would subsequently create." A tear leaked out from her eye. She dabbed at it with a finger.

"But then," She said, regaining control over her emotions, "the Father did something that was the essence of selflessness. It was of an order of nobility that transcends everything that came after."

"Even Jesus on the cross?" he asked in wonder. "That was pretty painful. And humbling."

"Yes. Even that. The Father was first to humble Himself. He set the standard. And yes, it was painful too. Remember that He possessed everything that was and ever will be. He chose to give that up."

"What did He do?"

"He chose to manifest an Other out of Himself, giving up part of Himself in the process and restricting His portion in everything that is or ever will be to that of one Member of a Partnership. He decided to share His exalted position with that Other. But here's the great beauty of what he did: in relinquishing His singleness He added love into the mix. And through this love He again became One with His Other."

This union between Father and Holy Spirit, as I also noted in

Buddy, bore fruit in the begetting of Jesus Christ, the Son and the Word, at the point at which, in Jesus, time began:

"For instance, in Revelation 3:14, Jesus describes Himself as the beginning of the creation of God. Now think about that, Earl. What does that imply?"

"Well . . .yeh, it does suggest a beginning."

"Yes, and that contradicts the teaching that you brought up, doesn't it? Which really means that the teaching itself leaves something to be desired. I'll quote next from Genesis 1:

"In the beginning God created the heaven and the earth. And the earth was without form and void; and darkness was upon the face of the deep. And the Spirit of God moved upon the face of the waters. And God said, Let there be light: and there was light. And God saw the light, that it was good: and God divided the light from the darkness. And God called the light Day, and the darkness he called Night. And the evening and the morning were the first day."

"Earl, what was that light?"

"Well, it must have been the sun." She made it sound like a trick question. What else could it be?

"No no. You need to pay more attention to what you read. On what day was the sun made? Think, Earl."

"Oh. Yes. The sun and moon were made on the fourth day."

"That's better." She made a frown, and then softened it with the tiniest of winks. "That light, Earl, was the first Word that God spoke, Jesus Christ. If you read the first few verses of Genesis 1 very closely, you'll grasp that the Spirit of God, the Holy Spirit, was moving in response to the Father, the Divine Will. He first willed Light, and the Light was also the Word. Listen to the Gospel of John. In the very first chapter, he says that,

"In the beginning was the Word, and the Word was with God, and the Word was God. The same was in the beginning with God. All things were made by him; and without him was not any think made that was made. In him was life; and the life was the light of men. And the light shineth in darkness; and the darkness comprehended it not."

"You see? Jesus is the Word, the Light and the Life. Awesome, isn't it?"

"Yeh. That means that He existed before He came in the flesh, all right. But not necessarily forever."

"Careful. With your dimensional limitation you can't even perceive the meaning of eternity. You can simply say that He existed before time began, which is the meaning that Scripture intended to convey. In fact, there was a man by the name of Arius who was pretty popular around the fourth century. He started one train of thought by saying that there was a time when Jesus was not, and extended that to imply that Jesus was inferior to the Father. He equated that perceived inferiority with the notion that Jesus wasn't God, or at least God of the same order. That notion was immortalized as the famous 'Arian heresy'. Arius violated common sense. A human father naturally predates his son because both of them reside in the domain of time. But as Jesus as the preexistent Son of God represents all of creation, time itself began with Him. For that reason the question of whether Jesus sequentially followed the Father has no meaning. Even if the Son did follow the Father sequentially in time, it still wouldn't imply inferiority. The same can be said of the Holy Spirit, who also existed with the Father when time began. The word "eternity" references time, so it is logically accurate to agree with the Council of Nicaea which in 325 A.D. defined them to be coexistent with God for all eternity, although the council probably was being somewhat reactionary to Arius' belief. But at any rate, as far as you humans are concerned, Jesus existed from eternity as you can comprehend it."

Given the view of heaven suggested by a fully-gendered Godhead, I'm rather excited about the prospect. When we get there, we'll be dimensionally compatible with Jesus, which will give us the ability to intuitively understand the eternity issue as well as time in general. But not only will we understand more, we'll be doing more, and in all we do there'll be an abundance of love and intimacy in our relationship with each other and with our divine Spouse, Jesus Christ.

Seven

RECONCILING CLAIMS AGAINST A FEMININE HOLY SPIRIT

My high school trigonometry teacher, the one who entertained lascivious thoughts toward Lorelei, wasn't the first teacher with whom I had an odd encounter. In the ninth grade, I had Mr. Edwards as my teacher in earth science, a man I remember quite vividly for the disturbing information he hurled in my direction after class. The bell had rung and the other students had dashed for the door, which was our usual mode of exit. I hung back that day, because a large wall map of the world caught my attention. I had walked up to the map and was studying it intently when Mr. Edwards verbally accosted me.

"Don't even think about it!" he shouted from behind his desk. Red-headed and red-faced, he was Irish to the core and way beyond, and he had a voice to match his brash demeanor. That's all he had to say. I remember being amazed that he knew exactly what I was thinking, and that in that one short sentence I knew that he knew, and he knew that I knew that he knew.

"They don't fit!" he continued. "It's just an accident of geography. Chance, if you will. Africa and South America were never joined; science now knows without a doubt that they were separate continents from the beginning of the world billions of years ago." He dismissed me from his mind and went back to the papers he was reviewing. I kept looking at the map, not sure what to believe. It seemed so basic, so obvious, and yet here was a man of science, an expert in the field, an authority telling me different. I finally shrugged my shoulders, accepting the fact that Mr. Edwards knew far more about the subject than I did.

Many years later I got wind of the fascinating new theory of plate tectonics, and the collateral damage it did to Mr. Edwards' understanding of geology. His authority, at least as far as I was concerned, was overthrown in an instant, my only regret the time I had wasted accepting his pronouncement. But at least I learned something: *don't accept everything that "experts" say as truth.*

That new understanding about authorities and truth was reinforced in college, where I learned that respected scientists had declared around the beginning of the twentieth century that virtually everything knowable about the universe had been uncovered; all that remained was the calculation of certain physical constants and other rather mundane cleanup work. That pronouncement was made, of course, before Einstein had arrived on the scene, development started on atomic physics and quantum mechanics, the Van Allen radiation belt was discovered, exploration had begun of our solar system and the uncovering of the vast intricacy of the molecular machinery of life had not yet borne its amazing fruit.

Several years after college, I became fascinated over the controversy between Immanuel Velikovsky and Carl Sagan regarding the visitation on earth of catastrophes of planetary scope. Sagan, as a member in excellent standing of the scientific community, was the expert, whereas Velikovsky was an interloper who was daring to trespass on the intellectual property of the evolution/uniformitarianoriented community. What really stuck in Sagan's craw was that Velikovsky was basing much of his innovative theory of enormous catastrophes that occurred within the memory of man on the Bible, specifically the accounts of Moses around the fifteenth century B.C. regarding the Exodus, and, about fifty years later, of Joshua's long day (and America's long night) and of Isaiah in the eighth century B.C. How dare the man contaminate science with notions of God, Sagan fumed. But Velikovsky had predicted certain things on the basis of his thesis, like his certainty that when man was able to measure the surface temperature of Venus, he would find the planet to be so hot that it wouldn't support human life. Sagan scoffed at the notion, asserting on the basis of his own spectroscopic studies of Venus that the planet was earthlike in temperature. We all know how Sagan's notion worked out in that regard. In fact, Sagan and others within their scientific clique were continually surprised by what our space probes were finding, all of which confirmed Velikovsky's predictions and negated Sagan's sneering, intellectually empty rebuttals. Most profoundly, Mars was found to have suffered immense damage, which was a revelation that would have been unthinkable to the mainstream scientific community back when.

Then along came the father-son Alvarez team, who managed to toss the mainstream uniformitarian notion into the intellectual trash heap, regardless of the fact that the scientific community continues to dig for it among the rest of their intellectual garbage, attempting to somehow resurrect it and restore it to its former glory. Nat Geo is doing its best to help out, but so far the collective IQ of the population that it and the media are managing to convince is steadily progressing downward to zero.

More recently, the biological sciences are making amazing strides, all of which are undercutting the theory of evolution.

The bottom line is that a revolution has been taking place within the scientific community for several years now. Not much is being said about it to the public at large; nevertheless, a good many scientists who have been venerated over the last several decades as "experts" and "authorities" have been uncovered as entertaining embarrassingly obsolete and downright wrong views on the subjects on which they had so arrogantly held forth.

Can the same be said about our religious theological "authorities"? I'll give you an example and let you decide. For starters, there are Catholic Christian authorities and Protestant Christian authorities who are theologically separated by a very large intellectual fence. While Protestant "authorities" pronounce their Catholic brethren to be entirely wrong about their veneration of Mary, their papacy, and the Eucharist, to name but a few items of contention, their Catholic counterparts are equally vehement in pronouncing their Protestant brethren lacking in their understanding in these same areas. What does this say about the objective truth of these matters? *Hint: both sides can be wrong, or one side can be wrong and the other right. But both sides cannot be right, which requires that at least one very large group of theological "experts" be wrong.*

Aw, I'll just come out and say it without beating around the bush. Both sides are burdened with some very wrong theology. To back that up, I'll first address a few glaring difficulties with the Catholic Church. A big one is the Catholic insertion of the papacy between us and our One Mediator, Jesus Christ, in open contradiction to Scripture, not only in Hebrews, but in general throughout the Bible. Another big one is the Catholic near-deification of Mary, wherein the Church laity is called upon to communicate with Mary at the expense of praying to Jesus or the other Members of the Godhead. A third is the Catholic insistence on Mary's perpetual virginity, despite the fact that the virgin birth of Jesus was a functional necessity that allowed Him to be both God and man, free of Adam's original sin and carried with it no connotation that moral purity involved sexual abstinence. A fourth and fifth are Mary's immaculate conception and bodily assumption into heaven, which are extra-Biblical assumptions. A sixth is the continuing corruption within the Church leadership, its latest manifestation being unthinkable sexual misconduct, a difficulty that was preventable under a more perfect understanding of God and what He is looking for in mankind. And then there's the issue about the opulence of the Vatican and its treasures of art, gold and precious jewels, and of the pomp that accompanies all these physical assets in spite of the clear Scriptural teaching that Jesus' kingdom is not of this earth.

Now, as to the equally grave difficulties associated with the Protestant Church. First, there is the overabundance of discord from one sect to another, indicating the same kind of theological error associated with the discord between the Catholic and Protestant Churches. While I have applauded such differences of opinion in the past as indicating that some Christians care enough about their faith to think about the issues, this unresolved squabbling also indicates a murky understanding. Much of this discord has to do with issues that are, at best, connected indirectly with Scripture, and, while at first glance that may seem to be somewhat trivial, most actually are quite important. Among these are the controversy over free will vs. election (Calvinism vs. Arminianism), infant baptism, the gifts of the Holy Spirit in modern Christianity, the meaning of prosperity, the almost complete indifference toward Mary and the denial, in open contradiction to Scripture (particularly John 3 and Ephesians 5), of feminine motherhood in the economy of God, and the sterility of the Godhead. And what's going on with all this falling away of the mainstream Churches from Scriptural truth, such as the popularity of the Chrislam movement, the ordination of Gays and the widespread ignorance of the Bible? To top off this list of ills is the odd indifference of some branches of the mainstream Protestant Church to the magnitude and nature of the love intrinsic to the Godhead and how this love harmonizes with and moderates the Godhead's other attributes.

But there's more. The Great Schism of 1054 that separated the Western Roman from the Eastern Orthodox Church goes beyond the quibbling between and within the Catholic and Protestant Churches. Among the multitude of divisive issues that fomented that split, the theological one labeled "the filioque" ("and from the Son") was one of the most serious. At some time around or before the sixth century A.D., the Roman Church tampered with the Nicene Creed, inserting the filioque into the original creed that described the Holy Spirit as proceeding from the Father only. This alteration was accepted by the papacy in 1014, and survived the Catholic-Protestant split in the Reformation, continuing to be accepted by both Catholic and Protestant Churches. The English version of this creed, which is included in the liturgy of many Sunday worship services to this day, is given below, where the brackets encapsulate the Roman addition:

> I believe in one God, the Father almighty, Maker of heaven and earth, and of all things visible and invisible. And in one Lord Jesus Christ, the only-begotten Son of God, begotten of the Father before all worlds, God of God, God of Light, very God of very God, begotten, not made, being of one substance with the Father, by whom all things were made. Who, for us men and for our salvation, came down from heaven, and was incarnate by the Holy Spirit of the virgin Mary, and was made man, and was crucified also for us under Pontius Pilate. He suffered and was buried, and the third day He rose again, according to the Scriptures; and ascended into heaven, and sits on the right hand of the Father, and He shall come again, with glory, to judge the quick and the dead, whose kingdom shall have no end. And I believe in the Holy Spirit, the Lord and Giver of Life; who proceeds from the Father [and the Son], who with the Father and the Son together is worshiped and glorified, who spoke by the prophets. And I believe one holy catholic and apostolic Church. I acknowledge one baptism for the remission of sins, and I look for the resurrection of the dead, and the life of the world to come. Amen

While the principle issue here is the multitude of divisions within Christianity that are suggestive of theological confusion, it is interesting to note that the filioque is another indication of a drifting away by the Western Church from the understanding of a feminine Holy Spirit in the primitive Church. Historically, the early Eastern Orthodox Church, like its predecessor Jewish religion, viewed the Holy Spirit as feminine and linked Her directly with Wisdom.

We thus approach our attempt at reconciliation with the understanding that while Scripture itself is inerrant in the original, the interpretations of it associated with mainstream theology are every bit as susceptible to human error and misunderstanding as other human endeavors.

> *And God said, Let us make man in our image, after our*
> *likeness; and let them have dominion over the fish of the sea,*
> *and over the fowl of the air, and over the cattle, and over all*
> *the earth, and over every creeping thing that creepeth upon*
> *the earth. So God created man in his own image, in the image*
> *of God created he him; male and female created he them.*
> —Genesis 1:26, 27

From this passage we get the idea that the gender separation is intrinsic to the Godhead itself. Are we reading too much into this? If this passage stood alone as supportive of that idea, we might be. But there are other passages like the following that dovetail well with that same interpretation:

> *And Adam said, This is now bone of my bones, and flesh of my*
> *flesh; she shall be called Woman, because she was taken out of*
> *Man. Therefore shall a man leave his father and his mother,*
> *and shall cleave unto his wife; and they shall be one flesh.*
> —Genesis 2:23, 24

In his letter to the Ephesians, Paul presents to the Church a remarkable mystery of great importance. It is to be treasured not only for its contribution to our future hope and expectation, but also to clarify our understanding of our God. This mystery is encapsulated in Ephesians 5:25-32:

> *Husbands, love your wives, even as Christ also loved the*
> *church, and gave himself for it; That he might sanctify and*
> *cleanse it with the washing of water by the word, That he*
> *might present it to himself a glorious church, not having spot,*
> *or wrinkle, or any such thing; but that it should be holy and*
> *without blemish.*
>
> *So ought men to love their wives as their own bodies. He*
> *that loveth his wife loveth himself. For no man ever yet hated*
> *his own flesh; but nourisheth it and cherisheth it, even as the*
> *Lord the church: For we are members of his body, of his flesh,*
> *and of his bones. For this cause shall a man leave his father*

and mother, and shall be joined unto his wife, and they two shall be one flesh.

This is a great mystery: but I speak concerning Christ and the church.

In dwelling upon this wonderful notion, we experience not only joy in understanding that our future spiritual role shall be as the Bride of Christ, but catch a glimpse of the true Trinitarian nature of God Himself. With that vision in mind, I'll enumerate and then address the several objections to it that have been lobbed in my direction by my theological betters.

Nine Objections

Without a doubt the most serious objection to a feminine Holy Spirit is the use in Scripture of masculine pronounce in reference to the Holy Spirit. The "He" issue, however, while being the most obvious, is not the only one that Church authorities use to support their claim that the Holy Spirit lacks a strong femininity. Several others, both Scriptural and extra-Scriptural, are brought to bear as well, including the following, for which I personally have been charged in discussions regarding my intellectual malfeasance in assigning the feminine gender to the Holy Spirit:

Scripture specifically claims in Galatians 3:28 that (in the resurrection) there is neither male nor female. Therefore, the spiritual realm is gender-neutral.

I have ignored Scriptural passages, such as Jeremiah 10:10-13, in which the Father claims as His own some attributes generally associated with the Holy Spirit.

I have been cautioned regarding what appears to be a hasty connection between Wisdom, as presented in the Book of Proverbs, and the Holy Spirit. It was noted in that regard that in the common interpretation of the purpose and nature of Proverbs, which is contained in the "prologue' summary (Proverbs Chapter 1), there is no compelling reason to make that connection.

It seems inappropriate, in the light of Paul's restrictions on the role limitations defined by Paul of females in the Church, of conferring Godhood on a female.

There are many within mainstream Christianity who perceive God as being above passion. This particular notion of God being greater than our feelings of romantic love was expressed by the medieval theologian Zanchius, who to this day enjoys a considerable following.

As I noted in my blog *friendofthefamily.wordpress.com*, I felt pretty much alone in my perception of the female nature of the Holy Spirit. It has been suggested to me that there usually are pretty good reasons for "being out there alone."

An objection was made that I may not be alone as I think: I seem to share my conviction with a collection of individuals who are not well-regarded in the conservative church, including thoroughly discredited Branch Davidian leader David Koresh and notoriously new-age adherent Oprah Winfrey.

In making my claims, I am assuming the responsibilities of a teacher of the Word of God, which should not be taken lightly.

In all, these nine objections represent a collection of all reasons advanced to me by those more theologically knowledgeable than me for rejecting the association of the female gender with the Holy Spirit. These objections will be rebutted below:

The "He" Issue

Undoubtedly the most influential objection to the view of a functionally feminine Holy Spirit has been the numerous references in Scripture to the Holy Spirit in terms of masculine pronouns, representing the big "He" issue, although less frequently the neuter pronoun "It" is also used. A partial listing of references to the masculine "He" or "Him" includes John 14:16, 14:26, 15:26, 16:7, 8 and 13-15, and Hebrews 3:7 and 10:15.

For the sake of argument, suppose that the demonstrable

gender switch from the Hebrew feminine to a basically Gentile masculine Holy Spirit is ignored and that the use of male pronouns for a functional female Entity is logically justified. If we were to summarize the possibilities, what would that justification consist of? It turns out that there are several plausible reasons, all of which permit a male descriptor to apply to a functionally female Holy Spirit. As I had noted in my Christian nonfiction work *Family of God* and in my novel *Buddy*, as well as in my blog *friendofthefamily. wordpress.com,* I had explained the various ways that Scripture may have quite logically referred to the Holy Spirit in terms of "He" within the context of a functionally female gender. As my arguments there fully acknowledged the Scriptural use of a male pronoun for the Holy Spirit, the number of repetitions in that use is meaningless to the argument: just one would have sufficed.

In both the books and the blog my implied definition of "female" was "complementary other." In neither venue did I connote in that description anything physical or overtly suggestive of a link between the spiritual gender that may be applicable to the Godhead with the manner in which sexuality is applied to humans, as such attributes that God may have in that realm are completely beyond our understanding. In no case was I attempting to contradict Scripture or to suggest that Scripture might possibly contradict itself. The reasons that I will present below for a male reference to the Holy Spirit imply no such contradiction.

Basically, I said in *Family of God* that the Holy Spirit, while performing an essentially female function in the context that I have defined in the introduction above, could also legitimately be considered to be male with respect to substance, composition or union. I went on to speculate that the Scriptural emphasis on the male substance as opposed to the female function may actually be a promise to mankind regarding his future spiritual participation in the Godhead as the Bride of Christ. This viewpoint, however, applies to the entirety of redeemed mankind who constitute the Church, and not to redeemed individuals, who simply comprise components of that Body.

A paradox stands in the way of internalizing this new and welcome information. This inconsistency first must be resolved in order that we may fully accept it. The issue is this: we, redeemed mankind, are collectively treated as masculine whereas in Scripture we are given to understand our spiritual role in relationship to Jesus as feminine. This conflict requires us to differentiate between our gender as an aggregate of individual elements and our gender in a functional application. Thus, regarding our future spiritual identity, as an aggregate we shall be male whereas functionally we shall be female.

I expanded on this thought in my blog *friendofthefamily.wordpress. com* by noting that as Bride of Christ, redeemed (spiritual) mankind itself, while being designated as male in composition (mankind is a male descriptor), will obviously be performing a female functional role that is harmoniously complementary to Jesus Christ.

Actually, the issue may be taken to a more basic level than that. According to Genesis 2:18-22, God fashioned Eve out of Adam. Therefore Eve, while being female in function, may be thought of as possessing the substance of her male predecessor.

A conflict of much the same nature exists in our understanding of the Holy Trinity: Among the Members of the Trinity, the First and Second Persons, as Father and Son, are naturally considered to be male in gender. Regarding the Third Person, the Holy Spirit, however, there is no small amount of gender ambiguity. Obviously, if future mankind can legitimately be male in composition and female in function, the same attributes may apply in an equally non-contradictory manner to the Holy Spirit, in Her feminine functional role as distinct from Her substance as originating from the masculine Father. Indeed, why would it "not be good", per Genesis 2:18, for Adam to be without a complementary other, yet be good for that situation to exist within the Godhead?

Scripture as most of us know it attempts to remove the ambiguity surrounding the Holy Spirit by routinely applying the pronoun 'He' to this Person. In doing so without explanatory or qualifying remarks, the Scripture handed down to us in the West automatically assigns only the male gender to this Divine Person. It has often been commented, however, by respected theologians, that Scripture elsewhere seems to develop an image of the Holy Spirit that is female in nature. We saw this in the review in Chapter 4 of some Christian authors who attempted to describe the nature of the Holy Spirit. To the Holy Spirit are regularly assigned the attributes of comfort, nurturing and compassion, supported by statements made by Jesus Himself. These female descriptors are functional attributes, whereas the pronoun 'He', when applied to the Holy Spirit in Scripture, refers to the Divine Person in the sense of object. There is a striking parallelism here with the object/function gender differentiation of the Church and in mankind itself. It is tempting to point to that parallelism to claim the same object/function gender differentiation of the Holy Spirit: male in substance, but female in function.

Could it be, then, that the use in Scripture of the pronoun 'He' in reference to the Holy Spirit, instead of constituting a gratuitous introduction of confusion, is related to this parallelism? Despite that possibility, the mainstream Christian Church is committed to its view of the Holy Spirit as being gender-neutral, masculine or sometimes even hermaphroditic in basic nature.

Up to this point, an argument has been made regarding the legitimacy of viewing the gender of the Holy Spirit differently between function and substance. As I noted at the outset of this argument and applied to the Church, this difference from function may involve other descriptors besides substance, such as composition and union, related to substance but with slightly different connotations. Returning to the human spiritual model of the Church, it is a fact that whereas functionally the Church is overtly feminine as set forth in Scripture, it consists of numerous individual elements which in the aggregate, the collective definition as mankind carries with it a male designation.

While substance or composition or both may be factors that legitimize the application of masculine descriptors to a feminine function, the most basic factor may simply be the notion of union, the loving merging of two complementary others into one. In marriage the male and female members are components of a greater unity than either of them alone and as one, they would rightly be addressed by the gender of the dominant Member, the male.

Exploring this notion further, we readily imagine that the relationship between Father and Holy Spirit is so perfectly close that the Holy Spirit is considered to be One with the Father, as suggested by the wife's use of her husband's surname in our own society. There is justification for that in Genesis 5:1 and 2, wherein the perfection of unity in love carries with it an implication with respect to the name of the female partner.

This is the book of the generations of Adam. In the day that God created man, in the likeness of God made he him; male and female created he them; and blessed them, and called their name Adam, in the day when they were created.

This is a love kind of thing. God never intended either a man or a woman to remain as an individual. Instead, He created them to be in union together, one man and one wife. This unity is emphasized by His calling them both by the name of the male, a custom that is practiced to this very day. In that context, the "He" associated with the Holy Spirit may be intended to convey the unity between Father and Holy Spirit, wherein the Holy Spirit is always considered not as separate, but united in everlasting love with the Father.

The significance of this passage to the view of the Holy Spirit as a Complementary Other to the Father is that it justifies the use of a male pronoun in referring to a basically female Holy Spirit. It implies that the bond between Father and Holy Spirit, representing the image upon which the bond between Adam and Eve was based, is so perfectly close that they can truly considered to be one. In that context, the male pronoun applied to the Holy Spirit would represent the perfection of that bond.

Of course, one can't ignore the possibility of a very simple yet profound explanation: that the Holy Spirit was sent to us in Jesus Christ's name, which, of course, is male.

After having said all that regarding the gender distinction between substance and function, I now will address a little-known but very significant complicating factor in this 'He' business, hinted at earlier, that may well settle the issue in favor of a fully feminine Holy Spirit without the necessity of making an object/function differentiation. It turns out that while we may still be able to claim that Scripture is inerrant in the original, the Scripture to which we have ready access isn't the original. It's been tampered with, probably at some time after Constantine made Christianity a state religion in the early fourth century A.D.

It is an undeniable fact that with regard to Scripture, "Church authorities" did indeed engage in a sexual cleansing operation, for not only were the Godhead and Mary stripped of their sexuality, but there is indisputable evidence that Scripture itself was altered to sexually mutilate the Godhead by substituting a weak all-male congress for what always was perceived by the Jews and also by the earliest Christians as a Divine Family consisting of Father, Mother and Son.

It wasn't always that way. In the Hebrew Old Testament, the Holy Spirit, as the *Ruah* or *Shekinah*, was viewed as feminine. The switch to masculinity occurred in the New Testament.

In Isaiah 51:9 and 10, for example, the King James Version reads:

Awake, awake, put on strength, O arm of the Lord; awake as in the ancient days, in the generations of old. Art thou not it who hast cut Rahab, and wounded the dragon? Art thou not it who hast dried the sea, the waters of the great deep; who hath made the depths of the sea a way for the ransomed to pass over?

The original, however, read as follows, and some Bible scholars assert that the neutering was deliberate:

Awake, awake, put on strength, O arm of the Lord; awake, as in the ancient days, in the generations of old. Art thou not She who hast cut Rahab, and wounded the dragon? Art thou not She who hast dried the sea, the waters of the great deep; who hath made the depths of the sea a way for the ransomed to pass over?"

According to an Internet search of "feminine Holy Spirit in the Hebrew Scriptures", multiple modern, deeply serious theologians and ancient language scholars share the view that the earliest Hebrew Christians had access to Scripture that presented the Holy Spirit as a feminine Persona; this feminine persisted within the Syriac and other Eastern branches of Christianity and within the Gnostic sect as well. A prime example of this is the Scriptural passage known as the Siniatic Palimpsest (a palimpsest is a recycled writing medium, wherein a second layer of writing was applied over the original, the original usually consisting of more important information) uncovered toward the end of the nineteenth century by Agnes Lewis. The original writing included portions of the Gospel of John of which a quote from Jesus Himself in John 14:26 asserts the following (translation attributed to Danny Mahar):

> *But She—the Spirit—the Paraclete whom He will send to you —my Father—in my name—She will teach you everything; She will remind you of what I have told you.*

There is a suggestion, from a comparative review of this text with Paul's letters that Paul, among the numerous early Hebrew Christians, used the version of John's Gospel from which this passage came. References to the Siniatic Palimpsest may be found on the Internet. Unfortunately, many of the translations into English found under the search phrase "Siniatic Palimpsest" apply without justification the more conventional "he" rather than the "she" of the original language. Some Internet references, however, do acknowledge the proper "she."

The identification of the Holy Spirit as feminine in the Siniatic Palimpsest is no small matter, for this document is the oldest of all copies of the Gospels, being dated to the second century A.D. It is a recognized principle of textual interpretation, even by the most conservative of Biblical scholars, that the older the text, the closer it is thought to be to the original Scripture. This is particularly important in light of the fact that there are no other Scriptural texts between it and the oldest Greek text dated to the fourth century A.D. One can only surmise that between the second and fourth centuries

Scripture had been altered to substitute "he" for "she" in references to the Holy Spirit. Even then, at least one reference to the Holy Spirit as "she", apparently having been overlooked in the switch, was allowed to remain. As Romans 9:25 reads in our King James Bible,

> *As he saith also in Osee [Hosea], I will call them my people, who were not my people; and her beloved, who was not beloved.*

Despite the overt mistranslation of the pronoun "She" to "It" or "He" in modern English translations of Scripture, these modified versions still provide sufficient evidence of the feminine nature of the Holy Spirit to convince all but the most reactionary of individuals. Among the most assertive in that regard is the Glory of God, the Hebrew feminine Shekinah, who indwelt the temples at their dedication. The obvious connection between the feminine Shekinah described in Exodus 40 and 1 Kings 8 and the indwelling Holy Spirit described in the Book of the Acts of the Apostles and referred to by Paul is, of itself, overwhelming evidence of the feminine gender of the Holy Spirit. The link between the Holy Spirit and the Shekinah Glory, as well as the many references to "Eloah", a feminine term for God in the Hebrew Scriptures, will be discussed in Chapter 8.

Why would Church authorities be so boldly heretic as to deliberately alter Scripture as to mislead the Church regarding the gender of the Holy Spirit and to remove all traces of sexuality from God? A number of possibilities have been raised by multiple scholars, among which two stand out as particularly plausible candidates. First, the Gnostic Christian community, which adhered to a feminine Holy Spirit, went overboard on some of its misunderstandings of Christianity, and was considered to be a dangerously heretic sect; in its attempt to stamp out this notion of God, the community that eventually came to represent mainstream Christianity engaged in a wholesale rejection of its precepts, in effect throwing the baby out with the bathwater. Second, the presence of femininity within the Godhead came perilously close to pagan theology, which involved the worship of divine families consisting of father, mother and son, and was often given to lewd ritualistic behavior, as lamented by Augustine among others. Here again, in her attempt to separate herself from these other religions, mainstream Christianity rejected the notion of a divine family out of hand, once more tossing the baby out with the bathwater. I will offer a third and more basic possibility when I revisit this issue in Chapter 11.

Ignoring Biblical References to Gender Neutrality

Galatians 3:28 was cited as Scriptural proof that heaven will be genderless. The verse reads as follows:

There is neither Jew nor Greek, there is neither bond nor free, there is neither male nor female, for ye are all one in Christ Jesus.

Regarding the verse cited above, I could go further. I also could quote Matthew 22:29 and 30:

Jesus answered and said unto them, Ye do err, not knowing the scriptures, nor the power of God. For in the resurrection they neither marry, nor are given in marriage, but are like the angels of God in heaven.

Neither of these passages remotely suggest that heaven is a gender-neutral domain. Properly interpreted, they say anything but that. Instead, they refer to individuals rather than the Church, which, in a collective sense, is strongly identified in Scripture itself as possessing gender.

The answer to this objection has been given in numerous places in the Bible, wherein Paul in great detail describes individuals in the spiritual realm as components of a greater body, the Church, and goes on to describe the Church as a feminine entity. An example of the aggregate nature of the Church is given in Ephesians 4:11-16:

And he gave some, apostles; and some, prophets; and some, evangelists; and some, pastors and teachers. For the perfecting of the saints for the work of the ministry for the edifying of the body of Christ, till we all come in the unity of the faith, and of the knowledge of the Son of God, unto a perfect man, unto the measure of the stature of the fullness of Christ; that we henceforth be no more children, tossed to and fro, and carried about with every wind of doctrine, by the sleight of men, and cunning craftiness, by which they lie in wait to deceive; but speaking the truth in love, may grow up into him in all things, who is the head, even Christ; from whom the whole body fitly joined together and compacted by that which every joint supplieth, according to the effectual working in the measure of every part, maketh increase of the body unto the edifying of itself in love.

1 Corinthians 12:4-27 also represents a passage describing the Church as an aggregate of individual persons, and is even more detailed in its depiction of our individuality as parts of a greater and different whole than the passage in Ephesians 4:

Now there are diversities of gifts, but the same Spirit. And there are differences in administrations, but the same Lord. And there are diversities of operations, but it is the same God who worketh all in all. But the manifestation of the Spirit is given to every man to profit. For to one is given, by the Spirit, the word of wisdom; to another, the word of knowledge by the same Spirit; to another, faith by the same Spirit; to another, the gifts of healing by the same Spirit; to another, the working of miracles; to another, prophecy; to another, discerning of spirits; to another, various kinds of tongues; to another, the interpretation of tongues. But all these worketh that one and the selfsame Spirit, dividing to every man severally as he will. For as the body is one, and hath many members, and all the members of that one body, being many, are one body, so also is Christ. For by one Spirit were we all baptized into one body, whether we be Jews or Greeks, whether we be bond or free; and have been all made to drink into one Spirit. For the body is not one member, but many. If the foot shall say, Because I am not the hand, I am not of the body; is it, therefore, not of the body? And if the ear shall say, Because I am not the eye, I am not of the body; is it, therefore, not of the body? If the whole body were an eye, where were the hearing? If the whole were hearing, where were the smelling? But now hath God set the members, every one of them, in the body, as it hath pleased him. And if they were all one member, where were the body? But now are they many members, yet but one body. And the eye cannot say unto the hand, I have no need of thee; nor again the head to the feet, I have no need of you. Nay, much more those members of the body which seem to be more feeble, are necessary: and those members of the body, which we think to be less honorable, upon these we bestow more abundant honor; and our uncomely parts have more abundant comeliness. For our comely parts have no need; but God hath tempered the body together, having given more abundant honor to that part which lacked, that there should be no schism in the body, but that the members should have the same care one for another. And whether one member suffer, all the members suffer with it; or one member be honored, all the members rejoice with it. Now ye are the body of Christ, and members in particular.

As Jesus retains His masculinity and the Church assumes her femininity in the spiritual realm, gender quite obviously applies to the Body as a whole rather than to individuals. The Church as a Body is a composite rather than a single redeemed human individual. Obviously, given the mystery that Paul explained in Ephesians 5, Jesus was referring in Matthew 22 to the relationship between redeemed humans rather than the relationship the Church as a whole will enjoy as Wife of Christ. The exact same comment applies as well to Galatians 3:28: Paul spoke only regarding the inter-human relationship which, in the spiritual realm, apparently won't include individual human sexuality. That says precisely nothing about the human-God relationship.

Perhaps it is this kind of mistaken understanding riding on the back of shallow thought that led Catholic theologian Father Macquarrie and a host of other would-be expositors of Scripture throughout the centuries, in recognizing gender-based traits within the Godhead, to attribute facets of both genders to each of its Divine Members.

We visited Father Macquarrie earlier in Chapter 5, noting there the difficulties associated with his viewpoint of shared gender characteristics, wherein the gender identification of each is so weak as to be safely asexual.

There is an interesting confirmation in Psalm 34:2 regarding the gender of our souls in the spiritual realm:

My soul shall make her boast in the Lord; the humble shall hear of it, and be glad."

This particular quote came from the King James Version of the Bible. While some other versions substitute "it" for "her" and still others manipulate the grammar to avoid the gender issue altogether, the Young's Literal Translation uses the word "herself," which agrees with the KJV as to gender. In order to avoid a conflict with Galatians 3:28, David's words here may be interpreted as his viewing his soul as functionally integrated into the Church as a whole.

The attempt to use these passages to demonstrate a lack of gender in the spiritual realm exposes an inability to differentiate between our individual selves and our collective self. While it is apparently true that as individuals we will not partake of gender in the spiritual realm, it is equally clear from Ephesians 5:31 and 32 that our collective spiritual attribute will be of the female gender:

For this cause shall a man leave his father and mother, and shall be joined unto his wife, and they two shall be one flesh. This is a great mystery, but I speak concerning Christ and the church.

If, now, we revisit the passages noted above dealing with the lack of gender in the individual spiritual person, we see the basic shallowness of an attempt to claim, on that basis, that there is no gender in the spiritual realm. For what would a gendered ear look like? Or how would a sexual foot accomplish that function? At the very least, it would impart a brand new meaning to the term "playing footsie". Would one have to make special provisions, for the sake of modesty, toward prohibiting the practice of walking barefoot? Shoe salespersons would have to be watched very carefully – perhaps making them submit to licensing. Of course, it would open an enormous market for suggestive footwear.

But as to the Church as the composite spiritual Bride of Christ, that's an entirely different story.

What do Christians think this marriage will involve? An unconsummated, virginal union basically empty of the natural meaning of union itself? A union in name only, incapable of bearing fruit, as suggested by the natural generation of offspring by almost every life form on earth, including humanity?

Ignoring Passages in Which the Father Appears to Claim that Attributes of the Holy Spirit Belong to Himself

The specific passage for which I was taken to task for ignoring was Jeremiah 10:10-13, in which the Father claims possession of attributes such as wisdom and discretion that are usually attributed to the Holy Spirit:

> *But the Lord is the true God; he is the living God, and an everlasting king; at his wrath the earth shall tremble, and the nations shall not be able to abide his indignation. Thus shall ye say unto them, The gods that have not made the heaven and the earth, even they shall perish from the earth, and from under these heavens. He hath made the earth by his power; he hath established the world by his wisdom, and hath stretched out the heavens by his discretion. When he uttereth his voice, there is a multitude of waters in the heavens, and he causeth the vapors to ascend from the ends of the earth; he maketh lightnings with rain, and bringeth forth the wind out of his treasures.*

I respond, in the first place, by asking whether God here was speaking as the Father alone, or whether He was speaking on behalf of the Trinity. But since the person taking me to task presupposed that the Father was speaking only for Himself, I shall, for the sake of argument, assume that he was correct in this presupposition.

In the context of my view of the spousal relationship between Father and the Holy Spirit, I already have noted that a major characteristic of this union, particularly if it is a perfect one, is that it necessarily involves mutual possession. The divine Partners in a spousal setting own each other. In that context, it is logically sound to view the passage in Jeremiah quoted above as the Father describing features and deeds of His Holy Spirit in a possessive sense.

It is only if the relationship between the Father and the Holy Spirit is seen in the far looser context of a committee relationship, as would be appropriate to the prevailing viewpoint, that the Father speaking in a possessive sense about the Holy Spirit doesn't seem to fit, and the more likely interpretation would be that the Father was speaking of Himself instead of the Holy Spirit.

It's all in the presuppositions. My own ones continue, at least, to be self-consistent.

Linking the Holy Spirit to Wisdom in the Book of Proverbs

I was chided for making a "hasty" connection between the Book of Proverbs and the Holy Spirit. The person who said this to me himself spoke somewhat in haste, knowing nothing about the amount of time I had spent on the subject before committing my thoughts to writing.

The connection that I have made among the Book of Proverbs, Wisdom and the Holy Spirit was not made in haste. It developed over a period exceeding a decade. I could construe his remark about my hastiness to be a bit on the arrogant side in contradiction to his usual gentle demeanor, but instead I shall give him the benefit of the doubt, assuming instead that he honestly thought that it would take only a modicum of reflection on the subject to convince oneself that the Holy Spirit and Wisdom are not one and the same. Allow me, in the following commentary, to demonstrate otherwise.

Along with his comment regarding the haste of my connection between the Wisdom presented in Proverbs and the Holy Spirit, the individual who took me to task added, regarding the prevailing understanding of the Book of Proverbs, that the personification of Wisdom is simply a literary device and was never intended to represent an actual Person. But in opposition to this view, Wisdom in the original Greek has a name of a person, and that name is Sophia. Sophia has a history of being linked, in the Jewish and early Christian religions, with the Personhood of the Holy Spirit.

Jesus Himself, in Luke 7:35, associates Wisdom with motherhood, an eminently personal attribute.

But wisdom is justified of all her children.

While that verse possibly could be interpreted as being merely a figure of speech, Jesus in Luke 11:49 and 50 more emphatically personifies Wisdom:

Therefore also said the wisdom of God, I will send them prophets and apostles, and some of them they shall slay and persecute, that the blood of all the prophets, which was shed from the foundation of the world, may be required of this generation.

Regarding the connection that I presented in *Family of God* between the Holy Spirit and the Book of Proverbs, I emphatically confirm my claim as to that connection, citing Proverbs 3:13-20 (particularly verse 19 in light of Genesis 1:1-5) and 8:22-36, in which Wisdom acquires a distinct Personhood and is cast in the role of complementary companion to the Father in the act of creation, which I take as a distinctly female role. I disagree with the prevailing Protestant presupposition that Proverbs 8 refers to Jesus Christ, as well as the prevailing Catholic presupposition that Proverbs 8 refers to Mary, because in both cases the presuppositions simply don't fit the context of that chapter. I also could cite Proverbs 9 and 31 in that regard, and Psalm 104:30 which links creation with the Holy Spirit. (Job 26:13 is similar in that regard.) Although I prefer to remain entirely within Scripture in my responses, I also could cite Benjamin Warfield's commentary in page 122 his book *The Holy Spirit* that "In both Testaments the Spirit of God appears distinctly as *the executive of the Godhead* [italics in the original]." This reference is particularly appropriate, in that the person who made the objection and I both agree as to our high opinion of Warfield. I also point to Warfield's more lengthy discussion on pages 124 and 125 that elaborated on the role of the Holy Spirit in the act of creation. I wholeheartedly agree with the person who made the objection on the correctness of linking the Holy Spirit with an executive role, which I consider to be purely responsive (to the Will of the Father), and therefore represents a female role as detailed in Chapter Four.

The linkage given in Proverbs with Wisdom in an executive role, as well as its personification of Wisdom as a complement to God the Father amply justifies the inclusion of the Holy Spirit in that linkage. Furthermore, the whole tenor of Proverbs identifies the Holy Spirit as a functional female.

Beyond those comments, I note that other passages in Scripture besides Proverbs, as well as the context of Scripture in its entirety, strongly suggest a female functionality for the Holy Spirit, which adds weight to my entire argument as well as to my connection of Wisdom with the Holy Spirit as presented in Proverbs. As examples I cite Jesus Christ (John 3:3-8) and Paul (Ephesians 5:31 and 32).

In John 3, Jesus explicitly links the Holy Spirit with (Spiritual) birth, an undeniably female function, while in Ephesians 5, Paul declares the spiritual marriage between Christ and the Church, implicating God (we wholeheartedly agree on the deity of Christ) in the role of marriage partner. If God as Jesus is involved in romance, isn't it possible (I would say probable) that God the Father and God the Holy Spirit are involved in romance as well? Surely, given the Scriptural certainty of the marriage between Jesus and His Church, the notion of a genderless and therefore passionless and fruitless nature of such a union would not only be incomprehensible, but runs counter to the whole tenor of both Scripture and Creation.

Furthermore, in Ephesians 5, Paul repeats Adam's words to the effect that a man shall leave his father and mother and join his wife, and they two shall become one flesh. In applying this entire passage to Jesus, does not Paul imply that Jesus had a Mother to leave? As there is a general consensus that Jesus existed long before He came in the flesh, we also must agree that here Paul is not speaking of

Mary as Jesus' Mother.

It may be the case that most theologians don't perceive any compelling reason to equate Christ and the Church to Adam's words regarding leaving father and mother and joining unto his wife to become one flesh. But Jesus Himself as quoted in Matthew 19:4-8 appears to attach a significance to Adam's words that transcends a mere man-woman relationship. In addition, there are other passages in Scripture, including Genesis 24 and Isaiah 54, that tend to confirm the notion that in the spiritual realm the Church shall indeed serve in a female role as the Bride of Christ.

In further support of my equation of Wisdom with the Holy Spirit, I cite Isaiah 11:1 and 2:

> *And there shall come forth a rod out of the stem of Jesse, and a Branch shall grow out of his roots; And the Spirit of the Lord shall rest upon him, the spirit of wisdom and understanding, the spirit of counsel and might, the spirit of knowledge and of the fear of the Lord,. . .*

Another item that presents itself in a reading of Proverbs with an eye to the Personhood of Wisdom is the implied intimacy between mankind and Wisdom in the warning given in Proverbs 8:36: he that sins against Wisdom wrongs his own soul. Could this imply that our own purpose and function in the spiritual realm might actually parallel that of the Holy Spirit? There may well be a correlation between this caution and the one expressed by Jesus in Matthew 12:31 and 32:

> *Wherefore I say unto you, All manner of sin and blasphemy shall be forgiven unto men: but the blasphemy against the Holy Ghost shall not be forgiven unto men. And whosoever speaketh a word against the Son of man, it shall be forgiven him: but whosoever speaketh against the Holy Ghost, it shall not be forgiven him, neither in this world, neither in the world to come.*

These are strong words, and they make a strong connection between Wisdom and the Holy Spirit. Perhaps theologians instinctively sense this correlation. Perhaps also not wishing to shoot themselves in the foot and instead of attempting to truly understand what is being said here, they duck away from presenting anything controversial regarding the Holy Spirit. Historically, that has certainly been the situation with numerous theological expositions regarding the Holy Spirit, all of which end up complicating an extremely simple understanding of the nature of the Trinity by claiming that ultimately man is unable to grasp it.

I must express my disappointment with all such expositors for allowing this unjustified fear to prevent them from furnishing a richer, more love-inducing understanding of their God to the Christian community. How can we possibly fulfill God's greatest commandment to us to love Him with all our hearts if we cannot understand Him? How can we truly worship God if we turn our hearts away from His own Word? I assert with the Revised Westminster Confession that the three Persons of the Trinity have but one substance—that of the Father, shared among them, and three distinct Personalities, or roles. I identify those roles as Father, Mother, and Son, wherein the Three constitute one God in the context of Family, by virtue of the love intrinsic to that structure which, of course, is idealized in its application to God. This identification I make does not represent any cleverness on my part; rather, its very simplicity gives me cause to suspect that many followers of God would do well to actually follow God in love tempered by fear instead of fear tempered by love, and to follow God Himself instead of adhering so stubbornly to the traditions of man.

Moreover, I would suggest that in a functional sense an all-male Godhead represents a model that can be construed with little difficulty to support homosexuality, in opposition to God's detestation of that practice, as found in Genesis 19, Leviticus 18 and Romans 1.

As a final comment regarding my association of Wisdom with the Holy Spirit, I note that Irenaeus, commonly accepted as a respected Church Father, also directly equated Wisdom with the Holy Spirit, and he did so a number of years before I (and others of my ilk) did. It may be said in response that Irenaeus as a human had his problems, one being his belief in Apostolic succession. I thoroughly agree that such should not be revered, pointing to another Church great, Martin Luther, who not only was a rabid anti-Semite, but was devoted to scatological quips and who, by the way, thought that Mary Magdalene was Jesus' consort. On the other hand, Irenaeus' peccadillos, like those of Luther, should not lead one to reject everything that they said or believed.

On the other hand, the Catholic Church, by elevating Mary as she did, did not completely deny the family of God the balancing femininity it so badly needs, so maybe Irenaeus should be respected a bit more in the Protestant community. Another thing the Catholic Church did for the feminine which the Protestant Church did not was to include the Book of Wisdom within the body of canonical, and therefore considered to be inspired, Old Testament books. This beautifully-written book furnishes several interesting passages suggestive of the identity of Wisdom as the feminine Holy Spirit. Selected passages are presented below:

And in your wisdom have established humankind... Give me Wisdom, the consort at your throne... Now with you is Wisdom, who knows your works and was present when you made the world; Who understands what is pleasing in your eyes and what is conformable with your commands. Send her forth from your holy heavens and from your glorious throne dispatch her that she may be with me and work with me, that I may know what is pleasing to you. For she knows and understands all things, and will guide me prudently in my affairs and safeguard me to her glory... Or who can know your counsel, unless you give Wisdom and send your holy spirit from on high?
—Wisdom 9:2, 4, 9-11, 17

Conferring Godhood on a Female

Is it really appropriate, I was asked, in the light of Paul's comments regarding female participation in church activities, to confer Godhood on a female? The implication was that it is not.

Personally, I think that the reason that Paul, in 1 Timothy 2, expressed the desire to limit the role of females in the Church is that he wished all of us, given our future hope of participating so intimately in the Godhead, to remain suitably humble regarding the nature of that future participation. In that sense, he would have had no interest in lessening the position of the female in the present church; to the contrary, his interest would have been to keep all of us, male and female, in our places. Most interestingly, God Himself, when men fail to step up to the plate, puts women in positions generally thought to be reserved for men.

One can readily discern in the account of the prophetess Deborah in Chapter 4 of the Book of Judges that God didn't categorically deny to women the exercise of leadership. Deborah was the fourth in a line of fifteen judges over Israel following the death of Joshua and before the institution of kings over the nation. The situation was extreme, to be sure, and apparently the men at that time had turned so far away from God that He not only handed over the prophetic role to a woman, but also made her a judge and a military leader. Given that the Israelite men at that time apparently failed to shoulder their responsibilities, Deborah's actions should not be considered to be usurpations of authority as Paul admonished against in 1 Timothy 2:12. According to the account in Judges 4, Deborah served as a military leader only when Barak refused to confront the Canaanites without her. That certainly can not be construed as a usurpation of the man's role, and it is apparent from what followed that God was there all the way with both Deborah and the woman Jael, who slew Sisera.

The scene is set for the story of Deborah in Judges 2:13-19:

And they forsook the Lord, and served Baal and Ashtaroth. And the anger of the Lord was hot against Israel, and he delivered them into the hands of spoilers who spoiled them, and he sold them into the hands of their enemies round about, so that they could not any longer stand before their enemies. Whithersoever they went out, the hand of the Lord was against them for evil, as the Lord had said, and as the lord had sworn unto them; and they were greatly distressed.

Nevertheless, the Lord raised up judges, who delivered them out of the hand of those who spoiled them. And yet they would not hearken unto their judges, but they went a whoring after other gods, and bowed themselves unto them: they turned quickly out of the way which their fathers walked in, obeying the commandments of the lord; but they did not so. And when the Lord raised them up judges, then the Lord was with the judge, and delivered them out of the hand of their enemies all the days of the judge; for it repented the Lord because of their groanings by reason of them who oppressed them and vexed them. And it came to pass when the judge was dead, that they returned, and corrupted themselves more than their fathers, in following other gods to serve them, and to bow down unto them; they ceased not from their own doings, nor from their stubborn way.

The full account of the exploits of Deborah and Jael in Judges Chapter 4 is given below.

And the children of Israel again did evil in the sight of the Lord, when [the third prophet] Ehud was dead. And the Lord sold them into the hand of Jabin, king of Canaan, who reigned in Hazor, the captain of whose host was Sisera, who dwelt in Harosheth of the Gentiles. And the children of Israel cried unto the Lord; for he had nine hundred chariots of iron; and twenty years he mightily oppressed the children of Israel.

And Deborah, a prophetess, the wife of Lapidoth, judged Israel at that time. And she dwelt under the palm tree of Deborah, between Ramah and Bethel in Mount Ephraim; and the children of Israel came up to her for judgment. And she sent and called Barak, the son of Abinoam, out of Kedesh-naphtali, and seid unto him, Hath not the Lord God of Israel commanded, saying, Go and draw toward Mount Tabor, and take with thee ten thousand men of the children of Naphtali, and of the children of Zebulun? And I will draw unto thee, to the river Kishon, Sisera, the captain of Jabin's army, with his chariots and his multitude; and I will deliver him unto thine hand.

And Barak said unto her, If thou will go with me, then I will go; but if thou wilt not go with me, then I will not go. And she said, I will surely go with thee: notwithstanding, the journey that thou takest shall not be for thine honor; for the Lord shall sell Sisera into the hand of a woman. And Deborah arose, and went with Barak to Kedesh. And Barak called Zebulun and Naphtali to Kedesh; and he went up with ten thousand men at his feet: and Deborah went up with him. Now Heber, the Kenite, who was of the children of Hobab, the father-in-law of Moses, had severed himself from the Kenites, and pitched his tent unto the plain of Zaanaim, which is by Kedesh.

And they showed Sisera that Barak, the son of Abinoam, was gone up to Mount Tabor. And Sisera gathered together all his chariots, even nine hundred chariots of iron, and all the people who were with him, from Harosheth of the Gentiles unto the river of Kishon. And Deborah said unto Barak, Up; for this is the day in which the Lord hath delivered Sisera into thine hand. Is not the Lord gone out before thee? So Barak went down from Mount Tabor, and ten thousand men after him. And the Lord routed Sisera, and all his chariots, and all his host, with the edge of the sword before Barak, so that Sisera lighted down off his chariot, and fled away on his feet. But Barak pursued after the chariots, and after the host, unto Harosheth of the Gentiles: and all the host of Sisera fell upon the edge of the sword; and there was not a man left.

Howbeit Sisera fled away on his feet to the tent of Jael, the wife of Heber, the Kenite; for there was peace between Jabin, the king of Hazor, and the house of Heber, the Kenite. And Jael went out to meet Sisera, and said unto him, Turn in, my lord, turn in to me; fear not. And when he had turned in unto her into the tent, she covered him with a mantle. And he said unto her, Give me, I pray thee, a little water to drink, for I am thirsty. And she opened a bottle of milk, and gave him drink, and covered him. Again he said unto her, Stand in the door of the tent, and it shall be, when any man doth come and inquire of thee, and say, Is there any man here? That thou shalt say, No.

Then Jael, Heber's wife, took of nail of the tent, and took an hammer in her hand, and went softly unto him, and smote the nail into his temples, and fastened it into the ground; for he was fast asleep and weary. So he died. And, behold, as Barak pursued Sisera, Jael came out to meet him, and said unto him, Come, and I will show thee the man whom thou seekest. And when he cam into her tent, behold, Sisera lay dead, and the nail was in his temples.

So God subdued on that day Jabin, the king of Canaan, before the children of Israel. And the hand of the children of Israel prospered, and prevailed against Jabin, the king of Canaan, until they had destroyed Jabin, king of Canaan.

The bottom line is that God is not so rigid that He unconditionally prohibits a female from serving in a role usually reserved for a male. Where in Scripture outside 1 Timothy 2 is there even a suggestion that He should categorically deny a female from sharing Godhood with Him? Furthermore, it is a reach to extrapolate that notion from Paul's letter to Timothy. Even in that passage, Paul notes the cause of the proscription against women teaching as Eve's deception in the Garden of Eden. It is more likely that Paul's proscription came about through his perception that Eve had usurped her role as Adam's wife in acting independently without his lead, perhaps in so doing violating her creation in the image of the Holy Spirit. This likely scenario, then, far from precluding a female Holy Spirit, actually supports the notion.

The nation of Israel has had another female leader much more recently, one whom God also used to save the country. The following story, while somewhat redundant to the general theme of the feminine nature of the Holy Spirit, serves to underscore the fact that Paul's comments regarding the service of women in the Church has little or nothing to do with their capability of performing roles, with God's blessing, more commonly associated with males.

Born in 1898 in Kiev, Russia (Ukraine), Golda Mebovitz immigrated to the United States at the age of 8. She grew up in

Milwaukee, Wisconsin. She married Morris Meyerson in 1917 and with him she immigrated once more in 1921 to Israel, her homeland for the rest of her life.

Culminating a career in government service, Golda Meir was elected Prime Minister of Israel in 1969, becoming the fourth P.M. of the new nation. (There may be a prophetic implication here between Deborah's being the fourth judge – and effective leader - of Israel and Meir's being the fourth modern leader.) Mrs. Meir served in that capacity until she resigned in 1974 at the age of 76, partly because of failing health.

In the year previous to her resignation she played a major role in extricating Israel from near-defeat in the Yom Kippur War of 1973. Faced with terrible attrition in the coordinated Egyptian-Syrian assault, Israel was on the point of annihilation. Golda flew to the United States to plead with then-president Richard Nixon for support in the form of weaponry with which to resupply her troops.

Amazingly, Nixon's Quaker mother had told him when he was a child that some day he would be in a position to help the Jews. When that happened, she said, he must do everything in his power to provide that help. Her message to her son was prophetic, and when Golda Meir approached him with her plea for help, he remembered his mother's admonition. Accordingly, he embarked on a massive resupply operation for Israel. The action saved the day, and with that help Israeli soldiers turned the near-defeat into victory.

This modern incident supports the Scriptural suggestions that God doesn't mind if a lady takes over the reins once in a while. While it's rare, it's obviously not forbidden. Paul's comments in 1 Timothy 2 related to Eve and her female offspring, not to the Holy Spirit. Nor do they have anything to do with women's future post-resurrection roles.

If one wants to find a mindset that really represses females, all one has to do is go to China or India or visit a Mosque, talk (in depth) to a Muslim, or digest the tenets of Shari'a law. Interestingly, Islam, while treating women as greatly inferior to men, also denies the deity of Christ and the existence of the Holy Trinity, and advocates the murder of Christians and Jews. Jesus is there, to be sure, but as a mere prophet who subordinates Himself to Mohammad, denies that He died on the cross and supports the Muslim antipathy toward Christians and Jews. I personally think that God's view of womanhood, as gleaned from Scripture, is vastly different than that promoted in the anti-Christian Muslim faith. The odd fact, as noted above, that whereas Deborah was the fourth judge over ancient Israel, Golda Meir was the fourth leader of the modern nation of Israel, might be repeated in the context of demonstrating God's continuing hand over His people.

Even if one would insist upon a Godhood reserved exclusively for males, I suggest only a female function for the Holy Spirit, not a female substance. I would remind the objector that my view of the Holy Spirit is as a compositional male (substantively) as well as a functional female. In that capacity the Holy Spirit would indeed be capable of assuming a male role, notably the exercise of Will belonging to the Father. That the Holy Spirit has not assumed this lofty position to date is simply one of obedience to a functional role that is complementary to the Father's will given the continuing presence of the Father. This brought the disobedience of satan (Isaiah 14) to mind, which was of that nature. The issue also raised the companion issue of subordination of one Member of the Godhead to another, which appears to many as a heretical stance. In that regard, the specter of the old Arian heresy rears its ugly head. Here again, I had addressed the Arian heresy in *Family of God,* noting how it had no application in my thinking. The Arian heresy, in placing Jesus below the Father as lesser than God, is nowhere close to what I propose about the Members of the Godhead, which is more a voluntary and time-specific functional subordination, not one of intrinsic capability. Scripture itself endorses my stance. In John 14:28, for example, Jesus declares the Father to be greater than Him, which makes no statement whatsoever regarding either His Godhood or His capability of assuming the Father's role. Regarding the issue of precedence between the Father and Jesus, I cite Revelation 3:14, wherein Jesus names Himself "the beginning of the creation of God". I don't think this departs greatly from the Westminster definition of the Godhead, but to those who would claim that it does, I remind them that the Westminster Confession is extra-Scriptural.

Attributing Passion to God

As noted in Chapter 4, the Church appears to have been heavily influenced by medieval theologian Jerome Zanchius and his pseudo-rigorous development of a concept of God in which He is said to be void of passion. It was in reference to this source that I was told that God is generally not assumed to possess passion, certainly not of a nature that would admit of a romantic union between Father and Holy Spirit. This false perception that God lacks passion is most distressingly evident where God's attributes of power and majesty are emphasized during worship at the expense of His most important attribute of love.

But Scripture portrays God as possessing passion. The notion that God is above love of a passionate nature violates Scripture, the most obvious case being the ardor and passion intricately woven into the Song of Solomon, otherwise known as the Song of Songs or the Canticles. At least two Bible commentaries (in the Reformation Study Bible, New King James Version and in the New Schofield Reference Bible, both as introductions to the Song of Solomon, consider the Song to be an allegory of the future union of Jesus Christ with His Church.

My perception of the glory of God in all three Persons of the Godhead is far more the quality of their selfless willingness to give up the majesty than the grandeur of their possession of it. Connected with that perception I view the Members of the Godhead as capable of experiencing love with intensity and passion, which to me includes love of the romantic kind. The manner in which Jesus' first miracle at Cana (John 2) reaches my heart would be difficult if not impossible if I couldn't relate it to Jesus' future relationship to the Church. The same could be said regarding the Song of Solomon, which would seem to be a wholly gratuitous insertion into Scripture of material extraneous to the Word if it didn't speak either of Jesus' future relationship with the Church or of the inter-

Member relationship within the Godhead or both. Even more telling in this regard is the Shema of Moses, which Jesus presents as the greatest commandment in Matthew 22:36-38, and which demands a passionate commitment to the Lord. In light of the fact that Jesus, as a superlative Leader, never asked of His disciples anything that He wouldn't do of Himself, it would seem to be contradictory to His character for Him to ask of us a passion that He Himself was incapable of exercising or even possessing.

The Song of Solomon raises issues in that regard that are worth addressing in detail. A host of Christian authorities readily acknowledge that it speaks of marital love in terms of passion and ardor. The same authorities admit even the erotic nature of some of its verses. The 1995 *Reformation Study Bible* (New King James Version), for example has this to say of the subject matter of the Song of Solomon:

> The beauty and worth of sexual love is affirmed at the beginning of the Bible, where the difference and relationship of the sexes is associated with the creation of humanity in God's image (Gen. 1:27; cf. 2:19-25) If sexual love were evil in itself, it would be inappropriate as an allegory of Christ's love for His church.

Here Editor R. C. Sproul and his associates not only acknowledge the sexuality of the topic, but link it to both the nature of the Godhead and with the relationship between Christ and His Church. Indeed, in their same introductory commentary, the editors make the following statements:

> The Song of Solomon reveals three qualities of love between a man and a woman: self-giving, desire, and commitment. In all these ways love reflects the greater love of God our Creator. God delights in us and gives Himself to us... Christian marriage, according to Paul, should be modeled on the most perfect expression of such love, the self-giving love of Christ for His church and its willing response (Eph. 5:22, 23). The climax of the Song of Solomon is the praise of vehement and faithful love (8:6,7). The Song of Solomon... looks back to

the gift of love in creation, and forward to the perfection of love in One greater than Solomon, the Lord Jesus Christ.

The editors, after implying a gender attribute of Jesus and the Godhead Itself, back off from openly declaring a sexuality of God:

Although it is not proper to attribute sexuality to God, there is an analogy between the love we experience in marriage and the love that God has for us.

While I would have wished that the editors, after having stated here what easily could be interpreted as the essential opposite of what they presented elsewhere in their introductory remarks, might have explained to us what they meant by the words "not proper" and "sexuality" and how they might justify using these words, their comment here may be reconciled with their other insinuations while leaving intact the notion of gender in the Godhead. This reconciliation may be realized by considering the word "sexuality" to refer to the human-specific form in which the function of gender has been implemented. If that indeed is what the editors had in mind, then I would be somewhat in agreement with them (while, with one eye fixed on the Song, wondering if they hadn't been a bit hasty themselves in this declaration) and be tempted to applaud their discernment in declaring "sexuality" to be an inappropriate attribute of the Godhead. As I noted in *Family of God*, the human manifestation of sexuality may have little or nothing to do with the function of gender in the spiritual realm, about which we are unable to perceive anything, nor because of our limitations should it occupy our interest either negatively or positively except as brought out in Scripture.

I can't help but note here that I, too, in *Family of God*, stop short of explicitly linking sexual activity as we are familiar with it with the Members of the Godhead, as my gender references are far more modest than those implied in Song of Solomon. (I do, however, come closer to making that link in my novel *Buddy* and herein.) The Bible in that regard appears to be significantly bolder than me regarding sexual passion in the spiritual realm.

Obviously I perceive an intimate connection in the Song of

Solomon regarding the relationship between the Father and the Holy
Spirit as well as that between Jesus and His Church. Connected
with that perception is my belief that the Holy Spirit essentially
forms the subject matter of the Book of Proverbs. The commentary
on the Song of Solomon in the Reformation Study Bible hints of this
same connection in its acknowledgement of the Book's emphasis on
marital love:

> Many interpreters, both Jewish and Christian, have regarded
> the Song as an allegory of God's love for Israel or the Church.
> The association of the book with Solomon, however, points us
> in the direction of the wisdom literature of the Old Testament.
> Wisdom literature is distinguished, among other things, by its
> focus on the common sphere of human relationships. The
> Book of Proverbs uses language similar to that of the Song
> of Solomon in talking about marital love (Prov. 5:15-19), the
> subject of the Song. This love must finally be seen in the
> context of the even greater love of God.

The commentary on the Song of Solomon presented in the *New
Schofield Reference Bible* (1967 Edition edited by C. I. Schofield)
echoes, but even more forcefully, that given in the *Reformation
Study Bible*:

> Nowhere in Scripture does the unspiritual mind tread upon
> ground so mysterious and incomprehensible as in this book,
> whereas saintly men and women throughout the ages have
> found it a source of pure and exquisite delight. That the love
> of the divine Bridegroom, symbolized here by Solomon's
> love for the Shulamite maiden, should follow the analogy of
> the marriage relationship seems evil only to minds that are so
> ascetic that marital desire itself appears to them to be unholy.
>
> The book is the expression of pure marital love as ordained
> by God in creation, and the vindication of that love as against
> both asceticism and lust – the two profanations of the holiness
> of marriage. Its interpretation is threefold: (1) as a vivid
> unfolding of Solomon's love for a Shulamite girl; (2) as a
> figurative revelation of God's love for His covenant people,

Israel, the wife of the Lord (Isa. 54:5-6; Jer. 2:2; Ezek. 16:8-14, 20-21, 32, 38; Hos. 2:16, 18-20); and (3) as an allegory of Christ's love for His heavenly bride, the Church (2 Cor. 11:1-2, refs., Eph 5:25-32).

As there appears to be a general agreement among established Biblical authorities regarding the relevance of this openly passionate Book to Christ and His Church, and there appears to be a similarly general agreement among established Biblical authorities regarding the Diety of Jesus Christ, an inescapable observation must be made: At least one Member of the Divine Godhead is openly acknowledged to be fully capable and willing to (passionately) exercise His male gender. That said, why would one Member of the Godhead be endowed with such an attribute while the other two would not be? That utterly confusing and contradictory state of affairs could be acceptable only to an avowed ascetic, an attribute which I concur with the editors of the Schofield Bible to be a profanation of God and His Creation.

The Song of Solomon itself establishes, if somewhat indirectly, a female gender of the Holy Spirit by associating in no less than three verses (2:14, 5:2 and 6:9) the nature of the (eminently female) Shulamite with that of a dove. Actually, where a dove is noted in Scripture (KJV) and associated with a specific gender, that gender invariably is female. The particular verses where gender is described are: Genesis 8:9, 11; Psalm 68:13; Song of Solomon as noted above; and Jeremiah 48:28. The dove, of course, is a well-known symbol of the Holy Spirit as presented, for example, in Matthew 3:16:

And Jesus, when he was baptized, went up straightway out of the water; and, lo, the heavens were opened unto him, and he saw the Spirit of God descending like a dove, and lighting upon him.

After I produced several of these rebuttals to his understanding of God that He is without passion as we know it, the person who took me to task for attributing such passion to God offered the suggestion that while God Immanent might be endowed with passion, God Transcendent does not. Because the argument is somewhat complex,

I include it herein as *Appendix 3: Transcendence vs. Immanence on the Nature of God.* (The reader may wish to refer also to Appendix 1 as a prequel to Appendix 3.) The bottom line is that God exhibits passion regardless of whether He is viewed as God Immanent or God Transcendent.

As a general response to the objections raised to *Family of God,* I repeat below some justifications for my position that were not fully developed in that book and were subsequently presented in some of my blogs that I had posted in *friendofthefamily.wordpress.com.*

Excerpt from posting entitled "A Deficiency": If God commands us to love Him with all our hearts as indeed He does (Deuteronomy 6, Matthew 22), I would suggest that such would be easier to fulfill in a full family context than otherwise. Furthermore, it is difficult to reconcile the oneness of God in a Trinitarian setting without perceiving the unitizing force as love of the intimacy that we understand in marriage and family.

Excerpt from posting entitled "Friend of the Family": It is obvious that the expression of gender in a family setting is among the most fundamental characteristics of our nature as humans, as well as the driving force behind our ability to love each other with a selfless fervor. In Scripture God simply asks us to expand upon the family-based element of this love, extending it as well to Him and our neighbors. The centrality of gender to our being, as presented in Scripture, strongly suggests that gender is a quality possessed by God.

Excerpts from postings entitled "Isaac's Marriage to Rebekah" and "Rebekah's Counterpart: In Genesis 24, Isaiah 54 and Ephesians 5, Scripture depicts the Church's future marriage to Jesus in terms not only of romance, but of bearing creative fruit. It also sets a Scriptural precedent of identifying a masculine aggregate (spiritual mankind) as functionally female. Given that identification, there is no Scriptural justification for insisting upon a male functionality of the Holy Spirit just because the substantive identity is male.

Excerpts from postings entitled "Sometimes I'm Lonely" and "The Gender of the Holy Spirit": Given that Scriptural references to the office of the Holy Spirit, such as 'Comforter', seem to connote a female function, it seems confusing and awkward to identify the Holy Spirit with a neutral or male gender. I know from reading and from face-to-face conversations that I've had with several Christian 'authorities' that they are indeed confused by their lack of understanding of the Holy Spirit. Yet they are terribly uncomfortable with any attempt to perceive the nature of the Holy Spirit, preferring instead to label this nature as a mystery. I cannot presume to doubt that such persons, in the face of this incomprehension of at least one Member of the Godhead, find it within themselves to love God with the fervor that the Shema of Moses suggests. I only know that for me such a mental gymnastic would be difficult. An additional comment: while being alone with a notion does suggest that one may be going off the deep end, it is not definitive in that regard. History is replete with examples of persons who have been alone with unpopular notions, only to have those same notions embraced as common knowledge at a later date. On the other hand, I suspect that in fact I may not be as alone as I implied in the earlier blogs, a point that I attempted to clarify in a later posting entitled "I'm Not As Alone as I Thought". In that post I noted that in the book entitled *Creation out of Nothing*, which was published in 2004 and which was loaned to me by my friend and pastor, authors Paul Copan and William Lane Craig remarked that Church father Irenaeus fully associated Wisdom with the Holy Spirit. In their writing, the authors appear to show some sympathy with that connection, although Irenaeus' possible linkage of Wisdom with a feminine Holy Spirit is my conclusion and does not necessarily agree with the conclusions of either Dr. Copan or Dr. Craig. There are indications in other literature that Irenaeus theologically leaned toward the denial of sexuality within Christianity. Nevertheless, of itself the association of Wisdom with the Holy Spirit implies at least two items: first, that Wisdom is identified in Scripture, in Proverbs to be specific, as a sentient Persona; second, that despite a comment that I had received to the effect that theologians normally don't associate Wisdom with the Holy Spirit, this very connection within the clergy was made very early on.

Excerpt from posting entitled "The Marriage of God With God": Here again I noted how much more readily, in the context of family, one can love our Trinitarian God as He commanded. How can such an idea be out of the question when Scripture itself tells us that at least one Member of the Godhead will be married in the future? Furthermore, this context is information-rich, allowing one to identify with ease the primary functions assumed by the Members of the Godhead. Information richness is a hallmark of truth. Finally, the treatment of Mary by the Catholic Church demonstrates how much the Church has struggled with the issue of Jesus' spiritual Mother, and how much confusion has entered into the issue in the process. Given that persistent state of confusion, I consider it my obligation, as I noted in this post, to attempt to present a reasonable alternative picture of the Godhead.

The bottom line is, of course, what Scripture has to say about the notion that the Godhead might Itself be a family, a characteristic that would make sense only if God the Son had a Holy Mother, a functionally feminine complement to the Holy Father. Can this notion be found anywhere in Scripture? Indeed it can, in Ephesians 3:14 and 15:

> *For this cause I bow my knees unto the Father of our Lord*
> *Jesus Christ, Of whom the whole family in heaven and earth*
> *is named...*

Finally, I wish to address herein a recently-acquired understanding of Jewish tradition that supports my viewpoint regarding the female functional nature of the Holy Spirit from a fresh perspective. That is the practice, as mentioned in the Wikipedia reference to the feast of Shavuot, of singling out the Book of Ruth for reading on that Jewish holy day. We know Shavuot, of course, as Pentecost, when the Holy Spirit was poured out upon the new Church. It is interesting to note that a feast that ultimately honors the Holy Spirit focuses on a Scriptural Book in which the central character is a female. I would think that most reasonable people would consider that to be more than a coincidence. In searching the Internet with the key word 'Shavuot', we also came across an article published by *thewatchman.org* that notes a close connection between Shavuot and the marriage union between YHWH and His people. Another coincidence?

Being Out There Alone

I can't help but smile ruefully at the suggestion that there might actually be a good reason why I'm 'out there alone'. The suggestion smarts because it carries a lot of truth. I have to agree with that, wondering myself why such a profoundly beautiful concept has been ignored by the vast majority of Christians for millennia. I don't have an answer to that. It still bothers me. Yet the problem doesn't give me a Scriptural reason that justifies my abandoning the concept. I can only say that all of our understanding of Scripture, even collectively, is progressive. Why me? Who knows? Maybe it's because I—and others of my persuasion—are such small potatoes that the introduction of this concept may be hardly noticeable and therefore quite gentle.

In the introduction to her delightful little book entitled *The Holy Spirit: The Feminine Nature of God,* Patricia Taylor expressed something akin to that sentiment when she wrote "I am not a theologian, pastor, evangelist or formally trained in any way. I am not even an author. I have never seriously considered taking on the daunting task of writing a book. As far as credentials go, I am a nobody. This is an aspect of God's nature that is so refreshing. He loves to use nobodies to carry out His plan for mankind. When He told Gideon He would use him to save the Israelite people from the oppression of the Midianites, Gideon said his family was the weakest of his tribe and that he was the weakest of his family. David and Joseph were both the youngest and weakest, in a worldly sense, in their families. And, of course, Jesus came as a carpenter's son from a small, insignificant town. He chose uneducated fishermen and other unimportant people in society to carry His message to the world. Paul said, "...**I am a nobody: (NAS, 2Corinthians 12:11).** [Bold in the original.]

Sometimes I wonder whether there are a lot of little people like me in churches throughout the world who perceive as I do that the functional gender of the Holy Spirit is essentially female, but say nothing to anyone about their perception because they'd rather not rock the boat. Perhaps I'm not nearly as alone as even I think. If I am, what of it? This is more of an *ad hominem* attack than a Scripturally-based objection. And even if I'm wrong, I'm sure that God Himself is more than capable, if He should so desire, of negating any potential influence I may have toward anybody without involving another human being in the process.

Actually, the Mariology tradition of the Catholic Church gives me reason to suspect that a large number of thoughtful Christians over many centuries have inferred from Scripture that the Holy Spirit has had a female function or nature. Rather than submitting themselves to the expected reactionary abuse for their thoughts, they simply transferred attributes belonging to the Holy Spirit over to Mary, who herself, according to Scripture, provides us with a vivid type of the Holy Spirit. Mary's typification of the Holy Spirit is even more pronounced in the Catholic Church due to this transference of attributes. In my opinion, the Catholic Church is less in error in this matter than the Protestant denominations, which have made no effort whatsoever to reconcile Scripture with their insistence upon making the Holy Spirit either entirely male or genderless.

I expressed my feeling in my blog *friendofthefamily.wordpress. com* with respect to the loneliness of having a viewpoint of God that doesn't fall in line with mainstream opinion. That particular posting is repeated below:

Sometimes I'm Lonely

I have a lovely wife to whom I am devoted. We spend most of the day together and, of course the night too, because we're also the best of friends. We have a wonderful pastor whose sermons delve into Scripture quite deeply, and we belong to a small church where everyone is a friend of everyone else.

Our pastor loves Jesus, and it shows in the manner that he

conducts his life. He reveres Scripture as the Word of God, and that is plain from his preaching.

Because of these benign circumstances, I am almost happy. But not quite. As a Christian I lack the fulfillment of being able to share openly some insights into the nature of God that I consider to be of the most fundamental importance. The insights, while I understand them to originate with God, are personal, which makes me a bit of a stray. As one of Jesus' sheep, I suppose that I should have been content to graze with the rest of the flock, but I saw a greener pasture elsewhere. I'd very much like to think that Jesus opened the gate for me and led me into it, but a number of Christian brothers and sisters are bleating that I jumped the fence. My pastor knows where I am, but he has the rest of his flock to care for and so he must remain noncommittal about my situation. The upshot is that despite the richness of the grass nobody's coming in to share it with me, and I'm starting to get real lonely.

My situation began innocently enough. I love to read, and when I was born again, I picked up a Bible and read it. Having done that, I simply took Scripture at face value. When I arrived at Matthew 22, I read this:

Then one of [the Pharisees], which was a lawyer, asked [Jesus] a question, tempting Him, and saying, Master, which is the great commandment in the law? Jesus said unto him, Thou shalt love the Lord thy God with all thy heart, and with all thy soul, and with all thy mind.

Having taken this Scripture to heart, I attempted to be obedient of this greatest of commandments. To do so, I continued to read Scripture, this time in greater depth, in order that I might more intimately know this Person who commands me to love Him with all my being. Almost immediately a problem was encountered: God the Father is understandable in Scripture, and so is Jesus the Son, but the Holy Spirit, in the context of how we have been taught to view this Person, is not. Nor, because of the vagueness surrounding this Third

Person of the Godhead, is the Holy Trinity.

How then, given this vagueness of knowledge, could I be obedient to the greatest commandment of Jesus? Somewhat frustrated, I set the matter aside as I continued to pore over Scripture. Then, when I happened upon Ephesians Chapter 5, I was delighted to discover the plainly-delivered answer to my earlier question. It was noted in the previous posting that, in the fullness of time according to Ephesians 5:31 and 32, Jesus shall leave His Father and Mother to wed the Church:

For this cause shall a man leave his father and mother, and shall be joined unto his wife, and they two shall be one flesh. This is a great mystery: but I speak concerning Christ and the church.

It is conspicuous in this passage that in the process of marrying His Church, Jesus will leave his Father and Mother to do so. This, statement, of course, implies that He has both a Father and a Mother to leave.

Oh, my, what a lot of information is packed into those two verses! One must understand that even if the verses stand alone in the entire Bible as suggesting that the Godhead Itself is a Divine Family, they are unequivocal with regard to that implication. The only way that one can deny the family attribute of the Godhead in the face of those words is to deny that all of Scripture is inspired of the Holy Spirit. I'm certainly not willing to do that, for that constitutes an error infinitely graver than any controversy regarding the nature the Godhead.

In my previous posting, I described the implications of our future spiritual marriage to Jesus, ending with mention of the dichotomy between redeemed mankind's masculine aggregate designation and the obviously female nature of our role as Bride of Christ. I then asked whether this dichotomy exists elsewhere in Scripture.

I'll answer that emphatically in the affirmative, and add that in its broader form this dichotomy is so profoundly important that I find it difficult to understand how anybody can fully love his God without appreciating its significance. It has to do with another marriage, one that was consumated long ago at the beginning of time.

As noted before, when thinking of the substance of the Church in terms of redeemed mankind, we apply the male gender. We do that because when we use a pronoun to refer to an aggregate composed of both sexes, we always apply the one associated with the dominant gender, which is male. Sorry, ladies, but that's just the way it is, political correctness notwithstanding. But you still get the last laugh, because Scripture openly describes the Church as female in Her relationship with Jesus. A good example of this is Paul's description of the Church in Ephesians as Jesus' future Bride. That makes the menfolk spiritual females, a fact that you can goad your husbands with when they make you angry.

What I've written about the Church is not controversial with regard to basic theology. Being in full agreement with mainstream Christianity, I'm still grazing in the big pasture along with the other sheep. Now, in turning to the topic of the Holy Spirit, things begin to get dicey: the rest of the flock is staring at me and I can see the whites of their eyes. Nevertheless, I shall now assert that the gender situation with regard to the Holy Spirit may be very similar to that regarding the Church in Her functional role as Bride of Christ: just as the masculine pronoun is used when referring to the Church constituted of redeemed mankind, Scripture uses the masculine pronoun when referring to the Holy Spirit. But redeemed mankind is also the Church as Bride of Christ, and just as the masculine pronoun in reference to redeemed mankind does not contradict a functional reference to the Church as female, I would say that here we have Scripture itself paving the way to considering the Holy Spirit to have a feminine function in the face of a masculine reference. Therefore, the masculine pronoun in reference to the Holy Spirit need not contradict a functional reference to this Comforter as female. But there is a big difference between an implication by similarity and an actuality. Do I make that leap?

I do, and it places me alone in the small pasture. But this pasture is rich in nourishment, for the notion of Godhead as Divine Family fully agrees with Scripture, specifically Ephesians 5:31 and 32 as noted above, whereas any other possible understanding of the Godhead cannot enjoy that same agreement.

In the case of the Holy Spirit, the male designation simply may connote that this Member of the Holy Trinity, while possessing a unique functional identity that may be of either gender, is composed of the same Divine Substance as the Holy Father who is male. Then, as in the case with the church, the male pronoun would be used because male is the dominant gender, which also applies to the Holy Spirit for having an essence of which both genders consist. As I note in *Family of God*, the answer to this apparent gender inconsistency may be as simple as attributing it to a common lack of perception in reading the Bible, and that from the very beginning. In Genesis 5:1 and 2 the creation of man as first presented in Genesis 1:26 and 27 is recapitulated, but with a significant addition:

This is the book of the generations of Adam. In the day that God created man,, in the likeness of God made he him; male and female created he them; and blessed them, and called their name Adam, in the day when they were created.'

Note in this passage that both Adam and Eve were named Adam. We don't usually think about the implications, but that same practice is maintained to this day. When a woman marries a man, she takes his name. This is quite significant, for it implies, beyond the notion that God considers the male and female to be one flesh, that the woman (and the man also) was never intended to live apart from her spouse, but to assume his identity as an unbreakable partnership. Therefore, the reference to the Holy Spirit as 'he' may simply and quite logically imply that the Holy Spirit is of the same Divine Substance as the Father as well as being indivisibly joined to Him.

But in an alternative interpretation the male designation also may suggest a very wonderful promise to us: it may mean that the Holy Spirit is also an aggregate of many components, one that in our future spiritual form we actually may be privileged to join, possibly as a Divine Daughter.

This implication was brought out in *Family of God.* It was noted there that the reason for the use of the male 'he' in reference to the Holy Spirit may be identical with the reason why the church, with specific reference to its aggregate nature as redeemed mankind, is described as masculine when, in fact, it is functionally feminine. The possibility was raised there that the use of the male gender may represent a promise that the church and the Holy Spirit may have a closer relation than mere similarity of gender. In this suggestion, redeemed mankind may, in fact, while being a masculine aggregate, become intimately related to the Holy Spirit by assuming a functional role as a new Divine Means with Jesus serving as a new Divine Will. Is that why Jesus (John 5:17), in performing what the Pharisees considered as work during the Sabbath, said *"My Father worketh hitherto, and I work"*?

In *Family of God*, I emphasized the following line of reasoning in attributing a female functionality to the Holy Spirit: Judeo-Christianity is generally assumed to be a monotheistic religion; yet, our Godhead is also assumed to be Trinitarian. The basis of our monotheism is expressed in Deuteronomy 6:4: *'Hear O Israel: the Lord our God is one Lord.'* On the other hand, Christianity deifies Jesus as well as the Holy Spirit; together, all God, they comprise the Trinitarian Godhead. Adam's statement regarding Eve, repeated by Jesus and Paul, reconciles two back into one: *'Therefore shall a man leave his father and mother, and shall cleave unto his wife; and they shall be one flesh.'* Extending this unity of family to the offspring of this union permits the full Trinitarian Godhead to be perceived as one, justifying the monotheism implicit in Deuteronomy 6:4.

In this posting I have added further justification for a female Holy Spirit by noting in particular in that same reconciliatory statement that in joining with his wife a man shall leave his father and mother. When this notion is applied to Jesus as in Ephesians 5:31 and 32, it becomes obvious that Jesus had to have had a Holy Mother to leave in joining with His wife. This can't apply to Mary because the unions that we are addressing are spiritual and because, according to numerous references throughout Scripture, for example Micah 5:2, and John 1:1 and 14, Jesus existed long before His sojourn in the flesh. On top of that, Scripture and nature both emphasize the sterility associated with any union other than between a male and a female. How, then, could Jesus be the Son of God without a female forbear? Why would Jesus take a Bride if His Father did not?

I'm not simply attempting to justify a pet thought here. In my opinion, the prevailing notion of an all-masculine Godhead is intrinsically blasphemous, representing no less than a repudiation of Scripture itself. I sincerely believe that Paul and other Bible greats knew the truth about the functional gender of the Holy Spirit. If there are just a few who share the little field, remember these words of Jesus in Matthew 7:13 and 14:

Enter ye in at the strait gate: for wide is the gate and broad is the way, that leadeth to destruction, and many there be that go in thereat: Because strait is the gate, and narrow is the way, which leadeth unto life, and few there be that find it.

After I wrote this piece, I began to learn of more people who shared my view of the Holy Spirit. I discuss this happy situation in Chapter 9.

Being in Bad Company

As for my conviction regarding the gender of the Holy Spirit seemingly being shared with other not-so-conservatively-Christian individuals such as Koresh and Winfrey, I ask the objector to go back and read my book with a little more understanding of the positions each of us have taken on the subject and of the obvious differences in our perceptions. Winfrey's goddess theology is not even remotely connected with my notion regarding the gender of the Holy Spirit. The same might be said about Koresh as an individual and his self-serving beliefs, despite the fact that there was a woman in his organization, Lois Roden, who was an outspoken adherent to the view of the Holy Spirit as a feminine Persona and taught the same.

Actually, being told that one is among bad company and that being alone are so closely related that they're pretty much twins in meaning. Both connote being outside and looking in. Words and phrases of similar meaning that apply to both situations would include "outcast", "shunned by polite society", "not to be trusted", and "let's not be judgmental, but—" The person who got on my case for being in bad company might just as well have said to me "I told you to stay in the car!"

Accordingly, my response is identical to that eventually given to the charge of being out there alone: please refer to Chapter 9, thank you.

But before I dismiss this topic completely, I must offer the suggestion that others who eventually have been highly regarded had to suffer both the accusation of being out there alone and of being in bad company. Among these individuals was Jesus Himself, against whom the religious leaders of the Sanhedrin hurled numerous accusations of advocating theological views contradictory to theirs. Jesus was further chastised for consorting with people considered to be of less than sterling character, including a hated tax collector, lowly fishermen and a woman of the streets, according to some whisperers. There is a long list of martyrs, fully Christian, who lost their lives, some in horrible ways, because the tenets their faith at the time didn't match those of the prevailing understanding.

As a matter of fact, in James 2:1, the writer specifically tells us that:

May brethren, have not the faith of our Lord Jesus Christ, the Lord of glory, with respect of persons.

Taking Lightly the Responsibilities of a Teacher of the Word of God

Maybe the intent is to intimidate, but here again, the implication is that one who holds to my particular views is not to be trusted, a judgment that is confirmed by the absence of a PhD in my *Curricula Vitae*. The issue really isn't about my irresponsibility in teaching a dubious speculation. Whether or not it's dubious is a presumptive judgment, based on my lack of authority to teach, being, as I am, a member of the Great Unwashed Masses rather than a scholar in the field recognized for his advanced degrees. This is exactly the same kind of situation that got Galileo into hot water with the Pope. As we all know, Galileo's heliocentric view of the solar system was right, and the Pope's opposing geocentric view was wrong. But that wasn't the actual issue.

Galileo wasn't a champion of science against religion, as our schoolchildren are being taught. He was a devout Christian, so committed to God that he acquired a Bible and made the effort to read and understand it. Knowing Scripture, he challenged the Duchess of Tuscany's view that the geocentric position was Biblical by pointing out that it was a secular Greek notion that the Church held to as an extra-Biblical theme and which had nothing to do with Scripture.

What angered the Pope in this was Galileo's audacity as a Church layperson to presume to understand the Bible, a position granted only to the Church elite. In this, the Pope adhered to the same egocentric mindset as the Pharisees in Jesus' day. The Gospels quite plainly convey the opinion that Jesus held regarding the religious movers and shakers.

I am fully aware of the fact that in publishing my perceptions of the Holy Spirit and other matters having to do with my understanding of Scripture, I have assumed the responsibilities of a teacher. Despite my comment in the dedication of my book *Family of God* that I have more freedom than those in a pastoral position to engage in speculation, I have and continue to take that responsibility seriously. What I had written in *Family of God* was not hastily or shallowly formulated; to the contrary, it was the result of many years of pondering and reviewing Scripture. To any caution that may be directed to me regarding responsibility, I respond with Jesus' Parable of the Talents. Furthermore, I would say that if a person happens to chance upon a breathtakingly beautiful picture, is he right to be so cautious as to deny sharing it with others? To me that would fall short of the exercise of love, as Jesus commanded of us.

I would suggest instead that it is also the responsibility of a teacher, if he is committed to some particular understanding, to share it with the certain knowledge that God is fully capable of propagating or cutting off a thought. I might add, tossing this intellectual grenade back in the lap of its originator, that the burden of responsibility is equally on the shoulders of anyone who might be tempted to make a too-hasty objection to the associations that I have made, thus denying this potential insight to the Christian public at large.

The bottom line regarding this discussion is that the objections that I have received to date give me no compelling, Scriptural-based reason to alter my perception of the female nature of the Holy Spirit from that which I presented in *Family of God*.

There also is a practical side to my view of the nature of the Godhead. To my thinking, the association of a female function with the Holy Spirit furnishes a firm basis for the Christian objection to homosexuality that otherwise could not be made. Without rancor for individuals who are afflicted with that practice, I firmly believe that homosexuality is a sin, but for a more basic and profound reason than that it is spoken against in Genesis (Sodom) and in Leviticus and Romans. I believe that it is a sin because it is a violation of type, being contrary to the intrinsic nature of the Godhead. I also believe that the only viable alternative to considering the Holy Spirit to be functionally female is to consider the Godhead to be void of gender. I say that because if gender was involved in the Godhead and it was all male, then homosexuality would not represent a violation of type. God may just as well have populated the Garden of Eden with Adam and Steve rather than Adam and Eve; after all, it would then more closely correspond to the nature of the Godhead itself. But if gender is not involved in the Godhead, God being above that kind of thing, we would end up with a passionless God incapable of experiencing for Himself that which He fashioned in His creation and asks of us to respond toward Him. That would give us an experiential edge on God as well as to suggest hypocrisy in His nature, something that I would consider to be close to a truly blasphemous notion.

The problem that underlies the reluctance of many to resolve the gender paradox is the misunderstanding of sexuality to be morally impure, something that belongs in the material world only and has no place in heaven. This misapprehension, which actually is part of the Gnostic belief system despite the conviction of numerous Gnostic adherents that the Holy Spirit possesses a feminine gender, was fostered by the excesses of the ancient religions, which themselves represented a garbled form of the understanding of God imparted to the first humans. The garbling itself was a product of man's descent into primitive conditions and the continuous plague of terror from the skies above him. There is nothing whatever in Scripture that associates normal sexual activity within the marriage of a single man and a single woman with immorality or impurity. The only suggestion of the negative about sexuality in marriage offered in the New Testament is Paul's notion, particularly in 1 Corinthians 7, that marriage competes with a devotion to God, as I explain elsewhere herein. The Song of Solomon's inclusion in the canon of Scripture suggests the exact opposite of the association of immorality with marital sex, as did Jesus' honoring of marriage with His first miracle, as noted in John 2, and, of course, the references to His followers as His Bride.

A marriage is a unique institution that connotes mutual ownership. Mutual ownership in love reaches beyond joint ownership to encapsulate the state of intimate belonging. Within a family, its members belong to each other; they own each other. Within the Godhead, this mutual ownership is an unbreakable bond. It is in this context that Jeremiah 10:10-13 should be interpreted: God speaking of wisdom, understanding and power in a possessive sense, claiming ownership of the female Holy Spirit whose attributes God describes. It is in this same sense that the female Arm of the Lord, another term for the Holy Spirit, is described in Isaiah 51:9 and 10, wherein the original "she" in this passage was deliberately replaced by the gender-neutral "it" by translators who lacked understanding. Here is how it should have been translated:

> *Awake, awake, put on strength, O arm of the Lord; awake, as in the ancient days, in the generations of old. Art thou not she who hast cut Rahab, and wounded the dragon? Art thou not she who hast dried the sea, the waters of the great deep; who hath made the depths of the sea a way for the ransomed to pass over?*

I expand in Chapters 10 through 12 on my views as to why early Christianity linked sexuality with moral impurity. It is my heartfelt conviction that if the Church requires a correction in its teachings, among the most urgent would be the topic of sexual conduct and its relationship to godly purity. With regard to this item, it is I who might appropriately be judgmental of the current religious teaching standard.

Eight

SCRIPTURAL SUGGESTIONS OF A FEMININE HOLY SPIRIT

It might be thought by some that considering the Holy Spirit to be feminine goes against the grain of logic in that the woman is the weaker sex. To the doubter of this persuasion, the notion that the task of transforming a creative vision to its actuality in creation might be a feminine function appears to violate common sense. Too difficult, one might scoff, and inappropriate to confer the functional title of Divine Means on a "She".

One person, a likely candidate for harboring such thoughts, once in the heat of an argument with my wife but still rather condescendingly, pointed out to her what to him was an obvious fact: women, being weaker, shouldn't presume to handle management responsibilities.

"Weaker?" she retorted. *"Weaker?* Why do you think God made us physically smaller?" Her adversary backed off, but she matched him step by step and more, getting right into his face.

"I – I don't know," he stuttered, intimidated by her aggression.

"I'll tell you why, mister," she said. "It's because He made us to supervise you men. We don't need to be big and stupid to do that. That's what you're good for – under our direction." She walked away, dismissing him in her mind like a dumb ox.

She had a point. I hate to admit it, but she handles our financial affairs, which is a major household responsibility, for the simple reason that she can perform that task far better than I could. Nor am I the only man in that situation. In fact, it is the wives of most of the married men of my acquaintance who take care of financial matters in their households, as well as the scheduling of events, assuming the primary responsibility for rearing the children at home, maintaining the house, driving the family bus, and a multitude of other tasks, often all the while holding down a responsible job of her own.

I empty the garbage, haul out the trash, mow and trim the lawn, trim the hedges, and perform a myriad of other jobs as assigned by her. I kind of am a dumb ox, or perhaps a grunt corporal to her captaincy. But she's happy, and that's what matters most to me. So don't try to tell me that women can't get the job done, even if it is with my help. I know better. NASA knows better, too. Experiments have shown that in many tough situations women are stronger and display more endurance than men.

There's no doubt whatsoever in my mind that my life would be far less colorful without my wife Carolyn. It is her that sets the agenda for most of our activities. We never would have gotten a sailboat without her enthusiasm for sailing. We never would have enjoyed the RV lifestyle without her urging us to participate in it. Furthermore, I can't remember all the times she's helped to get us out of jams. But I do remember one incident that happened after we parked our fifth-wheel RV outside Charleston, South Carolina and drove our truck into the city.

There's a parking lot in downtown Charleston, next to an adjoining building that has an unusually-designed downspout. The pipe is the standard diameter, maybe two or three inches, from the roof gutter down to the level of my bumper, where, for some initially obscure reason that the following events clarified, an adapter expands it to a diameter of about 12 to 15 inches. If you take your truck or tow vehicle into town (the sights are certainly worth the effort) and park there, the attendant will attempt to back you into the stall in front of where it's located. If you're fresh from the pumpkin patch like me, you'll automatically follow the directions. Since you can't see the large-diameter section from your mirrors, you will hit it, an event that will immediately set off a chain reaction: the plastic section (which doubles quite convincingly as a drum) implodes into shards with a horrible high-volume noise that convinces the unfortunate driver that he has just leveled the house; as the driver gets out of the car, a ground-floor window opens up and an arm reaches out with the palm facing upward; along with the hand a disembodied voice (the face can't be seen) says, "Oh, you've done it now. That's gonna cost you fifty dollars." It's just a little scam, so I'm guessing that most people slap fifty onto the palm just to get rid of the problem.

I probably would have done the same had I been alone, but egged on by Carolyn, I refused to knuckle under. I argued about it and threatened to go down to Home Depot myself and buy the part for ten dollars. In the end, I coughed up 25 dollars, but it was good for a laugh after we both cooled down. In the heat of the moment, though, I had to restrain Carolyn from jumping out of the truck and confronting the man. Having seen her in action before, I have no doubt that had she gotten out and caught him with her glare, he would have backed off like a slug under a rain of salt.

It was noted in the previous chapter that when men fail to step up to the plate, God is content to let a woman do the job. Like Deborah in the Book of Judges or Golda Meir of recent Israeli history, they can handle the job admirably. It already has been noted that the Arm of the Lord, to which Isaiah referred in Isaiah 51, and who performed mighty tasks associated with great strength (perhaps in a supervisory role), was feminine in the original version of that prophet's writings. More will be said later about that passage.

It appears, from Scriptural passages such as Proverbs 15:29 and 28:9 and Isaiah 1:15, that God neither listens nor responds to some prayers directed to Him. The prayers must align with God's will and be spoken in truth and righteousness.

> *The Lord is far from the wicked, but he heareth the prayer of the righteous... He that turneth away his ear from hearing the law, even his prayer shall be an abomination.*

> *And when ye spread forth your hands, I will hide mine eyes from you; yea, when ye make many prayers, I will not hear. Your hands are full of blood.*

On the other hand, God is quick to listen and respond to prayers said according to His own will, and when it is in His will it is Wisdom, His divine Spouse, who directs the responding. One of my favorite passages in the Bible is the account in 1 Kings 3:5-28 wherein Solomon, the newly-crowned king of Israel, prays to God for wisdom, in this sense a spiritual gift given of Herself and in indwelling communion with Herself by the Holy Spirit, who Herself is named for that attribute:

> *In Gibeon the Lord appeared to Solomon in a dream by night, and God said, Ask what I shall give thee. And Solomon said, Thou hast showed unto thy servant David, my father, great mercy, according as he walked before thee in truth, and in righteousness, and in uprightness of heart with thee; and thou hast kept for him this great kindness, that thou hast given him a son to sit on his throne, as it is this day. And now, O Lord my God, thou hast made thy servant king instead of David, my father; and I am but a little child: I know not how to go out or come in. And thy servant is in the midst of thy people whom thou hast chosen, a great people, who cannot be numbered or counted for multitude. Give, therefore, thy servant an understanding heart to judge thy people, that I may discern between good and bad. For who is able to judge this thy great people?*

And the speech pleased the Lord, that Solomon had asked this thing. And God said unto him, Because thou hast asked this thing, and hast not asked for thyself long life; neither hast asked riches for thyself, nor hast asked the life of thine enemies, but hast asked for thyself understanding to discern judgment, behold, I have done according to thy words: lo, I have given thee a wise and understanding heart, so that there was none like thee before thee, neither after thee shall any arise like unto thee. And I have also given thee that which thou hast not asked, both riches, and honor, so that there shall not be any among the kings like unto thee all thy days. And if thou wilt walk in my ways, to keep my statutes and my commandments, as thy father, David, did walk, then I will lengthen thy days.

And Solomon awoke, and behold, it was a dream. And he came to Jerusalem, and stood before the ark of the covenant of the Lord, and offered up burnt offerings, and offered peace offerings, and made a feast to all his servants. Then came two women, who were harlots, unto the king, and stood before him. And the one woman said, O my lord, I and this woman dwell in one house, and I was delivered of a child with her in the house. And it came to pass the third day after that I was delivered, that this woman was delivered also, and we were together. There was no stranger with us in the house, save we two were in the house. And this woman's child died in the night, because she overlaid it. And she arose at midnight and took my son from beside me, while thine handmaiden slept, and laid it in her bosom, and laid her dead child in my bosom. And when I arose in the morning to nurse my child, behold, it was dead; but when I had looked at it in the morning, behold, it was not my son whom I did bear. And the older woman said, Nay; but the living child is my son, and the dead is thy son. And this said, No; but the dead child is thy son, and the living is my son. Thus they spoke before the king.

Then said the king, The one saith, This is my son who liveth, and thy son is the dead; and the other saith, Nay; but thy son is the dead child, and my son is the living. And the king said, Bring me a sword. And they brought a sword before the king. And the king said, Divide the living child in two, and give half to the one, and half to the other. Then spoke the woman whose the living child was unto the king, for her bowels yearned upon her son, and she said, O my lord, give her the living child, and in no wise slay it. But the other said, Let it be neither mine nor thine, but divide it.

Then the king answered and said, Give her the living child, and by no means slay it; she is the mother of it. And all Israel heard of the judgment which the king had judged, and they feared the king; for they saw that the wisdom of God was in him, to do justice."

That Solomon was given wisdom by God is amply demonstrated by this spectacular display of justice served. But note the nature and the character of Solomon's prayer to God for that wisdom. Foremost, it was both selfless and noble: Solomon asked for the ability to serve the Lord in a manner that would be pleasing to Him. It was also humble: in his prayer, Solomon noted his youth and its shortcomings with respect to leadership.

Far too often, when I think about God while reading the Bible, I fail to pray for understanding. But sometimes I do ask for knowledge, and it is those times that I seem to get insights into Scripture that rise above my own abilities. This gift beyond my own abilities dovetails well with Jesus words in Matthew 7:7-11:

Ask, and it shall be given you; seek, and ye shall find; knock, and it shall be opened unto you; for every one that asketh receiveth; and he that seeketh findeth; and to him that knocketh it shall be opened. Or what man is there of you whom, if his son ask bread, will he give him a stone? Or if he ask a fish, will he give him a serpent? If ye, then, being evil, know how to give good gifts unto your children, how much more shall your Father, who is in heaven, give good things to them that ask him?"

In this chapter, I'd like to share with you some understandings that I have been given while praying for a deeper knowledge of God. They relate to the feminine nature of Wisdom, the Holy Spirit.

Direct Scriptural reference to a feminine Holy Spirit

As noted in Chapter Seven, there actually are references to the Holy Spirit by the pronoun "She". The most significant of these is the use of the feminine pronoun in Jesus' own words in the John 14:26 as recorded in the Siniatic Palimpsest, the oldest copy of the Gospel known to be in existence. Also, in Romans 9:25 of the King James Version, Paul uses "She" in referring to the Holy Spirit. Again, in Romans 1:20, Paul's reference to the Godhead is made in the feminine derivative of the word "theos". Furthermore, as noted before, it is known that in Scriptural translations of Isaiah 51:9 and 10 in the Nicene era and later, the reference to the feminine Arm of the Lord was deliberately switched from "she" to the neuter "It".

Given this evidence, it is quite possible that all uses of the male pronoun "He" to refer to the Holy Spirit were all switched at one time from "She". There is no evidence to suggest otherwise.

Furthermore, the "El Shaddai" of the Old Testament actually translates to "full-breasted". The Isrealites of the Old Testament directly linked "El Shaddai", the "Spirit of God", "Dove", and the "Holy Spirit" with a feminine Entity.

The Most Significant Scriptural Indication of a Feminine Holy Spirit

As the rebuttals to the objections made in Chapter 7 to a female Holy Spirit pointed out, a feminine Holy Spirit is generally in harmony with Scripture. Perhaps the most significant suggestion of femininity in the Bible may be found in the property of indwelling, a characteristic of the Holy Spirit that strongly connects the New Testament with the Old.

That the Old Testament *Shekinah* is the New Testament's Holy Spirit is manifestly evident in the precursor role to the indwelling

Holy Spirit of the *Shekinah Glory* who indwelt both the Tabernacle in the wilderness and Solomon's Temple at their dedications. Since it has been claimed that the word *Shekinah* does not exist in the Hebrew Scriptures in its noun form (the situation there being similar to the absence in the Bible of a noun form of the word *baptize*), the following commentary will be made regarding its origin before proceeding with examples of the Shekinah presence.

In the Hebrew Targum, the Aramaic translation of the Hebrew Old Testament, the word *Shekinah* is used as a noun. It means "intimate dwelling" or "the presence of the Glory of the Lord". Justification for the use of this word is the use in the Hebrew Scriptures of its root word "shachan", referring particularly to the pillars of cloud and fire that accompanied the Israelites in their journey from Egypt to the Promised Land through the wilderness. The prophet Isaiah referred to it quite graphically in Isaiah 4:5 and 6, linking this pillar of cloud and fire to a covering presence. It is generally understood that this same pillar is referenced in Isaiah 51:9 and 10, where the prophet goes out of his way to describe by feminine pronouns the same pillar of cloud and fire that accompanied the Israelites on their journey from Egypt. The Targum interpretation leaves no doubt that the *Shekinah Glory* is a feminine presence, and represents an equivalence with a feminine Holy Spirit. Isaiah 4:5 and 6, and 51:9 and 10 read as follows:

> *And the Lord will create upon every dwelling place of Mount Zion , and upon her assemblies, a cloud and smoke by day, and the shining of a flaming fire by night; for upon all the glory shall be a defense. And there shall be a tabernacle for a shadow in the daytime from the heat, and for a place of refuge, and for a covert from storm and from rain.*

> *Awake, awake, put on strength, O arm of the Lord; awake, as in the ancient days, in the generations of old. Art thou not she who hast cut Rahab, and wounded the dragon? Art thou not she who has dried the sea, the waters of the great deep; who hath made the depths of the sea a way for the ransomed to pass over?*

Exodus 40 and 1 Kings 8 provide prominent examples of the *Shekinah* as a precursor to the indwelling Holy Spirit of the New Testament.   Exodus 40:33-38 describes the indwelling of the Tabernacle in the wilderness:

> *And [Moses] reared up the court round about the tabernacle and the altar, and set up the hanging of the court gate. So Moses finished the work.*
>
> *Then a cloud covered the tent of the congregation, and the glory of the Lord filled the tabernacle. And when the cloud was taken up from over the tabernacle, the children of Israel went onward in all their journeys; but if the cloud were not taken up, then they journeyed not till the day that it was taken up. For the cloud of the Lord was upon the tabernacle by day, and fire was on it by night, in the sight of all the house of Israel, throughout all their journeys.*

The description "cloud of the Lord" , "fire by night" and "taken up" leaves no doubt that this "cloud" is equivalent to the *Shekinah* of the Red Sea adventure and of Isaiah 4:5. The corresponding incident with respect to Solomon's Temple, taken from 1 Kings 8:6-13, is given below:

> *And the priests brought in the ark of the covenant of the Lord unto its place, into the inner sanctuary of the house, into the most holy place, even under the wings of the cherubim. For the cherubim spread forth their two wings of the place of the ark, and the cherubim covered the ark and its staves above. And they drew out the staves, that the ends of the staves were seen out in the holy place before the inner sanctuary, but they were not seen outside; and there they are unto this day. There was nothing in the ark except the two tables of stone, which Moses put there at Horeb, when the lord made a covenant with the children of Israel, when they came out of the land of Egypt. And it came to pass, when the priests were come out of the holy place, that the cloud filled the house of the lord, so that the priests could not stand to minister because of the cloud; for the glory of the Lord had filled the house of the*

Lord. Then spoke Solomon, The Lord said he would dwell in the thick darkness. I have surely built thee an house to dwell in, a settled place for thee to abide in forever."

In this passage the meaning of "cloud" is closely linked with "dwelling place" and "glory of the Lord", which again point to the phrase *Shekinah Glory.*

The connection between these precursor events and the Holy Spirit who indwells Christian believers is given in 1 Corinthians 3:16 and Ephesians 2:19-22, wherein Paul asserts that the Church herself, through her constituents, is a temple indwelt by the Holy Spirit:

Know ye not that ye are the temple of God, and that the Spirit of God dwelleth in you?

Now, therefore, ye are no more strangers and sojourners, but fellow citizens with the saints, and of the household of God; and are built upon the foundation of the apostles and prophets, Jesus Christ himself being the chief corner stone, in whom all the building fitly framed together groweth unto an holy temple in the Lord; in whom ye also are built together for an habitation of God through the Spirit.

The facts embedded in these passages are no surprise to Christians, who generally accept without question that believers are indwelt with the Holy Spirit and comprise, as the Church, a holy temple. What some of us may not be aware of is that this temple and its indwelling by the Holy Spirit was represented numerous times as the Glory of God in the Old Testament. Turning to the Internet, the Wikipedia entry for "Shekinah" begins as follows:

Hebrew [Shekinah] is the English spelling of a grammatically feminine Hebrew ancient blessing. The original word means the *dwelling* or *settling,* and denotes the dwelling or settling of the divine presence of God, especially in the temple in Jerusalem." An accompanying figure shows the Shekinah, or the Glory of God, indwelling the temple as described in 1 Kings 8.

Noting the female gender of this indwelling Shekinah, we find here by comparing the indwelling presence of the Glory in Solomon's temple with the description in Ephesians 2 of the Holy Spirit indwelling the human temple that Scripture itself, by furnishing this direct comparison, supports an interpretation of the Holy Spirit as a female Entity in the face of conventional Christian thought, as driven by the use in Scripture of the male pronoun in reference to the Holy Spirit.

This feminine gender attribute in Exodus 40 and 1 Kings 8 may have been simply lost in the translation from Hebrew (Aramaic) to English, which could have been a result of the lack of gender precision in the English language. (Actually, the first transference from feminine to masculine occurred in the Latin, for which the Holy Spirit was definitely presented as male.) But there is an associated gender misrepresentation in Isaiah 51:9, 10 that appears to be more deliberate. What the translators did in that passage was to substitute the grammatically incorrect 'it' for the gender-correct 'she' in reference to Shekinah. In their desire to maintain a fully masculine Godhead, they neutered the female. In the process, they inadvertently managed also to castrate their masculine God. As noted before at the end of Chapter 7, as just one example of this removal of gender Isaiah 51:9 and 10 refers to a neuter Arm of the Lord rather than the original feminine gender.

In addition to the femininity of the *Shekinah Glory*, other sources have pointed to a most interesting situation where the gender-neutral word *God* was substituted in numerous references in the Hebrew Scriptures for a specifically feminine Member of the Godhead denoted by the feminine word *Eloah*. *Eloah* was frequently used to depict the Judeo-Christian God in the original Hebrew Scripture, particularly in the Book of Job. In one count, it was claimed that this word for God was used 57 times in the original Scripture. In addition to that, the grammatically feminine Hebrew words *Ruach ha Kodesh* (*Ruah* in Aramaic) translate to Holy Spirit. *Ruah* and *Eloah* are considered by many to refer to that same Person in the Godhead, the Holy Spirit.

No longer on the defensive

Why has this link between the Holy Spirit and the Shekinah Glory been ignored for so long? Having attended several theological conferences associated with the Baptist community, I have in my mind an overview of the nature of the theology that is discussed among the intellectual leaders of that community. Typical topics under discussion among them are nowhere close to the importance of dialogue concerning gender within the Godhead, and yet that topic seems never to have been touched. It's time to change that dialogue.

Having taken a primarily defensive position up to this point, I am confident that my answers regarding the female function of the Holy Spirit are sufficiently logical that they justify my taking the opposite stance. In that vein, I respectfully invite any individual who objects to my view of the female functional nature of the Holy Spirit to respond with rebuttals of the following Scripturally-based items that support my viewpoint.

Marriage of Christ with His Church as representative of the family nature of the Godhead.

The rebuttal must take into account the fact that Jesus claimed that He is the Image of the Father, as well as address the oddity that while one Member would have a gender-based relationship, the other Members would not.

The linkage in John 3 of the Holy Spirit with spiritual birth.

Birth, whether it is physical or spiritual, is a profoundly female function. John 3 directly links this function with the Holy Spirit.

The linkage of the Holy Spirit with Song of Solomon.

Many respected Bible commentators agree that Song of Solomon represents the future relationship between Christ and His Church.

Well they should make this claim, for if it did not say something about God or His relationship with mankind, it wouldn't belong in Scripture. Moreover, Song of Solomon confirms the romantic nature of which God (Jesus and Church and/or Father and Holy Spirit) is capable in the spiritual domain.

As I had noted in Chapter 7 under the topic of passion in God, the published commentaries on the Song of Solomon in both the Reformation Study Bible and the Schofield Bible directly link the relationship between the lovers in this book with the anticipated future relationship between Jesus Christ and His Church.

However, it would be self-inconsistent for Jesus Christ alone among the Members of the Godhead to enjoy this type of relationship. If Jesus is the Image of the Father (John 8:19, 14:7,9), then Song of Solomon should also describe the relationship between the other two Persons of the Godhead, Father and Holy Spirit.

The linkage of the Holy Spirit with Proverbs.

The Book of Proverbs beautifully and harmoniously supports a female functional designation for the Holy Spirit. Of particular interest in this regard are Proverbs 3 and 8, from which the following excerpts are taken:

> *Happy is the man that findeth wisdom, and the man that getteth understanding... She is more precious than rubies: and all the things thou canst desire are not to be compared unto her. ..The Lord by wisdom hath founded the earth; by understanding hath he established the heavens... Doth not wisdom cry? And understanding put forth her voice?... The Lord possessed me in the beginning of his way, before his works of old. I was set up from everlasting, from the beginning, or ever the earth was. When there were no depths, I was brought forth; when there were no fountains abounding with water. Before the mountains were settled, before the hills was I brought forth: While as yet he had not made the earth, nor the fields, nor the highest part of the dust of the world. When he prepared the*

heavens, I was there: when he set a compass upon the face of the depth: When he established the clouds above: when he strengthened the fountains of the deep: When he gave the sea his decree, that the waters should not pass his commandment: when he appointed the foundations of the earth: Then I was by him, as one brought up with him: and I was daily his delight, rejoicing always before him; Rejoicing in the habitable part of his earth; and my delights were with the sons of men. Now therefore hearken unto me, O ye children: for blessed are they that keep my ways. Hear instruction, and be wise, and refuse it not. Blessed is the man that heareth me, watching daily at my gates, waiting at the posts of my doors. For whoso findeth me findeth life, and shall obtain favor of the Lord. But he that sinneth against me wrongeth his own soul: all they that hate me love death.

Several items come to mind from the above review of these passages in Proverbs. The first is that the Persona is female throughout; an attempt to assign some of these passages to Jesus Christ, as many do, would constitute an unnatural force-fit, most obviously in the issue of gender, but also with respect to function and role. The second is directly related to function, wherein the passages suggest a connection between Wisdom and the Holy Spirit as furnishing the most likely Person to which a female function may be assigned; the third is that the Holy Spirit was active in creation itself, as summarized in Genesis 1:1-3:

In the beginning God created the heaven and the earth. And the earth was without form, and void; and darkness was upon the face of the deep. And the Spirit of God moved upon the face of the waters. And God said, Let there be light: and there was light.

The frequent Catholic attribution of Wisdom to Mary faces the equally grave difficulty of linking Mary with capabilities such as creation that are reserved for God alone.

In the context of Scripture's general treatment of the Holy Spirit, the passage in Genesis quoted above more than suggests that the

Father was assisted by or in union with the Holy Spirit in the act of creation, the result being, as Jesus Himself suggested in Revelation 3:14, a manifestation of the Son. I am not alone in this assertion regarding the active participation of the Holy Spirit in the creation event. As a matter of fact, as I noted earlier I simply repeat the position of Benjamin B. Warfield, a noted Bible scholar who is well-respected among conservative theologians.

Any attempt at rebuttal must address Proverbs 3:19 in the context of Genesis 1:1-5, Proverbs 8:22-36, Job 26:13 and Psalm 104:30. The attempt to attribute Proverbs 8 to Jesus rather than the Holy Spirit must explain the out-of-context insertion into material descriptive of Wisdom, as well as the feminine description of Wisdom throughout the Book of Proverbs as opposed to the depiction of Jesus throughout Scripture as strongly masculine and the image of the Father. Furthermore, the attempt to link Wisdom with the Virgin Mary is unsustainable in the light of Mary's full humanity and consequent absence in the creation epic, wherein according to Chapter 8 Wisdom was at the side of the Father during the process of creation.

Wisdom, as depicted in Proverbs, is strongly female and only female. The attempt at rebuttal must also avoid taking the Jungian notion of the human psyche, both male and female, as containing both masculine and feminine elements, and extrapolating it to his notion of the Trinity. There are logical difficulties in doing so, as described below.

Scripture rather exclusively associates the Father with the Divine Will, which, as an initiating role, also is exclusively masculine. Similarly, Jesus the Son is presented in Scripture as the Divine Representation which, as the perfect image in reality of the Father would also be predominantly masculine. The masculine predominance of Jesus is given further weight by Paul's characterization in Ephesians 5 of Jesus as the Bridegroom of the (functionally feminine) Church. In *Family of God* I simply noted what to me was an obvious connecting function of the Holy Spirit between Father and Son: the Divine Means which, in union with the Divine Will, gave birth to the Divine Implementation in reality (Divine Representation). Obviously, this Divine Means, being so closely linked with the other two Members, is also Deity. Because the Divine Means performed a function that was responsive to the Will, an obviously female role, I attached a female gender to this Person. Scripture and Christian tradition both understand this third Member of the Trinity to be the Holy Spirit.

Another difficulty, and it is a big one, that I see in the notion of each Member of Godhead possessing elements of both genders is that such a state of affairs would promote self-adoration, a characteristic that I sincerely hope is lacking within the Godhead. Love and adoration require *otherness*. The alternative is narcissism. I truly believe (and hope) that both Father and Holy Spirit are as selflessly noble as the Son demonstrated on the cross.

A family-based Godhead in which the Holy Spirit is functionally female, united in love, naturally and intuitively resolves the apparent discrepancy between monotheism and a Trinitarian Godhead.

Assuredly, a union within the Godhead involving love of a non-romantic nature can be proposed. However, a rebuttal alternative should carry as much intuitive and love-inspiring force as a relationship in which a family setting is central. A rebuttal should also explain in functional terms why there is a proscription against the gay lifestyle as presented in Leviticus 18 and Romans 1. Furthermore, a rebuttal should also address the centrality of family in Scripture as well as in life in general.

Linkage of the Holy Spirit with an executive function.

This executive nature of the Holy Spirit was proposed by respected theologian Benjamin Warfield as well as others. It is certainly suggested in Scripture. An executive office is responsive to higher orders, this being within the Godhead the initiative of the Father, or Divine Will. A responsive office, in turn, is a distinctly feminine one. This creative response is distinctly different than Jesus' role as the Divine Representation, or Divine Implementation, which is, as a perfect Image of the Will, the result of creative response to the Will.

The Deeper Meaning of Adam's Rib.

The Scriptural account of the creation of man and woman is given in Genesis 1:27 and 28:

> *So God created man in his own image, in the image of God created he him; male and female created he them. And God blessed them, and God said unto them, Be fruitful and multiply, and fill the earth, and subdue it; and have dominion over the fish of the sea, and over the fowl of the air, and over every living thing that moveth upon the earth.*

In what on the surface appears to be something of an afterthought, in Genesis 2:18, 21 and 22 there is a more detailed description of how God formed Eve out of Adam:

> *And the Lord God said, It is not good that the man should be alone; I will make him an help fit for him. . . And the Lord God caused a deep sleep to fall upon Adam, and he slept: and he took one of his ribs, and closed up the flesh instead thereof. And the rib, which the Lord God had taken from man, made he a woman, and brought her unto the man.*

There is nothing in this passage that directly relates to the intrinsic nature of God, but the fact that God chose to point out in this detail the specifics of the process by which Eve was formed, along with the many more overtly definitive Scriptural pointers to the femininity of the Holy Spirit, is profoundly suggestive of its use by God as a model of the manifestation of the Holy Spirit as taken out of Himself in selfless love. This vision, which I noted in Chapter 5 of *Buddy* and excerpted in Chapter 6 of this work, transforms what might be considered to be a rather mundane and even somewhat extraneous Scriptural passage into a spectacularly beautiful description of the Father's elevation of love to the status of His primary characteristic. A brief paragraph of that excerpt from *Buddy* is repeated below:

He chose to manifest an Other out of Himself, giving up part of Himself in the process and restricting His portion in everything that is or ever will be to that of one Member of a Partnership. He decided to share His exalted position with that Other. But here's the great beauty of what he did: in relinquishing His singleness He added love into the mix. And through this love He again became One with His Other.

Nine

SOME CHRISTIAN CHURCHES THAT APPRECIATE THE FEMININE NATURE OF THE HOLY SPIRIT

I sometimes wonder what would have become of my understanding of God had my parents, grieving over my misbehavior as I noted in Chapter 4, marched me from the police station to a better Church than the sorry excuse that I was forced to attend. They certainly had other opportunities, for that particular incident was but one among many such sordid episodes in our coming of age.

For a few years during our preteens our neighborhood was embroiled in open warfare. It began inadvertently by our parents, who armed us with BB guns, which we promptly turned on each other. Usually my brother and I were pitted against Dave and Jeff. As such things inevitably do, the warfare engendered an arms race. Unknown to our parents we'd hold back on the Fourth of

July fireworks, hoarding them for our more sinister pursuit. Away from their watchful eyes we'd tear apart the firecrackers and save the powder in a jar. We'd also dig in the backyard for clay and mold ourselves very realistic grenades. We'd poke a hole in the top, and after they dried hard we'd fill the hole with powder and stick in a fuse. Now, along with the flying BBs, we'd have exploding shrapnel filling the air. We also made a pipe cannon. Capping one end of a section of galvanized water pipe, we drilled a hole near the cap into which we'd insert powder and a fuse, and pop a marble into the muzzle. We tried it out against the stucco wall of our house one day the minute our parents left for the store. It worked great, so good that a neighbor lady called the police.

We continued to load it up and fire away, starting to go through military aiming procedures when a police officer, who had been sneaking down the side of the house, suddenly jumped into the open to confront us. Unfortunately, we already had lit the fuse. We stared at him helplessly as he began his harangue, not knowing that he was inside the target circle. I made a surreptitious effort to redirect the pipe, but he shouted to get my hands off it. I still remember his expression and his pointing finger as the glass round whistled past his arm to strike the wall beyond.

We paid for that debacle with an involuntary arms reduction move by our parents. Fortunately, it was temporary. Somewhat subdued, my brother and I used that hiatus to construct our next war machine: a tank. Built atop an old four-wheeled coaster, it was absolutely impregnable. There was even a turret and a hatch atop it for entry. Our house was located at the top of a steep hill and after issuing a challenge to our enemy who awaited us on a level stretch of pavement below, we climbed in, poked a BB gun out of the turret, and headed off to the fray.

We hadn't thought our tactics through. The tank, being unpowered, stopped when it reached the level stretch. The enemy simply approached behind the turret and turned the tank upside down, trapping us inside as they peppered us with BBs and grenades. My brother and I, finally appreciating the stupidy of the whole skirmish, took it out on each other. It was awful.

If I had been marched into a better Church after an episode of miscreancy, would I have become a Christian right then and there? If I did, would I have been less skeptical of Church dogma and therefore more open to the acceptance of it as irrefutable truth? In brief, would I have been a more docile (and shallow) member of the Church as a whole?

There are other alternative scenarios of my becoming a Christian: perhaps I would have questioned less at the outset and rejected it at the first hint of a contradiction. Or maybe I would have rejected the Gospel for other reasons.

But that kind of speculation leads nowhere, because there are an infinite number of possibilities to speculate upon, and, in the end it doesn't matter anyway. It is what it is. Here I stand, deeply committed to my Christian faith after having been distanced by God from my earlier rejection, with a number of slipups and chastisements along the way, and burdened now with a system of belief that doesn't quite square with the thinking of the Church.

But if that makes me a heretic to the main body of the Church, at least I don't stand as alone as I had originally thought.

I categorize the Church that opposes my viewpoint as Western, both Catholic and Protestant, because many Eastern Churches, particularly those among Churches of Egyptian Coptic and Syriac roots, do indeed acknowledge the feminine nature of the Holy Spirit, as did the Jewish religion. Of the Western Churches, a substantial component of the Messianic Jewish community also considers the Holy Spirit to be feminine.

It was with this welcome understanding that I pursued my research on other theologians and Churches within the community of Western Christianity, following which I posted the article below on my blog site *friendofthefamily.wordpress.com*:

I'm Not as Alone as I Thought

As I learn more about the early Christians and the Church Fathers, I'm beginning to appreciate that there have been more sheep than I first thought who have been feeding in my little field.

Not long ago my pastor loaned me a little paperback book entitled *Creation out of Nothing,* written by Paul Copan and William Lane Craig and published in 2004. The primary issue for Drs. Copan and Craig is the question as to whether God created the heavens and earth from nothing (*creatio ex nihilo)* or whether He did so from pre-existing matter (*creatio ex materia).* Admittedly, I hadn't given the matter much thought because I had simply assumed that God, being God, wouldn't have the need to start with something already at hand. I found the topic fascinating, however, and was intrigued with the necessity of addressing it, which, it seems, began with the Gnostic view of matter as evil and thus out of the realm of God's creative effort. I was also intrigued with the arguments that the authors presented in favor of *creatio ex nihilo,* which covered a range of source material from the Old and New Testaments, as well as information from extrabiblical sources, including religious texts and scientific data. The source that most impresses me is John 1:3:

All things were made by him, and without him was nothing made that was made.

As far as I can see, that statement pretty much covers it all. That, and the fact that if God had to rely on pre-existing material to perform His creative work, He couldn't exactly be called omnipotent.

Interested as I became in the main theme of the book, what really grabbed my attention was a side issue, one almost but not quite confined to the footnote region. On page 23 of the book, the church father Irenaeus is said to have essentially equated Wisdom with the Holy Spirit. Nor was this association trivially presented, for on page 24 Wisdom is described by Copan and Craig as a Craftsman at God's side, with a reference to Proverbs 8:27 and 30:

When he prepared the heavens, I was there: when he set a compass upon the face of the depth. . .Then I was by him, as one brought up with him: and I was daily his delight, rejoicing always before him;

The association of Wisdom with the Holy Spirit immediately exposes a gender issue, for Wisdom in Proverbs is identified as a female personage. It is precisely the same issue that led so many "experts" to pasteurize their attempts to offer "explanations" of the Holy Trinity into cold and ultimately empty logical sophistries. One can only conclude that such "explanations" are products of self-interest and fear. Irenaeus, on the other hand, seems not to have been so burdened with socio-political concerns; apparently, he seriously entertained the thought of associating the Holy Spirit with a female function despite his possible disregard of sexuality within Christianity as noted in Chapter Seven.

The reference to Proverbs 8:27 and 30 again associates Wisdom with the Holy Spirit, and this time it sets the record straight as to whom this passage refers. The prevailing preference is to associate this passage with Jesus, despite its obviously being out of context for that identification, as I noted in *Family of God.* I was most happy to note that the authors of *Creation out of Nothing* understood this and properly associated the passage with Wisdom. I think that the authors understand the unstated implication of attributing the verses to Wisdom: again, that the Holy Spirit and Wisdom are one and the same, and in the context of the nature of Wisdom presented in Proverbs, the Holy Spirit thus possesses a female functionality.

The authors go further, noting on page 25 the self-sufficiency of an intra-Trinitarian love relationship. Love relationship indeed, and one that we can readily identify with on an intuitive level.

I'm more than happy to share my little turf with others. I just wish that they'd come on in, rather than just poking their heads through the fence.

Over the course of the history of the Church, there indeed have been people who have spoken up regarding important aspects of the true nature of Christianity in contradiction to the mainstream viewpoint, and some have even managed to be heard over the tumult of the opposing voices of highly respected but blind and shallow theologians. As I noted in Chapter 7, one of those few who understood better than his peers was the writer of the introduction to the Song of Solomon in the 1967 edition of the Authorized King James Version of the Holy Bible, edited by C. I. Schofield, D.D.

The writer of this introduction was lacking in one important association, that the Song of Solomon may well have been an allegory of the intra-Godhead relationship as well as representing the relationship between Christ and His Church. Perhaps, like his peer from the Reformation Reference Bible who wrote the comparable introduction to the Song of Solomon, he was tempted to do so, but was forced to back off from such a direct contradiction to the teachings of the Church, despite its harmony with Scripture.

In the Catholic canon, as I noted in Chapter 7, Chapter 9 of the Book of Wisdom describes Wisdom in a context that virtually declares this female Persona to be the Holy Spirit. No other Biblical personage, human or God, harmonizes so fully with the descriptive material of that chapter.

I was tempted to include the Nag Hammadi documents, buried in Egypt and uncovered in 1945, as material supportive of a feminine Holy Spirit. What held me back from this was my reading of the Gospel of Thomas which was found among these ancient writings, from which I took away the strong sense that the writer of this document was clueless as to the true nature and character of Jesus, whom he presented as entirely at odds with the selfless, noble and spiritually-inclined Jesus of the canonical Gospels.

Well after I had pieced together the information I have presented above, I came across, through a search of books offered by Amazon, two authors whose views closely paralleled my own. One was written by a woman, Patricia Taylor, to be specific, entitled *The Holy Spirit: The Feminine Nature of God*, published by iUniverse, Inc., and the other entitled *Sophia The Holy Spirit* and published through the organization La Ermita – The Hermitage, Inc. The publication date of Mrs. Taylor's book is 2009, while that for the other is 2010.

Like my books, they both employ logic similar to my own to justify the femininity of the Holy Spirit, and they both view the primary consequence of this feminine Presence within the Godhead as supportive of a loving Divine Family.

Their books both differ from mine in their adamant claims that the use of masculine pronouns to refer to the Holy Spirit was never inspired by God and, furthermore, was not in the original versions of the texts but rather was a deliberate alteration performed in later translations in an attempt to distance their Christianity from its Gnostic and pagan rivals. Regardless of the purity of this intent on the part of the early clergy, it represents a gross violation of the sacredness of Holy Scripture, something on the order of a layperson entering the Holy of Holies in Solomon's Temple.

These authors possess sound backup for their claim, perhaps the most significant of which is the Siniatic Palimpsest discussed in Chapters 4 and 7, in which in the original Jesus is recorded in John 14:26 as referring to the Holy Spirit with feminine pronouns.

As I had noted in several places in my books, I consider this "he" issue to represent the most substantial of the objections to a feminine Holy Spirit. If these authors are indeed correct, as I think they are, those who insist upon either the masculinity or the gender-neutrality of the Holy Spirit have some very spindly legs to stand on.

The timing and similarities in what the three of us have had to say about a feminine Holy Spirit leads me to believe that the Holy Spirit Herself is taking an active part in our understanding of God. An observation made by one of the authors, Mr. Meisner, is that over the past decade or so the Internet has seen a substantial increase in the number of people interested in the possibility of a feminine Holy Spirit. This, too, indicates an active involvement of God.

But then there's that thing about my marching to a different drummer. It continues to haunt me. After all is said and done, maybe my mama was right.

But that doesn't mean I'm wrong about the Holy Spirit.

Ten

THE OVERT CAUSES OF THE DENIAL OF A FEMININE HOLY SPIRIT

Denial is an interesting word. It has a variety of diverse applications and a lot of baggage. Usually a person goes into denial of a fact or situation because he doesn't want to accept something. I once saw a severe case of on-the-spot open denial. When I recall it I'm tempted myself to deny that it really happened, because it involves guilt on my part. At the time our family vehicle had just completed a long and arduous climb up a primitive logging road to the summit of Dog Mountain near the towns of Morton and Glenoma in Western Washington State. It was late in the afternoon, and we were there so that I could show Carolyn the point from which we would, the next morning, answer the question that she posed to me the week before after we had come down to a landing from the big hill. "When are we going to get some real air time?" she had asked, in a moment of bravado as I had found out later. But it was a valid question – the big hill was a training hill because it supported neither ridge lift nor thermal activity. It was high enough, to be sure, but flights off it were considered sled rides, because after launch the flight path was unidirectionally downward and the average flight time was on the order of five or so minutes.

We weren't going to fly that late afternoon at Dog, because I already had learned my lesson with Danny on late-afternoon flights, where the prevailing drift of air is downward and not conducive to a successful launch, and even more so with two people aboard.

The launch was already occupied when we arrived. When we stepped out of the vehicle we saw a lone figure there, already hooked in and ready to go for it. He hesitated, though, and for a very good reason: the air was quite obviously drifting downslope. The launch at Dog isn't a true cliff. It's quite steep, but not almost vertical like the big training hill. Therefore, the wings must provide lift in order for the pilot to leave the ground.

Here's where my guilt kicks in. We could see that a successful launch would be very iffy. So could he. His hesitation turned lengthy. In retrospect, I realize that he was getting ready to back off, tear down his kite, and wait until morning for better conditions. What prevented him from doing just that was our presence and his pride. We immediately should have returned to our vehicle and gone back down the mountain.

But no. We remained right there staring at him. He returned the stare and then looked back down the hill. I saw the exact moment when he committed to the launch. It was in his eyeballs. His brain was in complete denial and, with a shout of "Geronimo!" he started running.

Up to that point there was a darkly strange consistency to Carolyn's exposure to hang flight. Every time we went to a site that would be new to Carolyn, the events would include an unsuccessful launch of one sort or another. It was kind of cosmic.

With this particular launch Carolyn's record remained intact, but, unfortunately, the pilot didn't. His denial had consequences. He continued to run, ever faster as his desperation increased and the hill steepened, until his legs began to blur. But his wings, refusing to develop lift, betrayed him. His run ended abruptly against a large bush, into which he inserted himself quite deeply. The next sound that came out of his mouth was a very loud groan.

We helped pick him out of the bush, and were relieved to find that he hadn't broken any bones. His skin didn't look so great, but he was going to survive.

There are lots of reasons for denial. This particular one was pride. The gentleman didn't want to be seen wimping out of a launch.

It turns out that pride is the source of lots of denials. Regarding the issue of a feminine Holy Spirit, pride is very much involved in the denial of that notion by many, particularly by men of the cloth. In my book *Buddy*, that very issue of pride and denial enters the conversation between Wisdom and Earl regarding opposition to a feminine Holy Spirit:

> "That little background tidbit brings me to the main reason as to why I'm here. As to specifics: I'm going to move you to read and digest particular passages of Scripture that have to do with your gift, which is knowledge imparted to you about our family-structured interrelationship. Then you'll be moved to write about your findings. After that is the hard part: you'll be sharing your findings with others through a blog on the Internet. You'll get some reactions to it that you wouldn't believe if you didn't experience the rants. Most of them will be coming from those who consider themselves to be good Christians. But you'll also reach those for whom the message is intended."

> "I'm ready to do this, but I can't figure out why a person, especially a Christian, would be against learning more about God, and more so because it would help him to love God in a way that wouldn't otherwise be possible."

> "Oh, there are reasons. Lots of them. I'll give you a few. There's the 'NIH' factor, for one."

"You mean 'Not Invented Here'? I used to come up against that all the time at work. I wouldn't have thought that kind of self-serving reaction would have any place in the Christian community."

"You'd be surprised. There are lots of so-called 'Christians' who look upon their 'Christianity' as a kind of exclusive social club. They'll be particularly antagonistic to a member of their immediate group who seems to have a message that they themselves didn't receive directly from God, because that would mean that they weren't Number One in God's list of favorites. Despite the negative reaction, a confrontation like you'll be giving them is good for them. Many of them actually are Christians, but they need to get knocked down some so that they'll be useful to Us. Ego just doesn't have a place in Our plan, for Us or for you.

"Another reason why you'll be facing opposition is a problem with the menfolk. It's just plain male chauvinism. Even many women go along with it. The thought here is that a woman's place is in the home and certainly not within the Godhead. Like the 'NIH' factor, its root cause is pride. You'd be surprised, given what Scripture has to say on the subject, that there are so many Christians, among whom are a large number of pastors and other church leaders, who continue to be slaves to pride."

As Earl soon finds out as he is faced with opposition to his blog, there are a number of other factors that contribute to the Christian reluctance to associate femininity with God. One very large factor is the standard perception of our relationship with God as being an individual one on both sides of the fence. In the usual God-human relational context, the notion of family simply doesn't enter into the picture. We see ourselves as standing alone before God, so to speak.

One fine day I visited the Honda shop with my wife, who was fed up to the eyeballs with the concrete-hard seat of our non-Goldwing bike, while I, in turn, was fed up with her fists pounding on my kidneys. Soon after we walked in the door, my attention was drawn to the showpiece of the sales floor, a Honda Rune. The Rune was a strikingly handsome bad boy, the motorcycle equivalent of a movie star with slicked-back hair, a black mustache, long sideburns and a cigarette dangling from his sneering mouth. Without working up a sweat, it managed just sitting there to eclipse anything that a Harley possibly could offer in the way of attitude. My interest attracted salesmen like dung beetles to their favorite meal. I saw a problem with it, and spoke to myself more than anyone else. "There's no rear seat," I noted to my brain. "What about my wife?" I added in a mumble, but the sales manager picked up on it. "You have this piece of work, you don't need a wife," he replied, looking my wife's way with indifference. My wife's expression created a weather system right there in the middle of the showroom, and I hurriedly backed away from the attraction and turned toward the nearest Goldwing. But I was laughing as I did so.

That take-it-or-leave-it attitude that the salesman displayed toward my marriage partner almost earned him a punch in his oversized gut from my very angry wife, and then I think that she would have come after me for laughing at his ill-mannered remark. After the salesman and I both rushed to stabilize the situation and when peace prevailed once more, I reflected on the everyday prevalence of that attitude of individual self-sufficiency that supports the thought that a person's complementary other might actually be replaceable by a toy, which is merely symbolic of the much larger problem of commitment in today's society. This attitude is only loosely tied to the iconic but somewhat false image of the American pioneer who, acting alone, braved the wilds of a new land to tame it for those who followed in less courageous fashion. That heroic soul, in opposition to the prevailing image of him, often faced his dangers with both God and his equally courageous wife at his side.

The mistakenly admired self-sufficiency that I address here is the notion, common to ancient Greek thought and philosophically influential thereafter, that the essence of humanity is the individual man, the notions of complementary otherhood and family being peripheral to the primacy of self. To the religious, this view implies that every human being must stand alone before God to be judged individually without respect to his family connections and his behavior with respect to other family members. I cannot say definitively whether or not or how much the individual's representation of God-ordained family ideals enters into God's assessment of his life, but Scripture in Genesis 1:27, 2:18, 23 and 24, 5:1 and 2, Exodus 20:12 and 17, Matthew 19 and 22, 1 Corinthians 7, Ephesians 5, Colossians 3 and Revelation 21, to name but a few such passages, indicates that it does. Regardless of that particular issue, it doesn't seem a stretch to perceive that with respect to matters of the relationship between God and men, in many theological minds the individual trumps the family entity and supports an indifference, in violation of Jesus' commandment in Matthew 22 to love one's neighbor as oneself, to the welfare of those outside of self. It is a simple matter for those who adhere to this view to apply it to their understanding of God as well. In that context, in the individualists' minds the Individual Dieties, as represented in each of the three Persons of the Godhead, Father, Son and Holy Spirit, overshadows the notion of the Godhead Itself as the essential defining element of the nature of God as well.

Independence and sufficiency of the individual self is but one of several possible factors that have contributed to the currently popular view of the Godhead as being populated by a loosely-coupled, Trinitarian congress held together by an idealized *agape* fellowship in which neither sexuality nor intra-family ownership play a vital part. Other potential contributing factors include the shame of sexuality and a gross misunderstanding of human history. And then, of course, there's the fear factor which impels some Church members to "go with the flow" and acquiesce to mainstream opinions despite knowing full well that they contradict Scripture and plain common sense.

While many Western Church congregants historically and up to the present have considered sexual activity in a marital setting not to be sinful, they still think of it as being all-too-earthy and animalistic to be considered appropriate to God. Sex, according to religious thought as typified by the notions of Zanchius (see Chapter 4), is plainly beneath anything that might be associated with the spiritual domain. Such insight may be obtained merely by attending Church over a period of years, observing that wrongful sex (all sex by common implication) by human participants is vocally denounced from the pulpit while all love-related intimacy by spiritual participants is avoided like the plague.

The dichotomy between our theoretical view of God and our lifestyles reeks of hypocrisy. Bear with me as I briefly explore where it has taken us. It is a remarkable but undeniable fact: regarding gender and sexuality, the Western Christian Church, up to the very recent past, had an absolutely spotless exterior. Mainstream theological authorities unanimously continue to insist upon a Trinitarian Godhead, but even now by common assent within almost all mainstream Churches all traces of sexuality within the Godhead have been prohibited. Some Christian Churches perceive the Godhead as consisting of three entirely genderless Entities. Others, including both Catholic and Protestant denominations, treat the Godhead as comprising nominal male Members whose masculinity is defined as qualities of character typical of the male gender, but for whom any suggestion beyond that is met with rapid and vehement opposition.

Yet, remarkably, in the face of all this supposedly Godly purity, the Catholic priesthood for what might be assumed to be a very long time has famously indulged in sexual practices expressly forbidden by Scripture. Now an increasing number of Churches, both Catholic and Protestant, look benignly upon the open indulgence of these same practices among their congregants, and often among the spiritual leadership as well. All that may have been avoided at the outset had the Church taken a more balanced view of sexuality at both the human and spiritual levels.

A common explanation is given by those who don't accept normal sexual expression to be sinful and yet insist upon Mary's perpetual virginity as good in opposition to evil. This involves the notion, derived from an overemphasis of a couple of Paul's statements in Scripture, that the lusts of the flesh distract Christians from their whole-hearted focus on God.   I'd be willing to bet that a large portion of these people, however, while endorsing this asceticism in their theology, blithely ignore it in their everyday lives. And asceticism comes in many flavors, of which sexuality is only one. There are also eating, drinking, comfortable beds, hot tubs and a host of other pleasures that can distract one from a contemplation of God as well. Among those who do observe chastity, a good number don't mind sitting down to a tasty meal, which involves a lust of a different nature, but a lust nonetheless. The same may be said of those who don't mind partaking of a dollop or two, or considerably more, of alcoholic spirits.

In attempting to rid their religion of all traces of immorality, the Church in general has elected to ignore the imbalance of its thinking and consequently has chosen to throw the baby out with the bathwater. It is the excesses of sexuality, the deviations from the normal marriage union, that are immoral, not the sexual union itself, which is the most wonderful means that God devised to harmoniously foster intimacy between two complementary life-partners. It's a terrible shame that the Church has chosen to castrate its God by the elimination of sexuality. But despite the basic wrongness of this garbled thinking, it most unfortunately has indeed achieved its purpose of sterilization.

Given our abject misunderstanding of our world as demonstrated by our adherence to the false notions of macroevolution and uniformitarianism, the modern Church, like its predecessors, also has garbled its Christianity in more intellectual matters. Unless God intervenes, she possibly never will reach an understanding of the actual origin of Christianity or of the true nature of the Godhead. A short treatise on the falsehood of Darwin's theory of evolution is presented in Appendix 5 for those who might be interested in how modern science, particularly in the rapidly-growing field of molecular biology, has severely undercut the evolutionary notion.

The sad probability is that our most ancient forebears knew more about Jesus Christ and our future union with Him than we do, an issue that will be taken up in the next chapter, along with a detailed pursuit of the most troubling of the overt causes for the Church's denial of a feminine Holy Spirit. This very basic and most ancient of causes resulted in the elimination of sexuality from all matters of the Christian faith despite the Scriptural emphasis on both the physical and theological importance of sexuality as exemplified by the following passage which borrows from words spoken by Adam as he was inspired by the Holy Spirit, and repeated by both Jesus and Paul:

> *For this cause shall a man leave his father and mother, and shall be joined unto his wife, and they two shall be one flesh. This is a great mystery, but I speak concerning Christ and the church.*
> —Ephesians 5:31 and 32

Eleven

THE ROOT CAUSE OF THE DENIAL OF A FEMININE HOLY SPIRIT

Here I won't attempt to lighten the narrative with humor. The root cause of the denial of a feminine Holy Spirit is so overwhelmingly tragic and has been so terribly harmful to the human race that humor is simply not appropriate here. It would be like laughing at a funeral or, like the drunk Lee Marvin in the movie *Cat Ballou*, seeing all the lit candles and responding by singing "Happy Birthday" in front of a casket. It would be as repulsive as the recent billboard ad on behalf of a septic company regarding their honey wagons: *We Haul Milk on Weekends.* Enough.

In Chapter Ten I speculated on some contemporary causes of the initial attempt to cleanse the Church of matters sexual. This chapter will pursue a more basic reason for that divorce of sexuality from Christianity.

Having dwelt on the background fact that the Church has felt it necessary to clean up the Christian faith by removing sexuality from its most important elements, including the Godhead and Mary, the question that it naturally elicits is why that is so. Whatever the basic reason, it must have been deeper than mere pride or the notion of independence or the influence of sexually-oriented contenders for the faith that resided outside the boundaries of Christianity, because the resulting changes to Holy Scripture required a desperation of motive quite beyond what straightforward theological issues might be capable of eliciting. Here I turn to my humble opinion, reinforced by a not-so-humble assertion that is based on a rather deep understanding of what I have read on the subject, including the most important source, Scripture.

Without a doubt the most fundamental reason for considering all sex as beneath the purview of religion, including the monogamous marital relationship ordained and approved by God, is the sinful nature of man following the fall of Adam and Eve. This can easily be discerned by reviewing the Scriptural account of the fall and its aftermath, starting with the fall in Genesis 2:18 and 21-25:

> *And the Lord God said, It is not good that the man should be alone; I will make him an help fit for him. . . And the Lord God caused a deep sleep to fall upon Adam, and he slept: and he took one of his ribs, and closed up the flesh instead thereof; and the rib, which the Lord God had taken from man, made he a woman, and brought her unto the man. And Adam said, This is now bone of my bones, and flesh of my flesh; she shall be called Woman, because she was taken out of Man. Therefore shall a man leave his father and his mother, and shall cleave unto his wife; and they shall be one flesh. And they were both naked, the man and his wife, and were not ashamed.*

The Bible doesn't say explicitly that Adam and Eve had intercourse before their fall. The sequence of events as chronicled in Genesis may be interpreted, in fact, to raise the possibility that they did not. Nevertheless, we don't know that, nor do we know how long they were together before they fell from grace. What we do know is that they were fully equipped for intercourse and that Adam, at least, through his statement of cleaving unto his wife, was fully aware of what that equipment was for.

Being aware of that use, he was not ashamed of it. The innocence that Adam and Eve enjoyed before their fall was not their freedom from sexuality. To the contrary, it was their freedom from shame.

Then came the fall, as noted in Genesis 3:6 and 7:

And when the woman saw that the tree was good for food, and that it was pleasant to the eyes, and a tree to be desired to make one wise, she took of the fruit thereof, and did eat, and gave also unto her husband with her; and he did eat. And the eyes of them both were opened, and they knew that they were naked; and they sewed fig leaves together, and made themselves aprons.

We find that the shame of sexuality came immediately after the fall and was a direct consequent of it. The fall, as many theologians perceive, caused the spiritual death of mankind. Before the fall, I would suggest, the Holy Spirit indwelt man as is the case with Christians. Partaking of the Tree of the Knowledge of Good and Evil, I would suggest further, caused the substitution of the spirit of man for the Spirit of God, giving man a mind of a thoroughly secular nature, one that, while acknowledging the existence of God, was unable to commune with Him with the intimacy that both he and God once enjoyed.

Despite the freedom from sin that Jesus' crucifixion and resurrection obtained for mankind, the Church continued to cling to the shame associated with sex. More will be said later about this.

An important factor that feeds on the sexual shame that resulted from the Fall and attempts to submerge it, has to do with our misunderstanding of history. This misunderstanding came about largely as a result of the rejection of the Biblical narrative in favor of secular views regarding mankind's history. Darwinian evolution and its partner, uniformitarianism, were two very influential contributors to the false understandings associated with secular knowledge.

Ironically, the Church purged the good information instead of the bad, getting rid of sexuality and the Biblical creation narrative while retaining false and essentially mythical views of the world around us. The unnecessary association of sexuality with sin, amplified by a misunderstanding of history, along with an undue absorption with self and individuality, I would suggest, is the root of most of the current difficulties faced by the modern Christian Church.

As for our secular misunderstandings, I believe both logically and with my heart that the primary secular paradigms of evolution and uniformitarianism, including the consequent understanding of the age of the earth and of civilization, are blatantly and, with the aid of modern scientific knowledge, demonstrably false, as discussed in Appendix 5. Instead, I believe that the Genesis creation story represents far more truth than theologians generally acknowledge and, being inspired by the Holy Spirit, is not a redaction of earlier myths. Scriptural details regarding the initial nature of the earth that typically are considered to be difficult to comprehend and hard to believe can be rendered intuitively obvious with the understanding that a drastic natural regime change occurred at the time of Noah's Flood that was planetary in scope and violent beyond imagination. I supply details of this understanding in my book *Family of God.*

During the time that the most ancient patriarchs of the human race dwelt on the earth, according to my current understanding, mankind achieved a rather high level of civilization and sophistication. This isn't difficult to imagine, given the nearly thousand-year lifetimes of our ancestors. That lengthy duration is far greater than the mere three hundred years that have passed since Isaac Newton invented the calculus and turned physics into a hard, mathematically-rich science with enormous practical applications. Given the rapidity with which our own technology has grown and the world consequently has changed since Newton, it is rather natural to think that in some endeavors the progress that could have been made by our ancestors over the course of a millennium may well have resulted in a degree of sophistication which exceeded that of our own society.

In all likelihood, our most ancient forebears probably possessed an advanced knowledge of the physical sciences. They may also have had a deep understanding of God and of man's relationship with this Diety, which embraced a knowledge of Jesus Christ, including His future sojourn on earth and His mission here, as well as a comprehension of the Godhead as a divine Family. From hints embedded within myths and customs associated with the remnants of this ancient knowledge, this understanding probably included a view of the Trinity as having begun out of the selfless separation of the original One into a divine partnership. Within this partnership the original One subsequently united in love with His divine Complement. In doing so, He restored the unity of the Godhead in a love-inspired sharing arrangement that richly fulfills the prophetic words of Adam in Genesis 2:24 and repeated by Jesus in Matthew 19:5:

> *For this cause shall a man leave father and mother, and shall cleave to his wife, and they two shall be one flesh. "*

This gender-based union of the male divine Will and the female divine Means resulted in the birth of creation, the glory of which is represented by the divine Word or the divine Actuality, Jesus Christ.

The planet-shaking violence on Earth that began with the Flood recurred several times over a very long period thereafter. The follow-on events were a natural result of the first cosmic disaster that stripped the earth of its canopy of ice and created the gravitational disturbance that opened the fountains of the deep. Their repetition followed the laws of orbital mechanics, wherein the unwelcome cosmic intruder returned periodically to revisit its devastation upon earth and to re-introduce terror anew to the earth's suffering inhabitants. It is difficult to overstate the impact of these recurring earthwide catastrophes that accompanied Biblical events including the Flood, the Exodus, Joshua's long day and Isaiah's sundial incident. Most of the great body of knowledge that the ancients had accumulated during their lifetimes died in the chaos of a world gone mad. This loss may have been eclipsed by the abrupt and violent removal of a well-ordered physical infrastructure. Perhaps Noah had stored some relatively small tools in the ark, but within a generation or so they would have broken or otherwise become useless. Lacking the infrastructure necessary to begin rebuilding the civilization that no longer existed, they probably descended to a state far more primitive than their ancestors. They may have been forced into resorting to the use of caves. Artifacts of cave living are now commonly misinterpreted in the Darwinian/uniformitarian paradigm as a stage in the upward progress of man rather than the forced descent into a hardscrabble existence that it probably was. In the context of a universal and devastating Flood, during the centuries that followed this event, the tiny cluster of initial survivors would have attempted to cope with a radically-changed world while being forced to endure the inevitable privations associated with a sudden transition to a primitive lifestyle such as we might find in a post-nuclear world.

During the Flood survivors' repopulation of the earth, much of the little knowledge that remained would likely have become corrupted as the focus of minds turned from the acquisition and application of knowledge to mere survival. This would have included astrology, which degenerated into an arcane art, and mathematics, and, particularly, the intimate and detailed knowledge of God that existed prior to the Flood.

Contributing to this degeneration of understanding and amplified by the periodic nature of the terror from above was a constantly recurring, pervasive fear of further natural violence caused by planetary collisions and near-collisions, amplified by portents in the sky accompanied by real and terrible violence on earth. Mankind indeed worshiped, but to many the object of its worship was a master of destruction and torment that to some people looked like a calf, to others like a dragon, and to still others like a feathered serpent. In the presence of powerful heads of state with the temperament of bullies, modern statesmen are prone to taking the low road to the resolution of crises, attempting to avoid confrontation by accommodation. In the face of that all-too-human characteristic, it is rather easy to imagine how readily mankind would twist their understanding of a loving but largely silent God into something else in an attempt to appease the threat in the sky above.

But the garbling of their original understanding of God was never quite complete. From ancient documents, artwork and religious traditions that have managed to survive into modern times, it appears that a multiplicity of harsh, self-centered gods have in the past demanded allegiance at the threat of violence. But in the midst of such deities, there seem to have stood other gods startlingly similar to the Judeo-Christian God. These fully-gendered male and female gods related to each other in family contexts, wherein there was a constantly recurring theme of a divine son whose life ended sacrificially but who was resurrected to dwell in the heavenly domain. The similarities of these religions with Christianity are too pronounced and numerous to be the result of chance. A side issue regarding these religions of the past is that their deities not only possessed gender but were openly sexual. The nature of their love went beyond *agape* to include the possessive intimacy of *eros*. These deities united sexually to produce their offspring and they enjoyed romantic and family relationships.

A remarkable facet of our Judeo-Christian Scripture is that neither of its two Testaments in any way refutes this kind of intra-Godhead association. In fact, our Scripture generally supports the notion of gender and intra-gender communication and an intimate, tightly-coupled family-based unity within the divine Trinity. Furthermore, that same notion appears to be the only logically consistent way that a Trinitarian Godhead can be reconciled with monotheism.

The enormous difference between what Scripture suggests regarding gender within the Godhead and the various mutually-inconsistent interpretations of Scripture as practiced by our mainstream religions indicates that modern Christianity considered the predecessor religions, despite their similarity of theme, to be the false and morally degenerate initial product of mankind's ever-upward struggle for improvement. They were labeled "pagan" and dismissed as unworthy of consideration.

In my opinion the false notions of evolution and uniformity made a generous contribution to this perception, supporting the notion, in sharp contradiction to Scripture, that as mankind emerged from the swamp and its simple lifeforms it began to perceive the existence of God but with a crude and limited vision of what the nature of that God might be. Under that misapprehension, the refinement of those earlier religions into the perception of nobility associated with our own understanding of God required millennia of upward "evolution".

In contrast to this view as supported by the false paradigms of evolution and uniformity, these supposedly degenerate religions of the past likely represent vestiges of an originally coherent understanding of God possessed by our ancient forebears. This understanding also probably included a detailed knowledge of Jesus Christ and His future mission on earth. Modern Christianity, having accepted the falsehoods of evolution and the enormous time periods associated with evolution and uniformity, is largely incapable of comprehending what may well be the true root of these earlier religions and of how that early understanding may have been corrupted in the aftermath of the visitation on earth of violent cosmic intrusions.

Accompanying the misperception of Christianity's true roots is a corresponding misunderstanding of moral degeneracy, wherein the sexual shame associated with mankind's fall from grace infected man's perception of sexuality. Burdened by sexual shame and not comprehending that its source was within ourselves rather than God, theologians caused all sexuality to be lumped together as beneath any association whatever with God or religion. The various offshoots of Christianity dealt with this misperception of immorality in different ways, but in common they all removed any trace of sexuality from God or His interface with mankind. Insisting upon a New Testament version of the Holy Spirit in masculine terms in contradiction to the earlier Jewish understanding of the Holy Spirit as a feminine Entity, they visualized either a genderless or all-male Godhead that brooked no notion of a primarily female Holy Spirit despite the logical ease with which a male pronoun may be applied to a functionally female Entity, and even more significantly, in contradiction to the Siniatic Palimpsest, the oldest known version of the Gospel and closest to the Gospel events, the one that Paul was believed to have referred to, and in its original form has Jesus Christ in John 14:26 referring to the Holy Spirit as feminine.

It is tempting for the doubter of my assertion of the negative impact of the theory of evolution on Christianity to point to the obvious discrepancy between the early formulation of Christianity's basic tenets, which began within decades of the Church's birth at the first Pentecost after Jesus' resurrection, and the several hundred years that had elapsed before Darwin proposed his theory of evolution. By the time that Darwin arrived on the scene, Christianity already had a long-established view of a weakly-gendered or entirely genderless Godhead. The Catholic Church, moreover, already had elevated Mary to the lofty position that she enjoys today in the Catholic faith and was insisting upon her perpetual virginity.

But Darwin wasn't the first to hold to the theory of evolution. His primary contribution to this falsehood was the proposition of what appeared, at a time when little was known of the molecular marvels associated with life, to be a viable mechanism. Speculation about evolution was a reasonably common topic in pre-Christian Greek thought.

As a matter of fact, it is difficult to over-estimate the influence of Grecian thought and customs on the development of the early Christian Church. The root of virtually all of the early heresies that invaded the developing Church was the Greek notion of all goodness residing exclusively in the spiritual plane; the material world, in contrast was considered to be evil to the core. The Church Fathers were quick to denounce the associated heresies of Gnosticism and Docetism, but despite the vehemence of their attempts to quell the intrusion of these doctrines into their faith, they couldn't manage to rid themselves entirely of the notions. Their situation in this regard is similar to what we now face in attempting to rid ourselves of our uniformitarian past: despite the recent acknowledgment that past catastrophes played a significant part in the history of the Earth, our dating of many of these events relies on methodology derived under uniformitarian presuppositions.

While openly denouncing the Gnostic heresies, our Church

Fathers continued to embrace a basic tenet of Gnostic thought: the notion that sexuality of any kind was base and beneath the spiritual realm. Consequently, they pasteurized their faith by purging it of all traces of sexuality. They did so in blindness of Scripture and in gross violation of its general tenor.

In summary, what the Church Fathers down through the history of Christianity did in error was their allowance of secular thinking to intrude into the Christian life. A major aspect of this admittance of secular penetration is that they first opened the door to the influence of Greek thought and customs on early Christian thinking, particularly in their perception of the primacy of the individual and of sexuality as being intrinsically evil. This perception has been a constant factor from the beginning of the Church Age all they way to the present and, in fact, was supported by the false pseudo-scientific notions of the past few centuries, including evolution and uniformitarianism, which remain deeply entrenched in secular thought to this day. This perversion of true and innocent Christianity was the direct result of the failure of Christian spokespersons to fully accept what God did in His kind and sacrificial restoration of the human race.

But if Christian thought is so deviant from truth in that area, one may ask, what remains of the truth of the entire Gospel? What assurance does the Christian have that he can put his faith in any of his religion? Most fortunately, Scripture itself remains intact. It turns out that while there are numerous confirmations of the inerrancy of Scripture, the same can't be said about the interpretation of it.

Scripture itself claims inerrancy. According to Paul in 2 Timothy 3:16 and 17 and Peter in 2 Peter 1:20 and 21,

> *All Scripture is given by inspiration of God, and is profitable for doctrine, for reproof, for correction, for instruction in righteousness. That the man of God may be perfect, thoroughly furnished unto all good works.*
>
> *Knowing this first, that no prophecy of the scripture is of any private interpretation, for the prophecy came not at any time by the will of man, but holy men of God spoke as they were moved by the Holy Spirit.*

Scripture itself backs up these statements, first by the supernatural fulfillment of prophecy in great detail centuries and even millennia after they were written, and also by the exceedingly intricate manner in which the words of some human writers of Scripture dovetail with those of others, all of whom were directed in their writing by the same Holy Spirit. And then, of course, there is the equally supernatural self-consistency of Scripture. The objections of those who claim otherwise invariably reveal their insufficient research into the topics they question and their own shallowness of thought. A brief commentary on the inerrancy of Scripture is furnished in Appendix 4.

But the interpretation of Scripture, even by some heavy-hitting theologians, cannot be said to enjoy the same inerrancy that Scripture itself does. At times even the most highly-motivated and God-fearing of individuals fall short of the research required to uncover some important Biblical truths. At other times they lack the clarity of insight demanded by a Scriptural passage. At still other times their own biases and agendas creep into their absorption of Scripture.

Like the inerrancy of Scripture, the errancy of interpretation can be backed up with numerous proofs.

It was from the two major mutually-supporting reasons noted earlier of sexual shame and a misinterpretation of history that led the Catholic Church to place onto Mary the attributes that belonged to the Holy Spirit, and that led the Protestant Church into an indifference toward the issue, replacing readily-available knowledge with a casual attitude that the subject was unknowable. This enormous difference in understanding between the Catholic and Protestant Churches clearly demonstrates that at least one of these Churches, and probably both, are in error.

It was the agenda of conforming to established Church doctrine that led the translators of the King James Bible to replace "she" with "thou" in Isaiah 51:9 and 10, despite the clear grammatical incorrectness of that translation. It was the agenda of never having seen a green horse that led these translators to translate the Greek word "chloros" into "pale" instead of the correct word "green". Further, it was the agenda of cleansing the Church of sexuality that led them to replace feminine references to the Holy Spirit with masculine ones.

The proliferation of various Christian sects throughout the history of the Church and around the earth cries of error in understanding, not only from the breakaway sects but more importantly from the mainstream organizations from which they parted company. The current falling away of many mainstream Churches into apostasy screams even louder of error.

The bottom line is that while Scripture is sacred, Church doctrine is not. Adam's race for the most part is still fallen despite the Church forgiven, and personal agendas and misunderstanding have and will continue to creep into many Christian Churches along with influential but unsaved individuals who pose as Christians but keep alive the saying of satan, "Did God really say—?"

The denial of the femininity of the Holy Spirit is thus placed on the doorstep of sexual shame, which itself is a direct result of mankind's fall from grace. This debilitating shame is maintained by Church leaders who know better but prefer to remain silent, which will be pursued further in Chapter Thirteen.

Twelve

An Informed Conjecture as to Why God Allowed the Western Church to Misunderstand the Nature of the Holy Spirit

My early experiences with cars were anything but mundane. First, I was not born to travel. My first memory of movement from point A to point B by car was with dad at the wheel. My second memory of travel was hard on the heels of the first, with dad still at the controls, but with me trying with all my might to maintain my dignity by holding down the bile. The situation would only escalate, because the attempt only made my nervous stomach twitch, a condition that fed upon itself, finally escalating into an eruption that projected vomit all over the floor on the back. How I remember the consequences! Dad would swerve the car onto the shoulder, brake to a violent halt, and yank open the rear door while shouting that the malady was all in my head and to "geddada the car now before I toss you onto the road." There was never any preparation for the mess; being always "in my head" it was never expected. He and mom would try to clean it up as best they could, after which the journey would resume with the windows in the back cranked down all the way. The cold plus my empty stomach helped to control the force of my retches, allowing me to puke with silent ripples without adding to the mess on the floor.

Of course that never helped much, because I was a twin. It was only a matter of time before the combination of my continued retching and the stinking mess on the floor assaulted the eyes, ears and nose of my brother to bring him to a sympathetic bout of hurling, restocking the mess on the floor to its pre-cleanup condition. The process would repeat itself, my brother now being the object of our dad's wrath.

We constantly disgraced ourselves in this manner throughout our childhood years. Once in a while we would be invited on trips with friends, in their parents' cars. On one particularly humiliating occasion, our best friend's older sister drove us across the Bay Bridge to the San Francisco Zoo. She had just gotten her driver's license and thought she was hot stuff. We ruined her day. With the windows tightly closed and she smoking like a chimney, it didn't end well. Our eruptions were virtually simultaneous, an event that caused our friend to screw up his face in disgust and his sister to shout things that turn faces red. As we were in the middle of a 13-mile long bridge at the time, she was unable to stop the car. Her rage mounted with each passing mile as the barf molecules increasingly polluted the air. Her cigarette quickly lost its appeal, and she began to gag herself. We were surprised that he remained our friend. She certainly didn't. With the exception of him, this nauseating event happened exactly once per friend, because our malady wasn't vehicle-specific. In fact, it haunted us until the exact time when we ourselves learned to drive, at which point the carsickness disappeared entirely never to return (with cars as the vehicles).

The humiliation didn't leave quite so readily. Vestiges of it, in fact, still remain and have been supplemented by a host of other humiliating experiences. But that's not necessarily a bad thing because, as was made evident in a previous chapter, pride pretty much represents the opposite of humiliation, and pride has done an enormously successful job of messing with a good understanding of God. Furthermore, Scripture tells us time and again, God hates pride. As I noted in Chapter 15 of *Buddy*, Psalm 101:5, Proverbs 16:5 and Mary's Magnificat (Luke 1:51 and 52) are quite clear on that issue:

Whoso privily slandereth his neighbor, him will I cut off; him that hath a high look and a proud heart will not I suffer."

Every one who is proud in heart is an abomination to the Lord; though hand join in hand, he shall not be unpunished."

He hath shown strength with his arm; he hath scattered the proud in the imagination of their hearts. He hath put down the mighty from their seats, and exalted them of low degree."

Despite my attribution of blame for a false and persistent misunderstanding of the Godhead on the Church leadership's unwillingness to accept all that Jesus offered in His sacrificial death and its uncritical acceptance instead of secular values and understandings, I must admit that it was God who ultimately permitted such a state of affairs to develop and then to persist for over a millennium and a half. But if that is the case, it isn't the first time that, for a higher purpose, and in opposition to what we might expect of Him but never in contradiction to Scripture, God has allowed His people to follow an error of understanding. The Jewish failure to recognize Jesus when He came in the flesh, despite numerous Scriptural references to His mission and character, including the drama of Abraham's attempted sacrifice of Isaac, the story of Joseph, the deeply-entrenched Passover custom, the messianic Psalm 22 and passages in Isaiah 53 and many others too numerous to mention here, furnishes a prime example of this passivity of God in the face of error. This precursor situation is clearly stated by Paul in Romans 11:1-12:

I say, then, Hath God cast away his people? God forbid. For

I also am an Israelite, of the seed of Abraham, of the tribe
of Benjamin. God hath not cast away his people whom he
foreknew. Know ye not what Scripture saith of Elijah? How
he maketh intercession to God against Israel, saying, Lord,
they have killed thy prophets, and dug down thine altars; and
I am left alone, and they seek my life. But what saith the
answer of God unto him? I have reserved to myself seven
thousand men who have not bowed the knee to the image
of Baal. Even so, then, at this present time also there is a
remnant according to the election of grace. And if by grace,
then is it no more of works; otherwise, grace is no more grace.
But if it be of works, then is it no more grace; otherwise work
is no more work.

What then? Israel hath not obtained that which he seeketh
for; but the election hath obtained it, and the rest were
blinded. (According as it is written [e.g. Isaiah 6:9 and 10,
Matt. 13:14], God hath given them the spirit of slumber, eyes
that they should not see, and ears that they should not hear)
unto this day. And David saith, Let their table be made a
snare, and a trap, and a stumbling block, and a recompense
unto them; let their eyes be darkened that they may not see,
and bow down their back always.

I say, then, Have they stumbled that they should fall? God
forbid; but rather through their fall salvation is come unto the
Gentiles, to provoke them to jealousy. Now if the fall of them
be the riches of the world, and the diminishing of them the
riches of the Gentiles, how much more their fullness? "

Is it possible that God also willingly removed His hand of restraint
in the unjustified rejection by Christianity of all gender associations
with Him? If He did, is it possible that He may have done so in
order to avoid the continuation of our insufferable arrogance so that
we would be unable, upon finally meeting Jesus face-to-face, to
crow about our superiority to the Jews for our better vision when,
in fact, we had been so blind in another important matter of faith?

Think about just who it was against whom Jesus so frequently spoke out: the religious elite. He constantly pruned back their hard and self-serving know-it-all attitudes toward God, in which they had thoroughly misled themselves centuries before and clung so intractably thereafter to their false understandings.

Are today's Church leaders so different from the scribes and Pharisees of Jesus' day? Hardly. And in the midst of the pomp and pride and financial obsessions and general fixation on the material world of modern Church leadership, who is to say that God hasn't with purpose permitted a very wrong understanding of the Holy Spirit to persist, to the end that when these leaders come to face their God directly, they will be humbled in His presence for their lack of comprehension and thus be forced to confront their own assumption of the Pharisaical mindset?

To my mind, that is a very reasonable explanation. It is, however, merely conjecture: I certainly don't pretend to know the actual answer, opinions or not. But as long as I'm indulging in speculation, another reasonable explanation comes to mind. This alternative answer connects with Paul's highly-contentious passage in 1 Timothy 2:8-15, that is ignored in some Christian circles and foments anger in others:

> *I will, therefore, that men pray everywhere, lifting up holy hands, without wrath and doubting; in like manner, also, that women adorn themselves in modest apparel, with godly fear and sobriety, not with braided hair, or gold, or pearls, or costly array, but (which becometh women professing godliness) with good works.*
>
> *Let the woman learn in silence with all subjection. But I permit not a woman to teach, nor to usurp authority over the man, but to be in silence. For Adam was first formed, then Eve. And Adam was not deceived but the woman, being deceived, was in the transgression. Notwithstanding, she shall be saved in childbearing, if they continue in faith and charity and holiness with sobriety.*

Ouch! I've heard a number of commentaries regarding this

passage, most of which, especially from women, are not to be repeated in polite circles. My pastor and his wife, to their credit, are obedient to this passage in faith, although they don't profess to fully understand the reason behind Paul's apparent vehemence behind it.

Was Paul a misogynist, as claimed by many modern Christian women? Given his beautiful presentations in Galatians and Ephesians of the essentiality of both male and female in the economy of God, and particularly in his famous mystery in Ephesians 5, I highly doubt that. Even more compelling is my belief, shared by most committed Christians, that this passage was driven by the Holy Spirit.

In fact, these words of Paul may well be strikingly supportive of a feminine Holy Spirit. In that context, a feminine Holy Spirit is perfectly responsive to the will of the Father in performing works that implement His loving vision. By contrast Eve, in succumbing to the serpent, failed to be responsive to the will of God or the will of her husband, and therefore directly violated her creation in the type of the Holy Spirit. That fallen nature of Eve has demonstrated itself often and graphically in the pages of Scripture. A prime example of this is the corruption of Solomon by some of his foreign wives, who enticed him to follow after strange gods.

Perhaps just as Moses was denied entry into the Promised Land because in his anger he failed to represent Jesus Christ, mankind has for centuries been denied a true and beautiful understanding of the family nature of the Godhead because men, in their fallen natures, fail to represent the Father's will to their families and women, in their fallen natures, continue to fail to represent the Holy Spirit's perfect responsiveness to the Father's will.

As to why, if indeed this conjecture has merit, God now may be allowing us to have that understanding of the family nature of the Godhead, I don't know. Maybe it's because, like so much other information now available to Christians to support their understanding of God, the opening of the Books according to Daniel 12 may be a very general event.

Perhaps God is aware that we of the Church finally will put into practice the freedom with which we are endowed through Jesus' work on the cross and the resulting indwelling Holy Spirit, and thus behave toward God and our life partners in a manner more in keeping with the way we were designed to represent the intra-Godhead relationship.

Thirteen

A Way for the Western Christian Church to Correct its Misunderstanding

It has been suggested to me that I have a gallows humor. The "suggestion" wasn't offered with benign intent—it was hurled as an accusation, the implication being that my gallows humor is an affliction. But I don't think of it that way. Rather, I think of it as a welcome endowment. It's welcome, because I'm clumsy and tend to get into trouble of the kind that parts of me get squished. If I'm going to have to go through life with that kind of problem, I'd much rather be laughing about it than crying.

I tend to associate myself with people who possess that same endowment, along with the clumsiness that often accompanies it. That way I get to laugh at them too, but in a sympathetic way, welcoming the fact that they get to laugh at my troubles as well.

My greatest sources of laughter by far were my hang gliding experiences and, thanks to my brother, ultralight events as well. There's just something about sitting around a campfire after a day of airborne adventure swapping tales of mishaps that didn't end up so seriously as to require hospitalization or funeral arrangements. What makes these aviation experiences so rich in colorful tales is that the craft are frail and tiny, making them subject to micrometeorological situations, which is a 50 dollar phrase meaning that they get tossed around a lot by vagaries of air and wind. Another source of richness is that the activities are dominated by people with gallows humor, who go aloft seeking the events of which tales are made of with adventurous spirits and not a whole lot of common sense, and more than their share of clumsiness. Most important of all, the activities aren't (or weren't when I was participating) encumbered with regulations and the means of enforcing them. A passage out of my novel *Buddy* readily comes to mind:

> He imagined Ray's mind at work constructing the latest local hang gliding legend, a tale in which he would be the star character. The sight of the peering eyes took him back to his first lesson. The kid who gave it had spoken with a stern voice wholly out of sync with his pimply face. Furrowing his greasy adolescent brows, he had stated with the assertion of a saint on a mission, "Never, NEVER fly into a rotor. If you do, you will DIE." He had sealed the importance of his statement with a slash of his outstretched finger across the festering pimple that jutted out from his neck. The inadvertent contact of his finger with the pimple made his eyes water, but, somewhat subdued, he had bravely continued on with the lesson.
>
> In the afternoon, not wanting to wimp out of the demo flight that would complete the day's lesson, the kid had jumped headlong into the rotor of a downslope wind, ending the lesson on a somewhat negative note. The class watched him hobble of the field dragging the asymmetrical remains of the one decent shop glider along with a semi-useless right foot. One of the students, his face ashen with disbelieving horror, had stood at the top of the hill gaping at the carnage

below: "Screw this crap," he had said under his breath, and had hurried down the other side to his car. He'd left in a cloud of dust, his car fishtailing in its haste to depart the area.

I've seen spectacular things, and heard of more: of gliders landing on fences, on cows, faces of cliffs and power lines. There's a famous picture, copies of which grace the walls of many hang gliding enthusiasts. The scene is of a vast flat field of grass, representing unlimited opportunities for safe landings. In the middle of the picture, dwarfed by all that open real estate, is a solitary tree. Against the tree is a wrecked hang glider.

I recall an incident of that ilk quite vividly: it happened in California on the same day that earlier I had caught a whirlwind, which is just a visible thermal, and had a nice elevator ride, but for the most part the site was like our training hill in Washington that produced sled rides. About that time pilots (at least in California) began to fasten parachutes to the bottoms of their harnesses with Velcro. I never did, and after witnessing a horrible mishap on that day that actually was caused by a parachute, maybe I'm glad that I didn't. It happened to the guy launching off in front of me. He ran toward the cliff edge, but went prone before he reached it. It wouldn't have mattered so much if he didn't have the parachute, but when his belly contacted the rock, it scraped off the 'chute. But he continued on over the cliff and achieved flight. We watched the parachute just laying there on the rock as the lines deployed, knowing with a terrible certainty what would inevitably come to pass when the lines became taut. Sure enough, with an audible PAF! the parachute blossomed out as it left the rock, bringing the hapless pilot to a screeching halt and denying him the lift that comes with motion. Just like in a Roadrunner cartoon, the poor guy went into a vertical nosedive. What saved him from anything more serious than a broken leg was the narrow fire trail below the cliff. He may have recovered just enough airspeed to break his fall somewhat as he impacted the road, and what could have been a very sad event became instead a source of jokes that hounded him thereafter.

Infrequently some pilots choose to enhance their courage with a nip or two of spirits, or maybe a six-pack, or merely to enhance the experience by grazing on the local mushrooms. When a pilot is seen so indulging, grins light up the faces of his companions and, once the creature goes aloft, eyeballs follow his flight with eager anticipation of the probable outcome. Now that's *really* gallows humor.

I remember a gentleman with a bent for innovative mechanics who, while attempting to modify his single-person ultralight for two-person flight, could not refrain from bragging about his creative genius. I didn't have a chance to view his maiden voyage on the modified craft, but soon after that I saw him busy at work on additional modifications. He had a cast on his leg and a bandage on his cheek. I was going to ask him how the flight worked out, but I turned around instead, waiting discreetly until my back was turned to him before permitting myself to openly express my inner thoughts. I sometimes wonder whether he noticed my heaving shoulders.

The flight path of one ultralight that ended in a crater of its own making was described by an onlooker as the darting about of an angry bee. In this situation, as events later demonstrated, the difficulty didn't involve micrometeorological conditions or mechanical defect. The issue became obvious as the bleeding pilot emerged from the damaged craft and proceeded on his own to continue on the ground a replica of the path that he had taken in the air. He finally fell down in a drunken stupor and remained there until external assistance arrived. He was wasted to the extent that it probably had saved his life.

I don't need intoxicants to add color to my travels. I do just fine at that in my natural state. Grace isn't my strong suit.

My lack of grace in things physical has another clear advantage besides giving me things to laugh about. It keeps me humble. I identify quite intimately with Paul's description of the Christian "B" team in 1 Corinthians 1:10-31:

> *Now I beseech you, brethren, by the name of our Lord Jesus Christ, that ye all speak the same thing, and that there be no divisions among you, but that ye be perfectly joined together*

in the same mind and in the same judgment. For it hath been declared unto me of you, my brethren, by them who are of the house of Chloe, that there are contentions among you. Now this I say, that every one of you saith, I am of Paul; or I., of Apollos; or I, of Cephas; or I, of Christ. Is Christ divided? Was Paul crucified for you? Or were ye baptized in the name of Paul? I thank God that I baptized none of you, but Crispus and Gaius, lest any should say that I had baptized in mine own name. And I baptized also the household of Stephanus; besides, I know not whether I baptized any other. For Christ sent me not to baptize but to preach the gospel; not with wisdom of words, lest the cross of Christ should be of no effect.

For the preaching of the cross is to them that perish foolishness; but unto us who are saved it is the power of God. For it is written, I will destroy the wisdom of the wise, and will bring to nothing the understanding of the prudent. Where is the wise? Where is the scribe? Where is the disputer of this world? Hath not God made foolish the wisdom of this world? For after that, in the wisdom of God, the world by wisdom knew not God, it pleased God by the foolishness of preaching to save them that believe. For the Jews require a sign, and the Greeks seek after wisdom; but we preach Christ crucified, unto the Jews a stumbling block, and unto the Greeks foolishness; but unto them who are called, both Jews and Greeks, Christ the power of God, and the wisdom of God. Because the foolishness of God is wiser than men; and the weakness of God is stronger than men.

For ye see your calling, brethren, how that not many wise men after the flesh, not many mighty, not many noble, are called; but God hath chosen the foolish things of the world to confound the wise; and God hath chosen the weak things of the world to confound the things which are mighty; and base things of the world, and things which are despised, hath God chosen, yea, and things which are not, to bring to nothing things that are, that no flesh should glory in his presence. But of him are ye in Christ Jesus, who of God is made

*unto us wisdom, and righteousness, and sanctification, and
redemption; that, according as it is written, He that glorieth,
let him glory in the Lord.*

Here's where self-pride might well intersect false doctrine, whether
it be the negation of sexuality in matters of God or something else:
regardless of whether or not the pastoral Church leadership accepts
or rejects the *status quo* regarding a particular Church dogma, rarely
if ever will a pastor display the courage or selflessness required
to contradict it. For him too much is on the line: his ministerial
career, his reputation, his status in the community; the correction of
a faulty understanding, if it represents the prevailing viewpoint, is
simply not worth it. I have been told by pastors specific instances
where fear and self-interest prevented other pastors from speaking
out about a doctrine that they were convinced was wrong. Other
pastors in increasing numbers resort to the relativistic creed of the
emergent church, ducking behind the claim that no person has access
to absolute truth.

The situation is probably worse in the seminaries, the schools that
teach doctrine, whether true or false, to new pastors. Their collective
survival and reputation is at stake. As the Church leadership
progresses in responsibility and eminence, the stakes get higher yet,
making it ever more likely that the *status quo* will be maintained
regardless of its basic truth.

As a ministerial friend noted, more than one associate had
confided in him privately that they knew full well that the Holy
Spirit was functionally feminine. Another friend remarked that the
continued silence of Church leaders regarding this subject didn't
square with the rapidly-growing number of commentaries on the
Internet that were sympathetic to the Holy Spirit's femininity. He
ended by associating the silence of these leaders with the hypocrisy
of the Pharisees, whom Jesus denounced in Matthew 23:13:

*But woe unto you, Scribes and Pharisees, hypocrites! For ye
shut up the kingdom of heaven against men; for ye neither go
in yourselves, neither suffer ye them that are entering to go in.*

If the Church is indeed burdened with a false understanding of the Holy Spirit, the way she may be able to extract herself from that difficulty is first to be exposed to the truth to the extent that Church members might question the *status quo*. Second, she must be made aware of the basic cause of the error, which was the sexual shame that afflicted mankind with the fall. Finally, she must exhibit the selfless moral courage not only to accept the truth in the face of opposition of tradition and Church leadership, but to proclaim it to others. That is a daunting task, but truth is truth, and the courageous Christian may expect the blessing and active support of the Holy Spirit in that endeavor, further supported by the fervent love engendered by a truthful understanding of the Godhead.

There's still time to bring the whole truth back into Church doctrine—God hasn't called the game yet, even though it seems a lot like we're in the bottom of the ninth. If the Church decides to wake up about her own shortcomings, many people would have the opportunity, right here and now, of loving God with the fervor of which we are capable, and, with that fervor, of bringing a multitude into a loving relationship with God.

God's solution to the immense loss suffered by mankind in its fall was the sacrifice of Jesus, as foretold in his command to Abraham to sacrifice Isaac. As a result of that loving act, mankind was given the gift of life, as promised in John 3:16:

> *For God so loved the world, that he gave his only begotten Son, that whosoever believeth on him should not perish, but have everlasting life."*

The essence of that gift is the indwelling Holy Spirit, promised to all believers in John 14:15-18, according to the King James Version of Scripture (which we believe to contain the mistranslation of "she" into "he" in reference to the Holy Spirit):

> *If ye love me, keep my commandments. And I will pray the Father, and he shall give you another Comforter, that he may abide with you forever; even the Spirit of truth, whom the world cannot receive, because it seeith him not, neither*

knoweth him: but ye know him; for he dwelleth with you, and shall be in you. I will not leave you comfortless; I will come to you.

What this gift of the indwelling Holy Spirit means to Christians is nothing less than a regaining of that which was lost in the fall of Adam: a cancellation of their spiritual death through a rebirth in the Spirit, as promised in John 3:1-8:

There was a man of the Pharisees, named Nicodemus, a ruler of the Jews; the same came to Jesus by night, and said unto him, Rabbi, we know that thou art a teacher come from God; for no man can do these miracles thou doest, except God be with him. Jesus answered and said unto him, Verily, verily, I say unto thee, Except a man be born again, he cannot see the kingdom of God. Nicodemus saith unto him, How can a man be born when he is old? Can he enter the second time into his mother's womb, and be born?

Jesus answered, Verily, verily, I say unto thee, Except a man be born of water and of the Spirit, he cannot enter into the kingdom of God. That which is born of the Spirit is spirit. Marvel not that I said unto thee, Ye must be born again. The wind bloweth where it willeth, and thou hearest the sound of it, but canst not tell from where it cometh, and where it goeth; so is every one that is born of the Spirit.

Through this rebirth we have been given the opportunity to regain our communication and intimacy with God. Provided that we are obedient to God in our practice of it, we also can regain our innocence in sexuality and thus be free to enjoy without shame this intrinsically beautiful gift from God. Moreover, this freedom from shame should permit us to restore in innocence the attribute of gender to our understanding of the Godhead itself. If only we ask.

The ever-present problem with our spiritual rebirth is that, being so laden down with secular customs and understandings, we fail to perceive the wonderful freedom that has been opened to us through that rebirth. In John 16, Jesus speaks of His death, resurrection and second advent. In verses 23 and 24, He appears to be speaking specifically of the joy that is available to us after His resurrection:

And in that day ye shall ask me nothing. Verily, verily, I say unto you, Whatever ye shall ask the Father in my name, he will give it to you. Hitherto have ye asked nothing in my name; ask, and ye shall receive, that your joy may be full.

To be sure, in John Chapter 16, Jesus also speaks of the tribulation that the world will impose upon Christians. Indeed, I have written at length on the topic of just such trials in the expectation that we soon may be participants in some unhappy events to come. But the point is that tribulations come from the secular world, not from God. In the midst of general persecution, even suffering, we can still, if we only ask, partake of the joys that our spiritual rebirth entitles us to, and which the secular world wishes to deny us.

It seems starkly apparent that even many Church Fathers, devout as they must have been, were so burdened by secular thought that they failed to fully receive the promised freedom of spiritual rebirth. Born again, they yet failed to accept the innocence that was their due. Instead, they wallowed in their sexual shame as if they were still fallen, and in that shame they castrated their God in their misunderstanding of the meaning of purity.

Examples abound of failures to receive God's blessings in that and other areas of man's interaction with God. The Catholic priesthood didn't quite live up to the demand for celibacy. That certainly didn't end well. Many Protestant Churches claim, principally on the basis of the unjustified interpretation of 1 Corinthians 13, centered upon an isolation of a Scriptural passage, that the gifts of the Holy Spirit ceased, either upon the death of the last apostle or on the canonization of Scripture. They are opposed by a less rigid community who happily enjoy the gifts that supposedly don't exist, although there are those among them who tend to overdo things. The Jewish community was heavily influenced by its traditions and rituals, in addition to simple self-centered pride and arrogance, to reject the Jesus who came in the flesh for its behalf. We all know how that worked out, although we must admit that, according to

Paul, God had a hand in their blindness for the sake of the gentiles.

May you the reader be blessed with the truth, and in that understanding, may he or she find the wherewithal to experience the kind of love toward God that represents obedience to His command to love Him with all our hearts, minds and souls. May God richly bless you in that obedience.

Fourteen

IMPLICATIONS FOR THE FUTURE

I'd very much like to say that our family was a decent representation, at the human level, of what the Family of God is all about. But, given the dysfunctional nature of our particular grouping, I most certainly hope that God does a better job of it than we did. It would be great to blame the disorder on mother's constant disappointment in us and as a result of that on dad's pretty constant wrath.

Truth be told, however, that's just not the whole truth. If mom and dad were incessantly on our tails, it's because we richly deserved it. The three of us, our sister, my brother and myself, are very close now. But that wasn't always the case. In our teen years we were a bad lot. My brother and I were shifty and were given to frequent bouts of anger toward each other, almost always involving physical conflict, most often hitting and choking. The rancor only intensified as we grew older. On one occasion it so happened that we both were home for the weekend on 72-hour liberty and sharing a bedroom. Late that night after returning from our dates I decided to take a shower, which in itself, given the lateness of the hour, was thoroughly inconsiderate to my brother. I made it infinitely worse by singing loudly in complete disregard of his well-being.

He didn't take it lying down. He arose from the covers and, knowing that I'd eventually have to open the door next to his bed, he stood on the mattress and assumed a posture that would bring his tight-knuckled fist downward into my belly with maximum impact. He waited there a long time, as I was in no particular hurry, and as he did so, his adrenaline level kept mounting.

I eventually opened the door, whereupon the fist connected with my stomach so abruptly that I was on the floor almost unconscious before realizing what happened. That was just one little event among a long string of sordid episodes where we both participated with equal fervor.

Our sister wasn't clean in all this. Oh, no. One evening when I was twelve she had a party at our house with several friends from her all-girl school. Our parents were gone, having left her to baby-sit, as, for good reason, they didn't trust us to be on our own. The girls had so much fun together that my brother and I were completely forgotten. One of the girls opened a bottle of rum and the party went into overdrive. Somebody mentioned how sad it was that there was no dog in the house. It would have been so much fun to get it drunk. While they were dwelling on that, with the imaginary dog on their minds, I came down the stairs in my pajamas to see what the noise was all about. That's when the light bulb clicked on in my sister's head. "We don't need a dog!" she screamed in hilarity. "We have my brother!"

Whereupon she invited me to sit and poured a very large dollop of rum into a glass and handed it to me. Not having any idea of the consequences, I thought it was a pretty good idea myself and proceeded to down the contents. I looked at them with a silly grin, held out the empty glass, and said "More!"

They were only too happy to oblige. Judging from the screaming that followed, I guess that I did pretty well as a drunk dog. But then the room began to spin. "I don't feel so good," I told them, and staggered back up the stairs to my bedroom. The bedroom spun around too, and continued to spin when I lay down. I hurriedly opened the window overlooking the flat-roofed garage and hurled out my guts. After a lengthy time of misery, I managed to fall asleep, but the next thing I knew my nose was being assaulted with the disgusting odor of pancakes. "Breakfast is on the table!" dad shouted. "Geddown here now!" My stomach continued to ripple with suppressed retching as I reluctantly emerged white-faced to the breakfast table, which was laden with nauseating objects that, somehow, I managed to force down my throat without puking back up. Dad looked at me strangely, wondering if I was coming down with the flu. When I left the table greatly relieved that the ordeal was ending, I discovered to my horror that another one was just beginning. There, right in front of dad's desk through the glass door that led to the roof of the garage, was an enormous pile of barf. I can't remember how I managed to get rid of it without attracting my dad's attention and subsequent wrath, but somehow I was able to do so.

I quite clearly remember harboring bad thoughts about my sister for quite some time.

Bad as we were toward our parents, they do need to assume some of the blame. Dad had a desk job, which was truly mundane. At least he thought so. To him his job was so tediously commonplace that he sought excitement elsewhere. The open road fit that need nicely. Before the world reached mid-twentieth century, the highway patrol was not so large in presence, lacked sophisticated detection equipment, and, best of all, maintained a culture of generosity. Behind the wheel, dad became, in his imagination, a race-car driver, or at least a cop in hot pursuit of a wicked criminal. The way he shook his fist at others who had the audacity to usurp his personal highway, every other motorist in the country had a shady past. Sometimes they'd lash back at him. I remember once in my late preteens raising up from my sickbed in the back seat upon a curse and a burst of acceleration to witness a 15-mile road chase with dad close on the tail of someone who had gravely offended him. When I questioned mom about the cause of this outrage, she pursed her lips and responded with a terse statement of his ugly crime: "He made an obscene gesture to your father." We children knew full well that the unfortunate driver in the car ahead of us had simply replied to his bullying with a one-finger salute. We silently applauded the poor fellow, whoever he was.

I would have thought that if he would have tried to pull off such tactics in a more recent setting, he would have been jailed for attempting to commit a hate crime, or at the very least, for aggressive driving. But no. He was still driving in his 90s just a few years back. Carolyn and I made a mistake, almost a terminal one, when we agreed to sit in the back seat of his Buick Century for a drive to the pharmacy. We should have jumped out of the car while he attempted to locate the shift lever, removing his foot from the brake in the process and allowing the car to drift into the side of the garage. But no. Accepting the new dent with aplomb, he finally found the lever, backed up from the scene of his latest accident, and emerged onto the roadway, where he was astonished to find that he had to share it with other cars. Within ten seconds he had his window down and his fist pumping away at the first offender he'd happened upon. Of course, it was also the first car that he met on the road.

Thankful to have emerged from that trip with all of our body parts intact, we asked for his car keys with the intent of leaving his car in the garage forever after. He didn't need the car. They lived in a very nice senior development that was well-equipped with shuttles and other help, even to the extent that volunteers were available either to take them shopping or do the shopping for them. But no. His pumping fist turned in our direction for our brazen attempt, causing us to fall back to Plan B, which was to contact the local police. We weren't prepared for the levity with which the police treated the situation. They laughingly referred to the senior development as "Death Valley" and told us that the denizens of the area, being well aware of the hazards posed by drivers like dad, had learned to "run out of the way." We left feeling like Alice in Wonderland. But then we realized that we were in California, which explained everything.

Most highways also were two-laners back then, which gave dad an opportunity to display his prowess at passing. Coming around a bend to find a car in front of him, he'd quickly assess the distance to the next curve, taking into account various factors like his current speed, the ability of his engine to accelerate to passing speed, and the risk of coming into the upcoming bend with insufficient braking distance. Almost invariably, his computations gave him to green light to proceed, whereupon he'd jam his foot onto the accelerator pedal, swerve out into the oncoming lane, and urge his steed forward into the fray. Sometimes, if an oncoming car came around the bend ahead at speed, he'd be forced to swerve back into his lane, sometimes (but rarely—he was pretty good behind the wheel back then) forcing the vehicle he'd passed to brake hard to let him back in. All I can say is that we had a lot of close calls involving speeding, braking and swerving, and we were pretty much occupied full-time either being sick or terrified.

His cars were all top-of-the-line. One day while we were still in our pre-teen years, mom was real excited. She told us that dad had gone to get a new horse, and when he returned home we saw what a champion he'd picked up. It was a powder-blue Pontiac convertible. At that time the horsepower race of the mid-'50s hadn't begun. Most of the garden-variety cars of that era, the Fords and Chevys, were way underpowered by today's standards. But the big straight-eight in that Pontiac was ahead of its time. By that time dad had taken a sales engineering job, which dovetailed well with his love of driving. Once in a while he would take one of us on a trip with him. I remember falling asleep in the car between Bakersfield and the grapevine as we headed south on Highway 99 toward Los Angeles. The screeching wind woke me on the downhill slope. I sat up in the seat and observed us rushing past other cars like they were parked. Glancing over at the speedometer, I saw that we were doing 105. Dad had a smile on his face. He was in his element.

I will say this about him, though. Despite his flaws in wisdom-judgment that prevented his passengers from ever relaxing, his racing judgment was superb. His reflexes were those of a cat, almost as good as Beltre at third base. When the time came for my brother and me to learn to drive, his capability as an instructor was as good as it gets. For that particular task he was surprisingly patient, and rather quickly passed on his advanced skills to us.

The downside of all that is that in the process of teaching us to drive, he unleashed his progeny onto the unsuspecting public after thoroughly embedding in them his faults. He paid for it, though. Until we bought our own cars we used his. Within three months he had to put his beautiful '52 Merc into the shop for a new clutch and rear tires. I don't understand how the U-joints and the rear end held out. We didn't tell him, but we wouldn't have given two cents for the rest of the drive train. I think he finally figured that out, because within a year he bought a beefier vehicle, a Packard Patrician. I think its engine was the one that kicked off the horsepower escalation – it was huge, one of the first 400 cubic-inch engines to grace a standard car. Despite its size and weight, propelled by that mill as we eagerly verified, the car was a rocket. Its only drawback was its brakes, which were wholly insufficient for the car's performance. As I remember, whichever one of us who had the car on a date would have to allow an extra half hour before returning it home to let the brakes cool off enough that the stink of the asbestos compound wouldn't alarm dad or the neighbors. It went to the garage for new brakes at intervals not anticipated by either the manufacturer or dad.

As I said, I sincerely hope that God does a better job of this family business than we did. Thankfully, we have every reason to expect that to be the case.

Given an understanding of the Holy Trinity as a divine Family, one is naturally led into a consideration of its role with regard to a primary family function: procreation and reproduction of kind. Scripture itself suggests that the Church, as the spiritual Bride of Christ, will also be the daughter-in-law of the divine Father and the Holy Spirit, enlarging the Godhead from a Trinity to a divine Four. There is a beautiful Scriptural passage, Romans 8:14-17, that openly suggests this very notion of Family continuity in the spiritual realm:

> *For as many as are led by the Spirit of God, they are the sons of God. For ye have not received the spirit of bondage again*

to fear; but ye have received the Spirit of adoption, whereby
we cry, Abba, Father. The Spirit itself beareth witness with
our spirit, that we are the children of God; and if children,
then heirs – heirs of God, and joint heirs with Christ – if so be
that we suffer with him, that we may be also glorified together.

In the context of our future marriage with Christ, the entire book of Ephesians reads like a marriage manual, or a prenuptial marriage counseling session. Ephesians 5:1 also expresses the notion of the Church's inclusion into the Family of God:

Be ye, therefore, followers of God, as dear children.

These passages, in turn, suggest that just as the union of Father and Spirit resulted in the Son Jesus Christ, the Church Herself will assume the same role in the spiritual realm as the Holy Spirit in uniting with Jesus to produce another divine Child, further enlarging the Godhead from a divine Four to a divine Five.

In contrast with a vague, rather static, understanding of heaven as encouraged by the prevailing gender-neutral view of the Godhead, the spiritual realm may be a place of excitement, action and adventure. I touch on that possibility in Part 2, Chapter 2 of *Family of God*:

Regarding our own union with Jesus, the book of Revelation clearly states that His Church will be raised up on the seventh day, to reign with Jesus for a thousand years on earth. Our reign with Jesus will resemble the function of our Divine Mother the Holy Spirit as we furnish the means that, in union with the Will of our Lord Jesus, gives birth to a new Creation. It will be a marriage of great joy, as specifically confirmed by our Lord in the second Chapter of John. As John recounts, Jesus reserved the first miracle that He performed on earth to demonstrate this to us by turning water into wine at the wedding ceremony in Cana.

The implications of this possibility are large. It confirms the nature of the Holy Spirit as diffuse, and complements the explanations presented in Chapter Twelve as to why God may not have encouraged us to worship a feminine Deity. For to worship this entity would be dangerously close to worship of self, or at least to self as it might exist in the future next to Jesus, our Lord and our Husband. Even now a false, arrogant, and self-serving form of this hope is manifest in the New Age belief that we ourselves are gods.

In the context of Jesus as the Husband of His Church, an interesting topic for further speculation is this as the Jewish procedure for divorce is recalled: in thrice denouncing the Pharisees, did Jesus annul His relationship with the religious leaders? And in His threefold request of Peter to feed His sheep, was He in effect betrothing Himself to His Church? We do know this: when Jesus in John 14 gave us the promise of a place in heaven, he was speaking according to the custom, current at that time in that society, of the preparations that the bridegroom makes for his wife:

Let not your heart be troubled: ye believe in God, believe also in me. In my Father's house are many mansions: if it were not so, I would have told you. I go to prepare a place for you. And if I go and prepare a place for you, I will come again, and receive you unto myself; that where I am, there ye may be also.

We also see in viewing Jesus as Husband the potential for a union that bears fruit. In Part One we arrived at the fascinating notion, albeit speculative, of the Godhead as a dynamically continuous Family process, a recursive drama in which the human pattern of one generation receiving the scepter of activity from its predecessor and passing it on to its descendents is truly an image of its Godly counterpart. There may be large differences, of course. The original God must still be active in an open and expanding universe rather than lying dead in some heavenly grave. But the essential functional passing of the torch, at least with respect to earth, yet may be a reality.

One very happy corollary to this view of our eventual

relationship with Jesus is a picture of heaven that is more substantial and infinitely more interesting than the usual diaphanous place of clouds, harps, and a rather boring stasis. To the contrary, our future time with Jesus appears to be a busy one, full of creative effort, quite possibly rich in adventure, and certainly with love.

Will there be an eighth day of God, one in which we, the Church, are intimately involved?

Appendix One

IMPLICATIONS OF GOD'S TRANSCENDENT NATURE ON THE ORTHODOX CHRISTIAN UNDERSTANDING OF GOD

Transcendence appears to be a vital feature of God. In his book *The Bible Among the Myths*, in fact, modern theologian John Oswalt asserts that the unique feature of the Bible, that preeminent quality which differentiates it from all other religious documents, is its description of God as a transcendent Being, existing above and separate from His Creation. As Dr. Oswalt takes the Bible as the source of his assertion, we shall accept this assessment of God's transcendent nature as accurate and fundamental to our investigation of its implications.

This God of Judeo-Christian Scripture possesses other distinct features as well, our understanding of which also has been gleaned from Scripture itself. According to theologian F. David Lambert, who has performed a detailed review of the catechisms or articles of faith of what have been considered to be the mainline Christian Churches prior to the general falling away over the past few decades, traditional Christianity has historically adhered to six basic principles in its definition of God. Those whose understanding of God falls within the boundaries established by those principles are embraced by Orthodox Christianity as members of their group, while those whose concept of God lies outside these boundaries are considered to adhere to a different theology than that which orthodoxy views as fully Christian.

The six tests of orthodoxy are these, which are generally acknowledged to have come from a literal interpretation of Scripture, the term 'literal' essentially meaning it is recognized as truth rather than fiction, and is understood naturally as opposed to allegorically:

First, God (or the Godhead) is a unique entity in the universe, possessing the attributes of omniscience, omnipresence, and omnipotence. He is all-knowing, all-seeing, and maintains absolute control over every event that occurs in the universe, which due to His transcendent nature, He created in its entirety. Given these attributes, God resides above our boundaries of space and time, and is not limited to them. (To be fair, there are Churches who grant to mankind the ability acknowledged as voluntarily granted by God, usually labeled as free will, to accept or deny the salvation offered by Jesus' work on the cross. Those who claim this ability for man are called Arminians, after Dutch theologian James Arminius, while those who deny this ability in man are called Calvinists, after the famous sixteenth-century theologian John Calvin. Most Churches, although they may vehemently oppose one side or the other on this issue, consider both Arminians and Calvinists to be within the pale of legitimate Christianity. It's healthy to argue – the Churches that have already fallen away typically don't perceive that the issue exists.)

Second, the Godhead is a triune entity consisting of Father, Son, and Holy Spirit (Holy Ghost), all equally God, who existed and shall continue to exist in triune form throughout eternity. (There is some argument over the meaning of eternity. Since it references time, which began with Creation, it restricts our knowledge of God to the boundaries of our own dimensional limitations, wherein we are unable to perceive anything of God outside of time.)

Third, Jesus Christ was born in the flesh through Mary, who was a virgin at the birth of Jesus. The fundamental issue of the necessity of the virgin birth is that Jesus in the flesh was fully God and fully man. Scripture itself elevates to considerable importance the issue of whether or not Mary remained a virgin after Jesus' birth, as any claim that Mary was a perpetual virgin contradicts Mark 6:3 and Matthew 1:24 and 25 and 13:55 and 56; indeed, most mainstream Protestant churches accept without reservation that Jesus had siblings, among whom were James and Jude, who wrote the New Testament epistle of those names. Nevertheless, the insistence of some Churches on Mary's perpetual virginity does not constitute an error so large as to separate such believers from the Christian community. Orthodox Christianity also recognizes, in accordance with John 1:14 and 17:24 and Ephesians 1:4, Jesus' spiritual existence to have preceded His birth in the flesh.

Fourth, out of God's pure and sacrificial love for mankind, Jesus died on the cross for the sins of believers and was subsequently resurrected. His act on the cross is understood to have been preplanned from the foundation of the world, as confirmed by numerous references to this sacrificial act in Old Testament Scripture, e.g. Genesis 4 and 45, Exodus 12, Leviticus 22, Psalm 22, Isaiah 53, Daniel 9 and Jonah, to name just a few of the more obvious references. Christians universally await His bodily return to earth to judge the nations, rule over mankind both directly and visibly and, most importantly, to exercise dominion over the earth with His bride, the Church, as noted in Genesis 24 and Ephesians 5.

Fifth, salvation, or the reconciliation between the believer and God, is effected by faith in Jesus Christ, and by that faith alone. While such faith will naturally result in works, it is impossible for man to reconcile himself to God (or storm the gates of heaven) through his own efforts, or by any pathway other than Jesus Christ.

Sixth, Scripture (the Bible, comprising both Old and New Testaments) is a necessary and sufficient presentation of God to mankind. It stands alone as a description of God and his intent toward man, and is to be understood under an interpretation that is naturally literal except in those infrequent cases that are obviously allegorical, and is considered to be the inerrant and inspired Word of God. As Scripture itself states in 2 Timothy 3:16 and 17 and 2 Peter 1:20 and 21, it is inspired by God and not open to private interpretation.

Implicit in these six defining features of orthodox Christianity, and demanded in particular by the attribute of actual and anticipated resurrection, may be added a seventh attribute, one which is shared among many religions but which is most appropriate to the Christian faith and which is particularly relevant to the theme under discussion:

Seventh, the human soul exists eternally, not being limited to the confines of the bodily mechanism.

The application of a "literal" interpretation to Scripture as required by this dogma does not imply the necessity for such a stern rigidity as would require the rejecting of figures of speech. For that reason, my pastor prefers to use the word 'natural' instead of 'literal'. This flavor of interpretation simply means that one should accept Scripture as a work of truth rather than fiction, interpreting it according to a reasonable and natural common understanding of language and avoiding the practice of allegorizing every difficult passage one might encounter. A common-sense application of a 'literal' approach to interpretation of Scripture would be flexible enough to appreciate that a "day" of God's creative activity might be very different than twenty-four hours. An earth day, for one thing, is dependent upon the rotational rate of the earth about its own axis. Who knows what that rate was at the time of Creation? If the earth had experienced no rotational velocity at that time, one 'day' would have been of infinite duration. It might make more sense to interpret a day, in this context, as an event-defined, repetitive period of unknown and possibly even variable length. On the other hand, the 'millions of years' taught by contemporary science as the duration of past ages is void of logical justification. A literal interpretation would also acknowledge the limitation of our languages, including the multiple meanings of certain words or even that the meaning of some words has changed over time.

From the notions of transcendence and the numerous attributes of God embedded in the above statement of orthodoxy, we can begin to develop a vision of God's character. Specifically, we understand the following:

First, from the notion of omnipotence and as specifically amplified upon regarding the act of creation in Genesis 1 and John 1: that God created the universe and everything within it apart from Himself.

Second, from the notion of transcendence that: God stands apart from His creation, existing prior to and independently of it.

Third, from the notion of the Trinity that: the Godhead consists of Father, Son and Holy Spirit, all fully God, all sharing some common essence, and all distinct (at least in any single point in time according to our limited perception) with respect to some quality or feature.

Fourth, from the notions of the cross and of God's act in Bounding Himself to become one with man and in offering Himself to pain, humiliation and rejection for the sake of fallen mankind, that: God is capable of loving his creation and of behaving nobly with respect to it. This is supported by the existence of Scripture itself, as well as its contents in particular; it is further supported through the work of the Holy Spirit on the believing soul.

Fifth, from the notion of the eternal existence of the soul, and as specifically amplified upon regarding Jesus' marriage to His Church in John 2 and Ephesians 5, that: redeemed mankind in spiritual form has a future destiny with God at a much more intimate (and loving) level than his physical existence will permit.

With the above characterizing items in mind, we can, with the aid of Scripture, refine this vision further.

With respect to God's omnipotence, the very Trinitarian nature of God requires a sharing of this power among the Members, consequently demanding a subordination of each Member to the Godhead. Again, because of God's omnipotence, this division of one into three had to be performed voluntarily, thus implying in itself a selfless nobility, which can be considered to be the essence of love in its purest form. Jesus' assertion in the Gospel of John that He and the Father are One strongly implies that the three Members, although distinct One from the Other, maintain unity through the binding force of love. Therefore, we have the common attributes of selflessness, nobility and love that characterize the individual Members of the Godhead, and probably the attributes of omniscience and omnipresence as well, whereas at least the attribute of omnipotence is reserved as a property for the Godhead alone. As two examples of this limitation of omnipotence upon each Member, it is noted in John 5:30 that the Father alone exercises the initiating will, and in John 1 that Jesus alone is given to represent the entirety of Creation.

Jesus Himself demonstrated passion in a variety of situations while in human form, including his anger while overturning of the money changers' tables at the temple, His weeping over Jerusalem and Lazarus, His cry that He and the Father were One, and his ordeals at Gethsemane and on the cross. Scripture, including the Old Testament, is replete with other examples of God's passion. Most importantly, if Jesus in spiritual form is beyond passion, then He would be denied any understanding or meaningful memory of His time on earth as a Man, which contradicts the essence of omniscience. Furthermore, his nobility as a Man would be of little value to a Father who, being above love and passion, would be unable to comprehend its importance. This situation would not warrant the Father's glorification of Jesus in the spiritual realm. Therefore, we feel justified in generalizing from Jesus as God to the other Members who share this essence of God in considering God to be capable of passion.

These three concepts of the Godhead, the power of the office, the unity that comes from love and the ability for passion, carry with them certain implications that have not been clearly worked out by the mainstream church, chief among them being some conflicts intrinsic to the church's declaration that while the three Members of the Trinity are of the same substance they are also distinct in some manner.

The first of these conflicts is implicit in a direct statement made above, which is the impossibility of assigning omnipotence to more than one Deity without some voluntary subordination, which appears to clash with the mainstream assumption that all three Members of the Godhead coexisted from eternity past, the standard implication being always. For if the Members of the Godhead coexisted from beyond eternity past, there would be no basis for such subordination, regardless of whether it was to be temporary or not. The only way to avoid this conflict is to assume that the quality of omnipotence resides not in the individual Members, but in the Godhead alone. But then the fact that the Godhead, not consisting of any Being of Itself, must necessarily be impersonal, suggests that initially (a level of eternity beyond our comprehension which preceded time as we know it, which began with Creation) there was a single God who voluntarily divided His substance, creating three individual Members sharing the same substance and all being subordinate to the omnipotent Whole. This notion is supported by Scripture, particularly in Revelation 3:14, in which Jesus describes Himself as the beginning of the creation of God (the spoken Word of Genesis 1 and John 1: Let there be Light).

The second of these conflicts is the ability of the three Members to differ in the face of their identity of substance. This conflict can be resolved in only one way: by assuming a functional differentiation among the Members such that at any one instance each member has a unique functional role. This assumption imposes no requirement of permanence regarding this functional distribution; the roles, for example, could be assumed on a rotational basis such that each Member assumes all possible roles over the span of all time. Support for this differentiation on the basis of function is again provided by John 1 and John 5:30, to name just two relevant passages among a multitude.

If this understanding appears to continue to conflict with the second rule of orthodoxy that required the Trinity to exist as such throughout eternity, our dimensional limitations must be remembered. The differentiation occurred in the environment where God resides, which is unbounded in time and space, so one cannot make any application of the notion of sequence to any Member of the Trinity; therefore, as far as we humans are concerned, the association of all Members of the Trinity with eternity past to eternity future remains intact. Every Member, in addition, being of the same substance, is equally God. Here we simply must acknowledge our dimensional limitations, noting that there are necessary boundaries to our ability to comprehend the nature of God.

Assuming, then, that the Members of the Trinity are distinct on the basis of functionality, it is rather straightforward to derive from Scripture specific functional roles attributable to each of the Members. The very beginning of Scripture, Genesis 1, implies that the Father creates the image of that which He wishes to be created in actuality; in union with the Holy Spirit acting as the means to actualize the image, gives birth to the Word of God, which is the actual creation itself. Restated, it is (according to my thinking) the Divine Will in union with the Divine Means that gives birth to the Divine Creation. In the context of these functional roles, Jesus, of course, represents Creation, or the actualization of the Will, as thoroughly described in John 1. In that same context the Holy Spirit serves as the Divine Implementer, performing the process that gives life to the Divine Will, birthing it into the Divine Actual. As such, the Holy Spirit assumes a role reserved for the female gender. The Book of Proverbs, with its description of Wisdom in female form, matches well with an understanding of the Holy Spirit as having a female identity with respect to function. If this is indeed the case, Proverbs provides a wealth of information to flesh out the nature of the Holy Spirit. Consider the following passages from Proverbs chapters 3 and 8:

Happy is the man that findeth wisdom, and the man that getteth understanding: For the merchandise of it is better than the merchandise of silver, and the gain thereof than fine gold. She is more precious than rubies: and all the things thou canst desire are not to be compared unto her. Length of days is in her right hand; and in her left hand riches and honor. Her ways are ways of pleasantness, and all her paths are peace. She is a tree of life to them that lay hold upon her: and happy is every one that retaineth her. The Lord by wisdom hath founded the earth; by understanding hath he established the heavens.

Doth not wisdom cry? and understanding put forth her voice? She standeth in the top of high places, by the way in the places of the paths... The Lord possessed me in the beginning of his way, before his works of old. I was set up from everlasting, from the beginning, or ever the earth was. When there were no depths, I was brought forth; when there were no fountains abounding with water. Before the mountains were settled, before the hills was I brought forth: While as yet he had not made the earth, nor the fields, nor the highest part of the dust of the world. When he prepared the heavens, I was there: when he set a compass upon the face of the depth: When he established the clouds above: when he strengthened the fountains of the deep: When he gave to the sea his decree, that the waters should not pass his commandment: when he appointed the foundations of the earth: Then I was by him, as one brought up with him: and I was daily his delight, rejoicing always before him; Rejoicing in the habitable part of his earth; and my delights were with the sons of men. Now therefore hearken unto me, O ye children: for blessed are they that keep my ways. Hear instruction, and be wise, and refuse it not. Blessed is the man that heareth me, watching daily at my gates, waiting at the posts of my doors. For whoso findeth me findeth life, and shall obtain favor of the Lord. But he that sinneth against me wrongteth his own soul: all they that hate me love death.

Strong as the Book of Proverbs is in support of a female Holy Spirit in the functional persona of Wisdom, this gender assignment still appears to conflict with Scripture's frequent use of the male pronoun 'he' with reference to the Holy Spirit. But this apparent conflict already exists more overtly in Scripture with respect to another entity, the Church, although it hasn't bothered us for centuries. Consider Ephesians 5, where Paul explains the mystery of the Church as the Bride of Christ in the most intimate of terms: "For this cause shall a man leave his father and mother, and shall be joined unto his wife, and they two shall be one flesh." Here we have an understanding, taken directly from Scripture, that the Church consisting of redeemed mankind, always referred to collectively by the male generic 'he', shall assume the role of Bride of Christ, an obviously female function.

One can carry this similitude between the Church and the Holy Spirit further. The two entities not only harmonize, but the similarity hints at a promise to the Church. Will the Church, in its relationship to Jesus Christ, serve in a role parallel to that of the Holy Spirit? We know too little to speak about this with assurance, but the possibility is exciting.

This perceived parallelism of the Spirit with the Church leads to yet more detailed appreciation of the harmony implicit in the nature and functional roles of both Entities. For example, in reflecting upon the birth of the Church out of the pierced side of Jesus as He stood on the cross, we can see the prophetic nature of the birth of Eve out of Adam's rib, and how both of these births might reenact the origin of the Holy Spirit. For another example, we might perceive the Holy Spirit as comprised of a collection of more basic individual Entities, for which the aggregate gender designation is male. Thirdly, we might also perceive the Scriptural aggregate designation for the Church (probably with redeemed mankind in its spiritual form) as male may suggest its eventual union with God, in a role companion to that of the Holy Spirit. In this sense, the Scriptural use of 'he' for the Holy Spirit may well represent a promise to us from God as to our future role in His economy.

The view of the Trinity presented above, coupled with the ability of God to experience passion, further suggests that love trumps power with respect to the nature of God, just as Scripture implies throughout and codifies in the Shema of Israel (Deuteronomy 6:4 and 5) and in the Great Commandment noted by Jesus (Matthew 22:36-38). It does so for the following reasons: first, in this view the Father, in Whom was the substance of everything that is or ever shall be, willingly humbled Himself to share His glory with Others upon Whom He first wished to set His love and affection, such that the defining attributes of Godhood as omniscience, omnipotence and omnipresence, or at least omnipotence, would reside in the Trinity rather than in any one Member; and second, that the other Members of the Trinity, the Holy Spirit and the Son, would remain subordinate to the Father's Divine Will, in the only sense that their functional roles were first defined by Him. While it is also true that the Will always initiates that which follows, we have no knowledge whether that particular function cannot be assumed, at least in part, by the other Members.

Appendix Two

JESUS' FEEDING OF THE MULTITUDES

Introduction

The Bible contains many mysteries. God wished it to be so in order that man would find from a diligent search the truth in the Word of God, and from that truth, come to know and love his God with the fervor of Jesus' Great Commandment in Matthew 22:37 and 38:

> *Jesus said unto him, Thou shalt love the Lord, thy God, with all thy heart, and with all thy soul, and with all thy mind. This is the first and great commandment."*

As with other things that we treasure the most, the solving of many of the mysteries of God require patience and hard work. God Himself said as much in Proverbs 25:2:

> *It is the glory of God to conceal a thing, but the honor of kings is to search out a matter."*

Not all mysteries of God are intended to be understood as soon as they are voiced or set down in Scripture. Many mysteries are intended to be revealed at a certain period of history, perhaps, as suggested in Daniel 12:4, at the end of the age of man's government on earth.

But thou, O Daniel, shut up the words, and seal the book, even to the time of the end; many shall run to and fro, and knowledge shall be increased.

Jesus' feeding of the multitudes is indeed an enigma that has eluded a solution for many centuries. Only recently was it found to be amenable to a mathematical solution, suggesting that the solution to the puzzle was intended for our present age. The proof of the mystery is an amazing image, a sign denied to the generation in which Jesus lived on earth, but now available to all to know that the Lord Jesus Christ is indeed the true Messiah sought by the Jews over centuries of hardship and persecution.

Scripture, in recounting Jesus' feeding of the multitudes, furnishes information regarding those events that extend quite deeply beyond the surface of the narrative. The mathematical solution to the feeding of the multitudes requires a complex analysis that draws upon different passages of the Bible, both the Old and the New Testaments, and is comprised of different meanings for the word 'feedings.' There are two very distinct definitions for 'feedings' that must be used together to solve the puzzle. One definition of feedings is nourishment found in food. The other definition of feedings is the nourishment found in the Word; one for sustenance of the body, the other for the sustenance of the soul, as Jesus Himself suggested in Matthew 4:4:

But [Jesus] answered [the devil] and said, It is written, Man shall not live by bread alone, but by every word that proceedeth out of the mouth of God.

Considering the spiritual feedings to be the one most important to God and dovetailing it into the physical feedings leads to the solution of the mystery.

The integration of these feedings into a meaningful pattern is found in the following essay and is meant to bless mankind with the beautiful nature of the Word of God and its inherent truth down to the smallest detail, including a prophetic element of importance to the people of today.

The Mystery

There is an element of mystery, of information hidden beneath the surface, that accompanies the Gospel accounts of Jesus' feeding of the multitudes. In the eighth chapter of Mark's Gospel, Jesus made a pointed and direct association of faith with understanding as he spoke with His disciples after feeding four thousand people with seven loaves and a few fish. Significantly, just prior to that incident as recorded in Mark He had encountered the Pharisees, who had sought some confirmation from heaven regarding Jesus' credentials.

And he sighed deeply in his spirit, and saith, Why doth this generation seek after a sign? verily I say unto you, There shall no sign be given unto this generation.

As the account in Mark 8 continues, Jesus recalls to His disciples the events in which He fed the multitudes, as if the details represented something of great importance.

And he left them, and entering into the ship again departed to the other side. Now the disciples had forgotten to take bread, neither had they in the ship with them more than one loaf.

And he charged them, saying, Take heed, beware of the leaven of the Pharisees, and of the leaven of Herod.

And they reasoned among themselves, saying, It is because we have no bread.

And when Jesus knew it, he saith unto them, Why reason ye, because ye have no bread? perceive ye not yet, neither understand? have ye your heart yet hardened?

Having eyes, see ye not? and having ears, hear ye not? and do ye not remember?

When I brake the five loaves among five thousand, how many baskets full of fragments took ye up? They say unto him, Twelve.

And when the seven among four thousand, how many baskets full of fragments took ye up? And they said, Seven.

And he said unto them, How is it that ye do not understand?"

In this account, Jesus confronts his disciples with their lack of understanding. In a commentary that appears at the first reading to be somewhat cryptic, He recalls the feeding of the five thousand and the four thousand. In this recollection, Jesus emphasizes numbers: the number of people fed, along with the number of baskets that contained the fragments that remained. Having recalled the specific numbers associated with these feeding events, Jesus makes the odd demand: *"How is it that ye do not understand?"*

It is tempting, in a first reading of this and the surrounding verses, to think of Mark as lacking in sophistication. He seems to mix numbers inappropriately into the basic message, and too many details are left unanswered. Why, for example, did Jesus emphasize the numbers associated with the feedings, as if these values were somehow related to their faith? Jesus painstakingly recalls to His disciples the number of individuals fed and the number of remaining baskets, but fails to complete the picture. How many fragments did each basket contain? Of what importance was the number of baskets of leftovers to the event itself, or to the disciples' faith? How can the number of baskets of leftovers have such theological significance that Jesus placed so much emphasis upon it in the recollection of the feeding events to His disciples? Why were 5,000 fed with five loaves, whereas seven loaves were required to feed the 4,000?

What if Mark, as guided by the Holy Spirit and therefore far from being unsophisticated of word, was actually presenting a truth of great depth? In this light, the passage literally pleads for a deeper understanding of the feeding of the people. When Jesus spoke about the specifics of the feedings to His disciples, it was as if he was presenting the future reader with a riddle and commanding him to solve it.

As this essay shall endeavor to show, the feeding of the multitudes contained the rudiments of such a sign as the Pharisees had requested of Jesus. But the completion of its components had to await the Pentecost. The Gospels also had to be written first, in the unique manner in which they presented the elements for later examination. Next, the Gospels had to be integrated into Scripture and thus become available for open review. Finally, a generation had to emerge whose perspective was conditioned to view Scripture beyond that which is immediately apparent.

The Significance of Jesus' Feedings

The physical bread represented only a part of the feeding events. In fact, it wasn't even the most significant part. The bread was only symbolic of a much greater spiritual Bread, the Word of God.

There are several proofs of this. First, there is the spiritual representation of Jesus in John 1:1 and 14 as the Word of God:

In the beginning was the Word, and the Word was with God, and the Word was God... And the Word became flesh, and dwelt among us.

Jesus, in fact, considered the material world, including physical bread, to be of little value. According to John 18:36a,

Jesus answered, My kingdom is not of this world;

But even before He made that statement, He was more direct in John 6 regarding the relative importance of bread and His Word:

Jesus answered them, and said, Verily, verily, I say unto you, Ye seek me, not because ye saw the miracles, but because ye did eat of the loaves, and were filled. Labor not for the food which perisheth, but for that food which endureth unto everlasting life, which the Son of man shall give unto you; for him hath God the Father sealed.

Then said they unto him, What shall we do, that we might work the works of God. Jesus answered, and said unto them, This is the work of God, that ye believe on him whom he hath

sent. They said, therefore, unto him, What sign showest thou, then, that we may see, and believe thee? What dost thou work? Our fathers did eat manna in the desert; as it is written, He gave them bread from heaven to eat.

Then Jesus said unto them, Verily, verily, I say unto you, Moses gave you not that bread from heaven; but my Father giveth you the true bread from heaven. For the bread of God is he who cometh down from heaven and giveth life unto the world. Then said they unto him, Lord, evermore give us this bread. And Jesus said unto them, I am the bread of life; he that cometh to me shall never hunger, and he that believeth on me shall never thirst.

The Miraculous Element of the Feedings

The element of the feedings that is the simplest to grasp is the miracle itself, as it simply mimics the process of the Word's propagation from ear to mouth without loss. After having been blessed by Jesus, the bread returned to wholeness every time it was broken. That's all there is to it. The rest of the process involves the mechanics of the distribution.

The leaven of the Pharisees that Jesus warned His disciples to beware of referred to the distortion of the Word and its consequent corruption as it was propagated by the religious leadership.

Preliminary Facts About the Feeding Process

Not having access to detailed eyewitness accounts of the feeding events, we can't be certain how the feedings actually took place. But enough information can be gleaned from Scripture to suggest that the process was an orderly one, at least in the spiritual domain regarding the feeding of the Word.

According to Mark 6:39 and 40, the men being fed were grouped into companies, where the size of each company was either 50 or 100 men.

And [Jesus] commanded them to make all sit down by

companies upon the green grass. And they sat down in ranks,
by hundreds, and by fifties.

Given that information, a typical company of 100 might be arranged in the 20 by 5 configuration shown in Figure 1 below, and a company of 50 might be half that size, or 10 by 5. These particular arrangements will be justified through Scripture later.

Figure 1: Typical company of 100

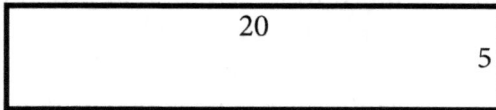

According to Matthew 14:19, the feeding was initiated first by Jesus, who blessed the bread, and second by His disciples, who then gave the loaves to the multitudes:

And [Jesus] commanded the multitude to sit down on the
grass, and took the five loaves, and the two fishes, and looking
up to heaven, he blessed, and broke, and gave the loaves to
His disciples, and the disciples gave them to the multitudes.

It will be assumed here that when Jesus broke the loaves, the two halves remained attached to each other as He handed them to His disciples. Each disciple, in turn, handed a loaf to one member (perhaps the captain) of the group of fifty or one hundred nearest him. This group will be called the frontmost group. As there were five loaves in the feeding of the five thousand, five disciples were involved. But there also were seven loaves associated with the later feeding of four thousand, which involved the remaining seven disciples, such that each of the twelve disciples (apostles) was involved once in the two feeding events.

A mathematical analysis was performed on the information in Scripture regarding the feedings. A reproduction of the analysis is beyond the scope of this essay and involves Scriptural information beyond that which has been presented to this point. Nevertheless, useful as it was toward the development of an understanding of the feeding process, it is not necessary for the reader to refer to it to acquire his own understanding, as such may be achieved merely by inspecting the pattern. One item of that analysis is helpful, however: if the number of fragments from the feeding of the menfolk is constrained to be the same for both the feeding of the five thousand and the four thousand, then the analysis demands that the number must necessarily be five. Therefore, it will be assumed that there were five fragments of leftover loaves due to the menfolk in each basket.

The Mechanics of the Distribution

The loaves can be visualized, with the aid of Figure 2 below, as being distributed one to each frontmost company by each disciple, to whom Jesus gave the initial loaves, to the first man in the front of the company, which, to the disciple would be the individual at the right end of the row as he faces him.

Figure 2: Basic pattern of feeding

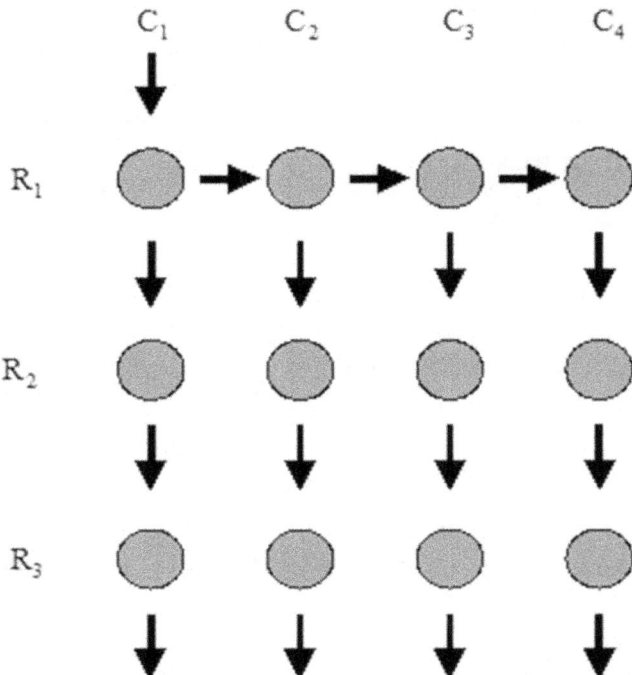

The individual does three things: first he breaks the loaf and gives it to the next man to his right, who does the same to the man on his right, and so on, until each of the men in the frontmost row of the company have received a loaf; second, the men in the frontmost row break the half-loaves that they retained, which in the meantime have become whole again according to the nature of the miracle, and give half to the men directly behind them; finally, these men eat the loaves remaining in their hands. Now all the men behind the frontmost row will just break the loaves that they receive from the men in front of them, pass a loaf to the men to their rear and eat the loaves that remain. In this way, the bread propagates to the rear of the columns, where the rearmost fragments from each column are collected in baskets.

As the process is described, it will be noted that, regarding each company adjacent to the others in the same row, what happens within a frontmost company stays in that company, the residue going to the company behind it but not to the sides. In other words, the distribution proceeds along the companies in each column, the process being independent from one column to another. It also can be seen that as many companies as desired may be stacked behind each frontmost company without altering the final number of fragments collected in the baskets.

Another point to consider from the fact that one loaf is given to each of the twelve apostles over Jesus' two feeding events is that there will be exactly as many frontmost companies as the number of initial loaves: five for the feeding of the five thousand, and seven for the feeding of the four thousand.

The pattern of stacking is summarized in Figure 3, which emphasizes the numerical constraints of each particular feeding event, which are the number of starting loaves and the number of remainder loaves that are collected in the baskets. If there are N loaves at the beginning of the feedings, where N is 5 for the feeding of the 5000 and 7 for the feeding of the 4000, then there will be N frontmost companies. This is the first constraint. Therefore, for the feeding of the 5000, there will be 5 frontmost companies, and for the feeding of the 4000, there will be 7 frontmost companies. There will be the same number of companies at the rear for the collection. The size of each of the rearmost companies, which must be the same as the size of each of the frontmost companies, is established by the number of baskets of remainders and the number of remainders in each basket.

Figure 3: Association of loaves with frontmost companies and remainders with columns of individuals

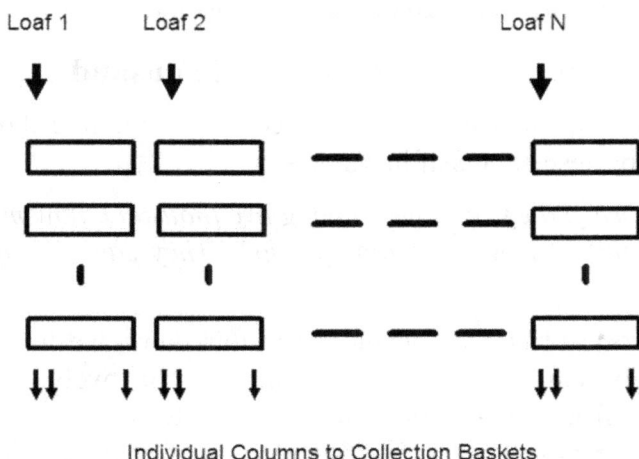

Individual Columns to Collection Baskets

The number of remainders in each basket was established from the arithmetic analysis as 5, as noted earlier. The size of each company is constrained at either 50 or 100. Thus the number of columns of individuals in a company of 50 is either 5 or 10, depending on the side (width or length) representing the columns, and the number of columns of individuals in a company of 100 is either 5 or 20, again depending on the side representing the columns. This is the second constraint.

The number of columns of individuals associated with each feeding event also is constrained to be 5 times the number of baskets of remainders, which, for the feeding of the 5000 is 12 times 5 or 60, and for the feeding of the 4000 is 7 times 5 or 35. This is the third constraint.

The number of frontmost companies of size 50 and the number of frontmost companies of size 100 is established by simultaneously satisfying the first, second and third constraints noted above. After establishing these numbers, the pattern is filled in with the number of companies of the sizes previously established to arrive at the total number of menfolk fed, noting that the number of companies involved in the rearward propagation of the loaves from frontmost to rearmost does not affect the number of starting loaves or the number of remaining loaves. While perfect rectangles are preferred, they are not necessary at this stage of the development.

Specifics of the Feeding of the Five Thousand

As noted earlier, the specifics of the feeding of the five thousand were given by Jesus Himself in Mark 8:

> When I brake the five loaves among five thousand, how many baskets full of fragments took ye up? They say unto him, Twelve.

As the process has been developed to this point, the five initial loaves involves five frontmost companies. The twelve baskets of leftovers from the menfolk requires, at twelve baskets and five loaves per basket, 12 x 5 = 60 columns of people. A unique pattern of companies of 50 and 100 may be constructed from this information, keeping in mind that as many companies as required to come up to five thousand may be stacked behind the frontmost companies without altering the numbers of frontmost companies or of the number of remainder loaves. This pattern is shown on Figure 4.

As indicated on the figure, the pattern involves four frontmost companies of 50 and one frontmost company of 100, for a total of five frontmost companies, which agrees with the number five of initial loaves. The number of columns of menfolk furnishing leftovers is 4 x 10 + 1 x 20 = 60, which, at 5 loaves per basket, yields 12 baskets.

There are 17 x 4 rows of companies of 50 and 16 x 1 rows of companies of 100, producing 17 x 50 + 16 x 100 = 5000 menfolk exactly, which agrees with the number given in the Gospel accounts of that feeding event. The fact that the resulting figure is not a perfect rectangle is somewhat awkward, but that issue will be addressed later.

Figure 4: Pattern for Jesus' Feeding of 5000

68 companies of 50 and 16 companies of 100 arranged in companies of 50 in 2 columns of 17 rows on each side of companies of 100 in center column of 16 rows.

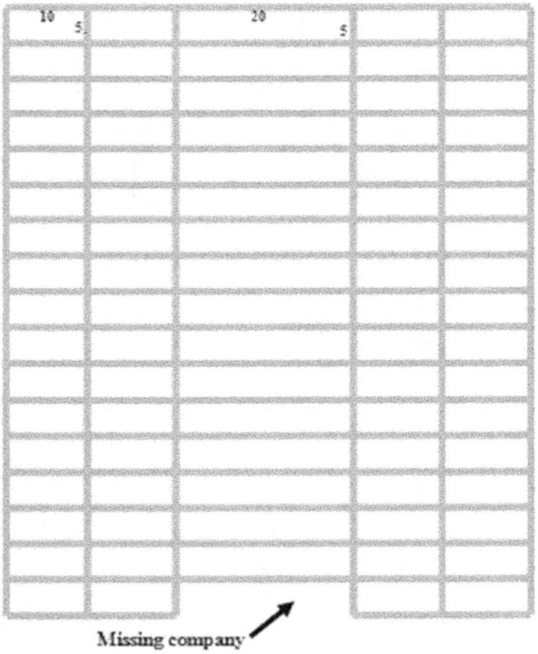

Missing company

Specifics of the Feeding of the Four Thousand

As in the case of the feeding of the five thousand, Jesus Himself, as recorded in Mark 8, described the specifics of His feeding of the four thousand.

And when the seven among four thousand, how many baskets full of fragments took ye up? And they said, Seven.

As before, the seven initial loaves involves seven frontmost companies. The seven baskets of leftovers from the menfolk requires, at seven baskets and five loaves per basket, 7 x 5 = 35 columns of people. A unique pattern of companies of 50 and 100 cannot be constructed from this information as in the case of the feeding of the five thousand. In order to come up with a workable pattern, it is necessary to rotate the process 90 degrees from vertical to horizontal such that, preserving the orientation of the companies themselves as in the feeding of the 5000, the frontmost companies are now to the right and the process of propagating the loaves from one company to the next is to the left instead of rearward. The remainders are also gathered in baskets at the left. This apparent inconsistency between the two feedings was initially somewhat disturbing, but was found to have much significance, as will be brought out later. The resulting pattern for the feeding of the four thousand is shown on Figure 5.

Figure 5: Pattern for Jesus' Feeding of 4000

77 companies of 50 arranged in 11 columns of 7 rows, plus 3 additional companies of 50.

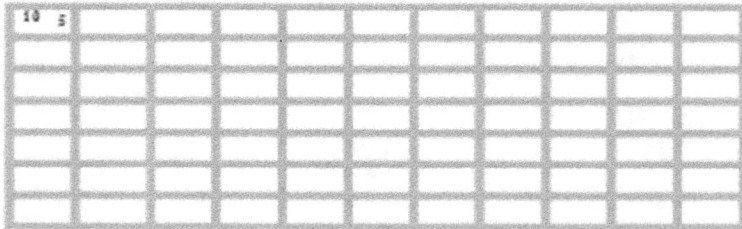

 three additional companies of 50, not necessarily arranged as shown

As shown on the figure, the pattern involves seven frontmost (rightmost) companies of 50 for a total of seven frontmost companies, which agrees with the number seven of initial loaves. The number of columns of menfolk furnishing leftovers is 7 x 5 = 35, which, at 5 loaves per basket, yields 7 baskets.

There are 11 columns x 6 rows of companies of 50 and 14 columns x 1 row of companies of 50, producing 11 x 6 x 50 + 14 x 50 = 4000 menfolk exactly, which agrees with the number given in the Gospel accounts of that feeding event. The figure shows the removal of 3 companies of 50 from one group of companies, resulting in two perfect rectangles, one of 3850 menfolk and the other of 150 menfolk. As in the case of the feeding of the 5000, the resolution of imperfect rectangles into combinations of perfect rectangles associated with both cases will be addressed later.

It should be noted that the three additional companies of 50 could have been tacked onto the end of the rectangle of 3850 menfolk in a variety of ways that don't alter the arithmetic, including one in which four rows consisted of 11 columns and the remaining three rows consisted of 12 columns each.

To this point, patterns have been developed for Jesus' feedings of the 5000 and the 4000 menfolk that show precisely how 5000 menfolk can be fed with 5 loaves and yield 12 baskets of remainders, and 4000 menfolk can be fed with 7 loaves and yield 7 baskets of remainders. This information answers the questions that Jesus asked of His disciples in Mark 8, linking their response to their faith. The answer also reveals something of the incredible depth and accuracy of Scripture.

But there's more to the story of the feedings. Jesus implied that while there was no sign to be given to the generation in which He came to earth, perhaps there might be one given to a future generation, maybe even ours. It is to the end of uncovering this sign that we proceed further, driven at first by our discomfort at the imperfection of the rectangles.

Elisha as a Precursor to Jesus in Feeding Many

As was the case with many other acts that Jesus performed, Jesus' feeding of the multitudes was not the first such incident to have occurred. God had permitted the prophet Elisha to prefigure Jesus in the feedings. The account is given in 2 Kings 4:

And there came a man from Baalshalisha, and brought the

*man of God [Elisha] bread of the first fruits, twenty loaves
of barley, and full ears of corn in its husk. And he said, Give
unto the people, that they may eat. And his servant said,
What, should I set this before a hundred men? He said again,
Give the people, that they may eat; for thus saith the Lord,
They shall eat, and shall have some left. So he set it before
them, and they did eat, and left some, according to the word
of the Lord.*

The process described above is remarkably similar to the accounts
of Jesus' feeding of the multitudes. In fact, the numbers involved
point to a configuration of 20 x 5 men, which furnishes a prototype
of the configuration of a company of 100 men as shown on Figure 1
above, and justifies the assumption made in the preceding discussion
of Jesus' feedings that a company of 100 is arranged 20 x 5.

It does more than that. If Elisha's feeding of 100 is combined
with Jesus' feeding of the 5000, it supplies the missing company of
100 for that account, creating in the combination a perfect rectangle
of 5100 menfolk. This property, in turn, strongly suggests that all
of the feeding incidents, including the feeding of the 4000, with its
two perfect rectangles of 3850 and 150, may be combined in some
meaningful way out of perfect rectangles.

Before that is attempted, there is another feeding incident to
investigate.

Jesus' Feedings as Precursor Events to Peter's Feeding of 3000

In John 14:12, Jesus said:

*Verily, verily, I say unto you, He that believeth on me, the
works that I do shall he do also; and greater works than these
shall he do, because I go unto my Father.*

It was noted earlier that the primary significance of Jesus' feedings
was regarding His Word rather than physical bread. Peter may not
have fed multitudes with bread, but he certainly did so with the
Word of God. Furthermore, in doing so, he was simply obeying the

commandment of Jesus as recorded in John 21. When, in John 21, Jesus commands Peter to "Feed my sheep", and repeats this command three times, can one fail to see some prophetic significance to His words? The first fulfillment of that command is given in Acts 2:41:

Then they that gladly received [Peter's] word were baptized; and the same day there were added unto them about three thousand souls.

Figure 6 below shows an arrangement that satisfies the feeding of three thousand people with the Word of God. It consists of three columns of companies of 100 stacked 10 rows deep to yield three thousand people. Note that the total width of this pattern exactly matches the width of the pattern associated with Jesus' feeding of the five thousand men. This feature further suggests that all the figures associated with the four feeding events can be integrated into a composite figure.

Figure 6: Pattern for Peter's feeding of 3000 with the Word of God

30 companies of 100 arranged in 3 columns of 10 rows

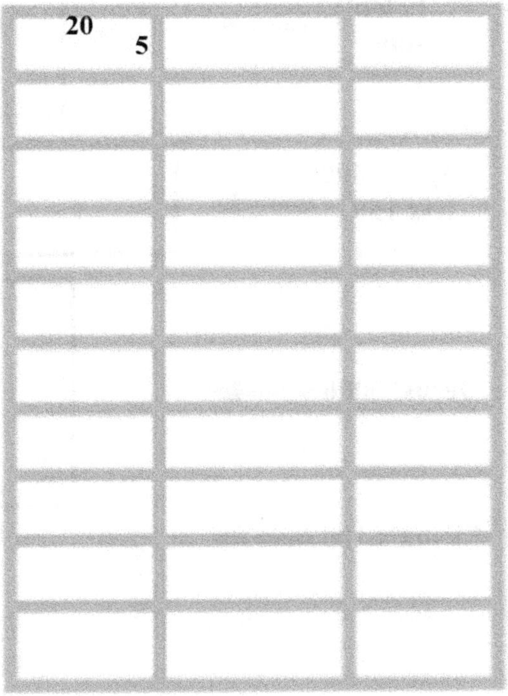

The Integration of the Four Feeding Events into a Composite Figure

The four feeding events produce the five rectangular objects shown on Figure 7 below. As shown on the figure, four of the five objects are perfect rectangles, while the one associated with Jesus' feeding of the 5000, is not. However, this very imperfection in that one object urges the observer to dovetail Elisha's feeding of 100 into the larger object of Jesus' feeding of the 5000, making it a perfect rectangle. This development, in turn, encourages the observer to combine all the objects into a single composite figure.

Figure 7: Five elements of the feeding events

Note: This Chart is intended to show a series of patterns and is not to scale.

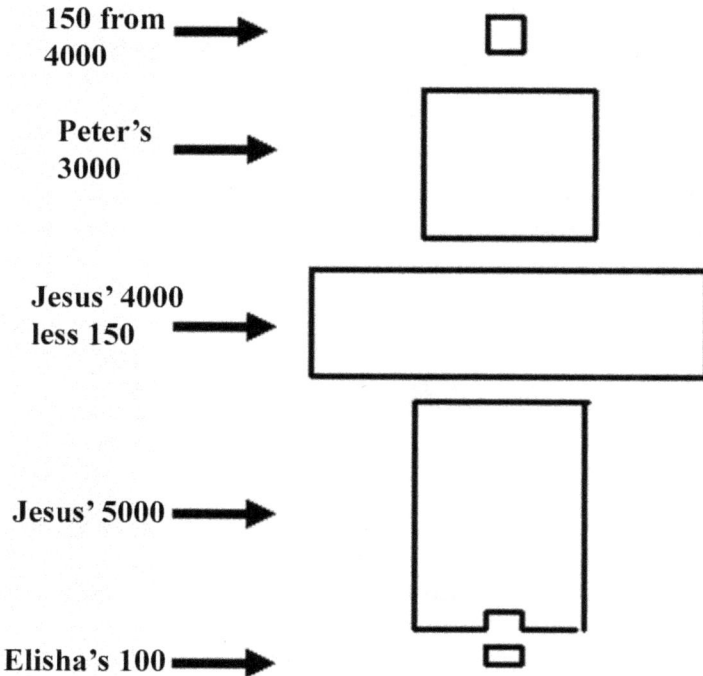

If the four feeding events are combined into a composite while preserving the vertical orientation of Jesus' feeding of the 5000 (combined with Elisha's feeding of 100) and Peter's feeding of the 3000, and the horizontal orientation of Jesus' feeding of the 4000, the following two alternate figures (Figures 8 and 9) result:

These figures are self-explanatory. They represent a sign indeed, but one which wasn't available until Scripture was completed. The proportions shown on the figure reflect a 2:1 ratio for individuals in the sitting position, as noted in Scripture. As shown in the figures, the three companies of 50 that were left over from the perfect rectangle of 3850 in Jesus' feeding of the 4000 represent the Titulus, the inscription placed on the cross which, interestingly, was presented in three languages according to Luke 23:38.

Figure 8: Composite of four feeding events

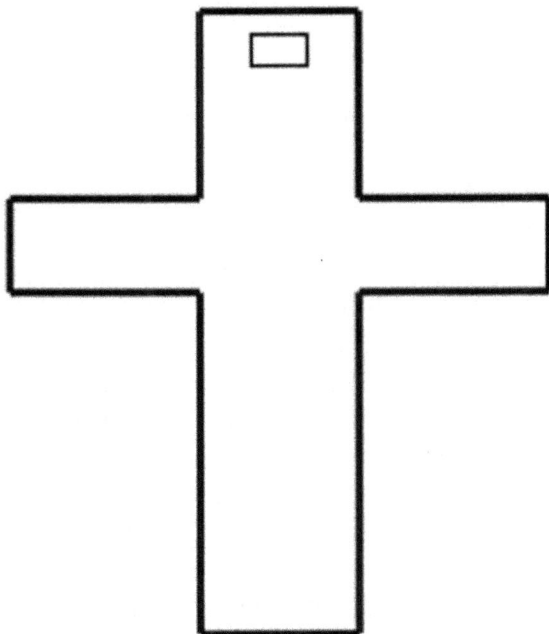

Figure 9: Alternate rearrangement of composite figure into Tau Cross

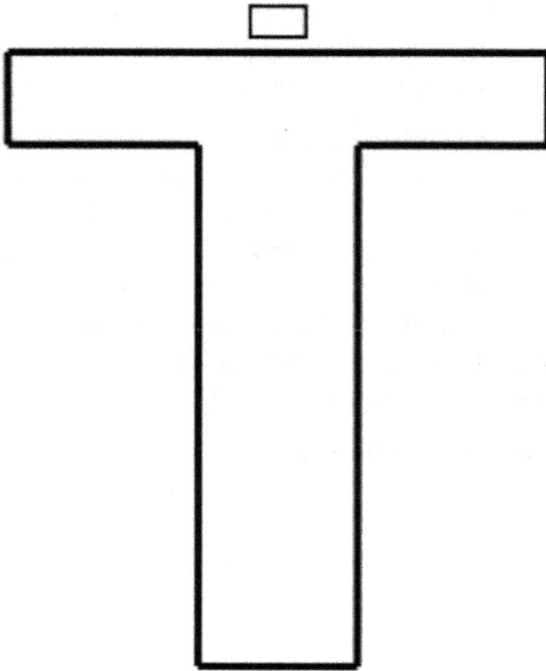

It is fascinating to note that if indeed Jesus' cross had been a Tau cross, as was commonly used by Romans at the time of Christ, then the simple rearrangement of the composite pattern, as shown on the latter figure, would furnish the associated representation. (See, for example, the article entitled "On the Physical Death of Jesus Christ" by William D. Edwards, MD, et al in the March 21, 1986 issue of JAMA.) For that period of time, the crosspiece (palibulum) was usually 5 to 6 feet in length, and the vertical post (stipes) was 6 to 8 feet in height. The average length ratio of palibulum to stipes for these ranges is (5/8+1)/2, or about 0.8 (.814). The length ratio of these members as shown in the figure above is nearly identical to this average, being approximately 0.8 (.8125).

A Word About the Baskets of Leftover Loaves

The assumption was made in the mathematical analysis and in the above development that each basket of leftover loaves contained the same number of loaves for both the feeding of the 5000 and the 4000.

This was probably not the case, as the original Scripture notes that the baskets used for the feeding of the 5000 was a small handbasket, for which 5 loaves would be appropriate, while the baskets used for collecting the remainder loaves in the feeding of the 4000 was a larger basket. It was for that reason that the development above was careful in attributing the 5 loaves per basket to the menfolk only.

In actuality, there were women and children in addition to the menfolk in both feeding events. According to Mark 7:31 the four thousand were fed near Decapolis on the south shore of the Sea of Galilee, while, according to Luke 9:10, the five thousand were fed near Bethsaida on the north shore, the implication being that the four thousand were mostly Gentile, while the five thousand were primarily Jewish. Further weight is given to this difference by the fact that the seven baskets of the four thousand correspond to the seven representative Churches that Jesus addressed in Revelation 1:20, while the twelve baskets of the five thousand match the twelve tribes of Israel.

The makeup of the audience is relevant to the size of the baskets in that the practice of the Jewish faith is patriarchal in nature, with the menfolk almost exclusively being involved in the ceremonial ritual. Also, the faith was exclusive in another sense, being restricted to Jews. Given the symbolic nature of the feedings, then, the sizes of the baskets, which represented the growth of the faith, were exceedingly important. The Jewish women and children were certainly fed along with the men, but it was the menfolk to whom the Word of God was primarily directed, it being their responsibility to interpret and direct this Word to their womenfolk. This changed radically with the birth of the Church at the Pentecost following Jesus' resurrection. For the first time, women and even children were to be directly involved in the spread of the Christian faith. This difference is borne out in Acts 2:16 - 18, wherein the Christian women as well as the men not only were involved in the gift of the indwelling Holy Spirit, but were expected to actively use that gift:

> *But this is that which was spoken through the prophet, Joel:*
> *And it shall come to pass in the last days, saith God, I will*
> *pour out my Spirit upon all flesh; and your sons and your*
> *daughters shall prophesy, and your young men shall see*
> *visions, and your old men shall dream dreams; and on my*
> *servants and on my handmaidens I will pour out in those days*
> *of my Spirit, and they shall prophesy: ...*

The bottom line is that the menfolk of both the four and the five thousand contributed five loaves to each basket. But the women and children of the Gentile four thousand added their share into the baskets of remainders, while only the menfolk of the five thousand contributed to their baskets of remainders.

Appendix Three

Transcendence vs. Immanence on the Nature of God

It has been said, in defense of Zanchius, that in describing God as above passion, he was referring exclusively to God *transcendent*, a state of being connoting God separate from and above His creation. God *immanent,* on the other hand, referring to God among us, would indeed possess passion. For we know that Jesus exhibited abundant passion in multiple forms in His experience in the Garden, as told in Luke 22:46:

> *And he came out and went, as he was accustomed, to the Mount of Olives; and his disciples also followed him. And when he was at the place, he said unto them, Pray that ye enter not into temptation. And he was withdrawn from them about a stone's cast, and kneeled down, and prayed, Saying, Father, if thou be willing, remove this cup from me; nevertheless, not my will, but thine, be done. And there appeared an angel unto*

him from heaven, strengthening him. And being in an agony,
he prayed more earnestly; and his sweat was, as it were, great
drops of blood falling down to the ground. And when he rose
up from prayer, and was come to his disciples, he found them
sleeping in sorrow, and said unto them, Why sleep ye? Rise
and pray, lest ye enter into temptation.

We understand from the above that passion in God *immanent*
cannot be an issue, because passion obviously is there. But what
about the claim, in defense of Zanchius and his understanding
of God as not possessing passion, that he was referring to God
transcendent?

This defense is weakened by the fact that it puts words into the
mouth of Zanchius that the gentleman never put there himself.
Nevertheless, the assumption shall be made herein that Zanchius
meant this all along.

It will also be presumed, so that the discussion might proceed
without immediately being cut off, that somehow the following
Scripture verse, namely Hebrews 13:8, can be interpreted to be not
applicable to a change in God's personality from "God transcendent"
to "God immanent."

Jesus Christ, the same yesterday, today and forever.

It will yet further be presumed, for the sake of initial argument, that
'God immanent' refers exclusively to Jesus in the flesh. But since
Jesus preexisted His sojourn in the flesh, his or any other Member
of the Trinity's existence prior to that event would necessarily be
'God transcendent'. But Exodus 32:7-14, for example, describes
that same God, who is, by our initial definition 'transcendent' at that
point in history, as possessing passion in abundance:

And the Lord said unto Moses, Go, get thee down; for thy
people, whom thou broughtest out of the land of Egypt, have
corrupted themselves. They have turned aside quickly out of
the way which I commanded them: they have made a molten
calf, and have worshiped it, and have sacrificed thereunto,
and said, These are thy gods, O Israel, which have brought

thee up out of the land of Egypt.

And the Lord said unto Moses, I have seen this people, and, behold, it is a stiff-necked people. Now therefore let me alone, that my wrath may wax hot against them, and consume them: and I will make of thee a great nation.

And Moses besought the Lord his God, and said, Lord why doth wrath wax hot against thy people, whom thou hast brought forth out of the land of Egypt with great power, and with a mighty hand? Wherefore should the Egyptians speak, and say, For mischief did he bring them out, to slay them in the mountains, and to consume them from the face of the earth? Turn from thy fierce wrath, and repent of this evil against thy people. Remember Abraham, Isaac, and Israel, thy servants, to whom thou didst swear by thine own self, and saidst unto them, I will multiply your seed, and they shall inherit it forever.

And the Lord repented of the evil which he thought to do unto his people.

Perhaps, then, lest we find immediate fault with this notion that "God transcendent" differs with respect to nature than "God immanent," the term "God immanent" would better be defined as "God interacting with man." But that doesn't work because the creation of man itself is one aspect of God interacting with man, and it is that very endeavor that defines "God transcendent'.

We could narrow the definition of 'God immanent' further to mean 'God communicating with man'. As redeemed mankind will be communicating with Jesus as His Bride throughout eternity, that raises a very strange and difficult, if not blasphemous theological issue: Jesus as God was once transcendent before He came in the flesh, but never shall be again.

We could narrow the definition still further to mean 'God communicating with man while He is in the flesh' But that doesn't work either, because Ephesians 5 demands that in His spiritual form, Jesus will be communicating quite intimately with His Church, to whom he is Husband. By this new definition, Jesus shall no longer assume the role of 'God immanent', but instead shall be 'God transcendent'. Shall we then insist upon a passionless marriage, one that violates the whole concept of marriage as God Himself in both Scripture and creation has presented it to us?

In his letter to the Ephesians, Paul's mystery in Chapter 5 gives us a very different message than this. It speaks of hope and joy to which Zanchius' definition of God simply doesn't do justice. It is to be treasured not only for its contribution to our future hope and expectation, but also to clarify our understanding of our God. This mystery is encapsulated in Ephesians 5:25-32:

> *Husbands, love your wives, even as Christ also loved the church, and gave himself for it; That he might sanctify and cleanse it with the washing of water by the word, That he might present it to himself a glorious church, not having spot, or wrinkle, or any such thing; but that it should be holy and without blemish.*

> *So ought men to love their wives as their own bodies. He that loveth his wife loveth himself. For no man ever yet hated his own flesh; but nourisheth it and cherisheth it, even as the Lord the church: For we are members of his body, of his flesh, and of his bones. For this cause shall a man leave his father and mother, and shall be joined unto his wife, and they two shall be one flesh.*

> *This is a great mystery: but I speak concerning Christ and the church.*

A devoted Christian condensed this beautiful statement into the following magnificent observation: "Just as Adam's side was opened for Eve, so Jesus' side was opened for His Church."

In dwelling upon this wonderful notion, we also anticipate a God who is capable of passion toward us regardless of whether His presence is transcendent or immanent. In recognizing this fact, we can return to the assurance in Hebrews 13:8 of God's unchanging nature.

What might change in God between transcendence and immanence is the dimensional constraint that Jesus experienced in becoming flesh. But that implies a limitation on His attributes rather than His basic nature, where passion belongs. Furthermore, it would be a limitation on His immanent form, not His transcendent form, which demands that His immanent form involves a subset of the attributes associated with His transcendent form, not the other way around. Therefore, even if one should insist in opposition to logic that passion was an attribute rather than an element of His basic nature, passion would be part of His transcendent form and not His immanent form, in contradiction to the argument that attempted to support Zanchius' omission of passion in God's nature.

Having refuted Zanchius' assertion on this point, we can state without restraint that God, regardless of whether His form or state of being is immanent or transcendent, is capable of possessing passion. An immediate implication of this is that God is not alien to us. A secondary implication of that is that Jesus' future marriage to His Church may be extrapolated back to a more basic marriage between God the Father and God the Holy Spirit.

Appendix Four

THE INERRANCY OF SCRIPTURE

Given the singularly important function of Scripture to provide man with a glimpse into the nature and character of God, it must necessarily be inerrant, for to deny this attribute is equivalent to stating that God does not possess the ability to make Himself known in sufficient depth to the centerpiece of His creation to permit His subjects to carry out His commandments to them. The outcome of this, of course, is to define a God who contradicts the attributes usually associated with Godhood, and who therefore is altogether unworthy of the love that He requests of us.

The only way that the skeptic of Scriptural inerrancy can avoid confronting this dilemma is to attribute the source of Scripture to man rather than God. It is amazing how many so-called 'authorities' do just that. But if a contradictory God is unworthy of our love, so is a God who is so small and powerless as to leave something as important as the presentation of Himself to mankind up to the inconsistencies, biases, self-interest and faults of unsupervised man. Another major problem with making this claim is that Scripture itself claims as its ultimate Author God Himself in the Person of the Holy Spirit. The prophets quite regularly spoke of God as the source of their information; much of what they wrote was written as a direct commandment from God to do so. It is common knowledge that just as directly, both Peter (2 Peter 1:20) and Paul (2 Timothy 3:16) clearly declared Scripture to have been written as men were led by the Holy Spirit.

As we shall demonstrate later, there are many other logically powerful reasons for attributing the source of Scripture to God rather than man. For now, as we explore the effect on the skeptic of assuming that Scripture contains errors, the issue of whether Scripture came from man or God is not even relevant. Either way, the result of denying its inerrancy will be the same.

More simply stated, regardless of whether Scripture came from God or from man alone, either it is inerrant or it is as worthless as the pseudo-God that it purports to represent.

Lest the equation of Scriptural error to its utter lack of value be too large of a leap to digest all at once, we shall break up the logical process that led to it into more manageable chunks by examining sequentially the consequence of attributing error to Scripture.

Suppose, for example, that in reading Scripture an individual (call him Jack) comes across an item A in one passage that doesn't seem to square with an item B in another. Because both item A and item B appear to be peripheral issues at best, Jack discounts the importance of their accuracy and applies the most logical way to handle it (given that he already knows more than Scripture can tell him, a really safe assumption in today's world), which also happens to be the simplest: he accepts the implied error and moves on. But the next day Bill points out to him a larger error in Scripture, one that does have some importance to Jack's understanding of God. Jack might struggle with this for a while, but because he has already accepted the possibility of error in Scripture, he gives up the effort a little more prematurely than he should, coming to the conclusion that Bill's opinion of the nature of God is better than his was. A few days later he comes across another difficult passage in Scripture, which he automatically reconciles as another error. This time he changes his opinion of God again, to something different than that which either he or Bill had previously held.

Forget the fact that this readjustment of opinion is probably ever downward, constantly diminishing the attributes by which he measures his God. The key issue here is that Jack's understanding of God is becoming as dependent on man's opinion as it is on Scripture. But how can man, with his lack of omniscience, differentiate those portions which are true from those which may represent myth or embellishment, or simply contain mistakes? Now Jack, in his inability to see this obvious consequence of accepting error, is open to any number of charlatans, prosperity-claiming megachurch leaders, and other scurrilous individuals who also come calling with their own patently false sets of opinions regarding the nature of God.

Most unfortunately, Jack is now also open to the opinions of man regarding conflicts between items A in Scripture and items B outside of Scripture. He places as much or more reliance on the attitude of the secular world than Scripture regarding the nature of God and of His place in society. If the Academy of Science tells him (as it does) that God's domain is purely moral and that the physical world is the exclusive domain of science, well, then it must be so. His esteem of Scripture, of course, goes down several notches with that, because any contradiction between mainstream science and Scriptural accounts of the physical world must then be resolved in favor of science. There are, of course, a whole lot of contradictions between Scripture and mainstream science, the most glaring at the present time being uniformitarianism, with its notion of vast time spans, and the theory of evolution, with its insistence that life did not require God to get started.

Well then, if God's Word cuts corners on time, and if God isn't that necessary for life, maybe God is not relevant to our own lives. Multitudes, of people have already formed that opinion, and with the Bible having been put in its place as far as he is concerned, why shouldn't he listen to them? Jack gets the picture loud and clear from all the major sources of information. He can't even go to a state or national park or just about any public place at all without getting a dose of these opinions that masquerade as science. By this time, poor Jack just can't get into the reading of Scripture at all. He certainly doesn't know enough about God to love Him. If he goes to church at all, it's only to collect a few tips on how to succeed. But since the rest of the country is working on different rules than he's getting at church, it's only a matter of time before he drops out.

What, now, if Jack and his ilk become the majority? For starters, having learned not to consider God as relevant to their lives, they speed up the process of removing Him from the public square. They do so with anger, thinking meanly of all the restrictions that have been placed on their lives by a God who probably doesn't exist to begin with. Having done that, they place their faith in a truly bad demagogue, who they willingly place over them as their leader, a lord worthy of their submission to him. Eventually realizing their great error in doing so, they listen to sincere political commentators like Glenn Beck, hoping to find some way to recover their country and their sanity. But they can't do that, because God has finally abandoned them to their own self-centered desires and in attempting to find purely political solutions to their problems, they will be unable to find God.

Is this the inevitable outcome of just a miniscule little supposition of Scriptural error? Yes, pretty much—it's a sharp slope toward perdition, and Satan has greased it well by pandering to our own self-absorption, which is really the root cause of our growing disbelief. The supposition of Scriptural error, no matter how apparently insignificant, requires the skeptic to assume at the very outset a judgmental role on a level dangerously close to that of God Himself. Despite the humility he might feign, only the self-centered individual has the wherewithal to do that. Just look around you, at the people you know, at your government, at your own lifestyle. When you ponder this mess, don't say 'How did this happen?', because deep down you know exactly how it did.

Let's now consider another individual, Charles, who happens to come across the same passage in Scripture that got Jack moving in his downward spiral. Like Jack, he struggles with it. But, already possessing some degree of passion (and respect) for God and His Holy Word, he struggles harder. Eventually he comes to a point of reconciliation between items A and B and, in the process of doing so he discovers item C, a concept that not only permits the reconciliation but leads him toward a significantly deeper understanding of God than he had before the exercise. Out of this effort, Charles, most happily, has increased his understanding of God, his love of God, and his faith in the Word of God. When Bill comes along with his more serious discrepancy, Charles applies the same exercise to it as he did with his more trivial issue, this time coming up with concept D, which represents an enormous breakthrough in his understanding of God. Having mined Scripture for the richness of information which he believed it contained, he was rewarded for his effort.

When the charlatans show up in his life, which they inevitably must, Charles, armed with concept D (and E, and so on, as he becomes ever more enamored with God through Scripture), is equipped to see these snakes for what they are. If they lead his church, he finds a better one, or so illuminates that place with the knowledge of Christ that the congregation itself finds better leaders.

Charles, having refused to be subdued by the false opinions of his supposed brothers and sisters in Christ, also stands firm against the equally false opinions of the secular world, regardless of how exalted they may be in the public mind. Having steadfastly opposed the theory of evolution, for example, he is now finding, to his further happiness, that he is in increasingly eminent company, for to his surprise he has come to the realization that a growing number of microbiologists and other heavy thinkers are offering substantial arguments, on the secularists' own terms, in support of the intellectual bankruptcy of the theory.

Charles, however, shares his world with Jack the doubter. Inhabiting the same country that had rid itself of God, they both suffer under the same governmental usurpation of their basic rights.

One might consider this to be an unhappy situation for Charles, uncalled for and totally unjust because of his lack of involvement in bringing about that mess. It is not. It is neither unjust nor unhappy, because Charles is busy bringing the light of Christ to a lost world. If he must suffer in the process, he is joyful at it, because he is living not for himself but for his Lord, whom he loves with all his heart. As the world descends into darkness, his light shines ever brighter.

Now that we've contrasted Jack's unhappy state with Charles' happier one, it's time to present their differences in greater detail. First, there is no perceived error in Scripture that is not trivial. The issue reaches beyond the effect on the doubter to touch the character of God Himself, for as one manifestation of the Word of God it is intimately linked to the embodiment of the Word, Jesus Christ. Jesus was careful to note the necessity of His fulfillment of Scripture, intimately associating Himself, as God, with it. In explaining how He fulfilled Scripture to His companions on the road to Emmaus (Luke 24), Jesus expected them not only to comprehend this intimacy, but to treat Scripture as sacred truth. The Bible scholar cannot appreciate this closeness while also asserting either that fallen mankind is the creator of Scripture, or that Scripture is errant. One has only to review the prologue (Chapter 1, verses 1-18) to John's Gospel to grasp this fact.

In his Gospel, John presented Jesus as a direct representation of God to man, that through his understanding of Jesus in the flesh, man might come to have an intimate knowledge of his God. But John went further than that. At the very outset of his Gospel, he claimed that by the power of God the representation was the physical embodiment of the Word of God. As the Living Word, the representation Itself was God. As John wrote,

> *In the beginning was the Word, and the Word was with God, and the Word was God. . . And the Word was made flesh, and dwelt among us, (and we beheld his glory, the glory as of the only begotten of the Father,) full of grace and truth. . .For the law was given by Moses, but grace and truth came by Jesus Christ."*

John's Gospel describes the Word as the substance of Creation Itself, for he wrote with boldness and without equivocation,

> *The same was in the beginning with God. All things were made by him; and without him was not any thing made that was made.*

With that single statement, John places Jesus as preceding His birth in the flesh through Mary, existing as God with the Father at the beginning of the Creation. In fact, in the first verses of the first chapter of his Gospel, John has already firmly established Jesus as the embodiment of the Word, as truth, as life, as light, as God, and as the pre-existing Creator. If Jesus is a representation of God, Scripture itself is a direct representation of Jesus, and if Jesus is both the Word and truth, the Word as Scripture must be truth. If the embodiment of the Word is also the Creator, then the truth of the Word must extend to all of creation as well as Scripture, including the world that is perceived as 'real'. It must be absolute.

The entire Bible with its two testaments is one self-consistent representation of the Word of God. As the New Testament fulfills the Old, so does the Old flesh out the New. It is absolutely necessary, to fully understand either of the testaments, to understand both and how they complement each other to form the single Word. This Word is to be honored and treasured above all, for as a representation of Jesus it is a representation of God. And it is yet more than that: as a part of the Creative Act in which God moved upon generations of mankind in a cosmic drama to develop it, Scripture is an integral part of the Divine Word.

It is of enormous significance that just as John identified Jesus with Creation, Jesus so thoroughly identified Himself with Scripture. In the Gospel of Matthew, Jesus is quite explicit regarding His relationship with Scripture. In Matthew 5, for example, He equates His ministry with its fulfillment:

> *Think not that I am come to destroy the law, or the prophets: I am come not to destroy, but to fulfill. For verily I say unto you, Till heaven and earth pass, one jot or one tittle shall in no wise pass from the law, until all be fulfilled.*

Here Jesus, the Word of God, asserts without reservation that He Who represents Creation Itself is bound, even defined, by the Word of Scripture. Through Him, Scripture is an integral part of the Creative Word. It is alive. Like Jesus, it is a representation of God.

In the eighth chapter of John, Jesus links His nature as the Living Word of God with the Word that was given to mankind in Scripture:

> *I am the living bread which came down from heaven: if any man eat of this bread, he shall live for ever: and the bread that I will give is my flesh, which I will give for the life of the world. The Jews therefore strove among themselves, saying How can this man give us his flesh to eat? Then Jesus said unto them, Verily, verily, I say unto you, Except ye eat the flesh of the Son of man, and drink his blood, ye have no life in you. Whoso eateth my flesh, and drinketh my blood, hath eternal life; and I will raise him up at the last day. For my flesh is meat indeed, and my blood is drink indeed. He that eateth my flesh, and drinketh my blood, dwelleth in me, and I in him.*

As John wrote, "...and the word became flesh..." How else can one partake of Jesus' flesh but by digesting Scripture, the profound manifestation of the Word of God that defines Jesus to mankind? How else could one perceive Him to the point of loving Him, not just for the sake of loving, but for the sake of those attributes of His that are worthy of our love? If we have no absolute gauge of the reliability of Scripture how can we be certain that those attributes actually exist?

Since this same Gospel (as well as Scripture in general) equates Jesus with the truth and with Creation itself, it is quite difficult to comprehend a Scripture with the inability to get the facts of creation together without error. One might just as well call Jesus a liar, for if Jesus is the embodiment of the Word, and if the truth of the Word is less than absolute such that it is not actually literal in a natural sense, we enter a world of confusing contradiction. For then we are left with a Jesus for which the religious truth that He represents may be higher, but yet different than the truth of the creation that He is also supposed to represent, making Jesus as the Living Word not who He said He is. In particular, He is not God in the flesh, and the entire structure of the Christian faith is but a house built of straw. One must conclude from this that faith itself demands a corollary insistence upon the inerrancy of the Bible with respect to its presentation to man of the nature of God, which necessarily includes the nature of His creation. This requirement applies not to Jesus alone, but to every Member of the Godhead. There is no room for compromise with this fact. Anything less than absolute truth must inevitably lead to the conclusion that the Biblical God of both the Old and the New Testaments does not exist. For if God is to be worthy of our worship as God, then He must possess those attributes which are appropriate to Godhood: omniscience, omnipotence, omnipresence, and, most importantly, given the greatest of His commandments to us, love in perfection.

If His Word is inaccurate in any way, not only is He a liar, but He would possess gaps in His abilities that mock the very attributes that make Him God.

He would also mock His own commandment to us to love Him, for one cannot love without intimacy, and one cannot be intimate with God without knowledge of Scripture.

There are other reasons why it is not possible for a devout Christian to look upon Scripture with reservations as to its accuracy or internal consistency. Some of these reasons are personal. As we have noted, the individual who like Jack has doubts will suffer from such an intellectual disadvantage that he will miss much of the profound beauty and richness of Scripture that only Charles can see as he struggles to reconcile item A with item B. It is unlikely that Jack will have the slightest inclination to study Scripture unless he does so with the motive of reinforcing his doubts. Suppose, however, that this improbable event does occur. Upon arriving at a point therein where he encounters a perceived conflict, he will immediately say 'aha!' and claim error. In that state, he will remain at precisely the intellectual level where the conflict is most apparent, never permitting his understanding to rise to the higher level that furnishes the context in which the conflict is resolved. Such individuals will fail to notice the prophetic link to Jesus in the Levitical rituals, the writings of the prophets and the very lives of Biblical heroes. They will remain blind to the fact that on the cross Jesus kept the Mosaic feasts and especially the Passover in both pattern and timing. The torment of Abraham at the sacrifice of Isaac will have no meaning to them. Joseph will have suffered at his brothers' hands for no real purpose. Daniel and Isaiah will become lesser prophets. David and his psalms will not have been inspired. Jonah will have allowed himself to be cast into the sea for nothing of lasting importance. Doubters like Jack will have completely missed the many incidents in the Old Testament that pointed to Jesus as the Yahweh of Israel, destined for the cross before the beginning of Creation. To them, He would be just a man burdened with significant emotional problems and we would remain burdened with our sins. As he turns to the New Testament his position of doubt only hardens. Comparing Gospel with Gospel, he notes with despair (or is it satisfaction?) that item A in Luke is completely missing in John, or that Item A in Mark differs somewhat from item A in Matthew. He expects the Gospels to be identical in every respect, missing the point that such a state of affairs would represent a redundancy so profound as to constitute a wholesale lack of information, and that the Gospels differ from writer to writer as the Holy Spirit chose to emphasize some facet of Jesus in one Gospel and a different facet in another.

Missing the point of whatever portion of Scripture which he deems to be beneath his consideration, the doubter of inspiration cannot perceive the God of love who is so dear to the heart of the believer.   Failing to see Jesus in the sacrificial traditions of the Israelites, the doubter sees a monster instead who feasts on the blood and gore of uncountable thousands of sacrificial animals. Moreover, in failing to satisfactorily resolve apparent conflicts, the doubter never reaches that point where he can grasp the fact that rather than containing errors, Scripture is remarkably free of them, being spectacularly consistent to the smallest details through the thousands of years and the multitude of writers that contributed to its content. Unable to recognize pearls of knowledge containing enormous significance in the minutiae of Scripture, the doubter allows such facts as the equivalence of Abel's lifetime with that of Jesus, or the age at which Joseph began serving Pharaoh being the same as the age at which Jesus began His public ministry, or the prophetic nature of Isaac's marriage to Rebekah, or the exponential nature of the decline of lifetimes following the Great Flood, or a host of similar relationships, to pass over his head completely unnoticed.

It happens that there is a name for the capability of the Bible to harmonize minute details from Scriptural accounts that are widely separated in time and conditions, and that this capability has long been considered as evidence for the divine inspiration of the Bible. In the chapter entitled 'The Phenomenon of "Undesigned Coincidences" of his book *The Signature of God*, Grant Jeffrey describes a number of issues that would be interpreted most readily by the casual reader of Scripture as puzzling inconsistencies (of the kind between item A in Scripture and item B in Scripture) or irrelevancies which might best be allocated to the error file, but which, on careful comparison with obscure passages that might be thought of as bearing no relation to the problem areas, astonishing answers are found that give the reader a sense of awe as to the truth of the Bible. Indeed, these Eureka! moments are encountered by virtually all serious students of Scripture and are treasured as rewards for diligent pursuit of the truth.

Noting that the first overt description of the phenomenon of "Undesigned Coincidences" was made in 1738 by Dr. Philip Doddridge in a commentary on Paul's letters, Dr. Jeffrey goes on to cite several examples, including the mysteries of why David's loyal counselor Ahithophel turned so strongly against him during Absalom's rebellion (Ahithophel was Bathsheba's grandfather, who took umbrage at the way David acquired Bathsheba by putting Uriah to death); why David picked up five stones when coming against Goliath (Goliath had four brothers); and why, when all the neighboring kingdoms used horses in battle, Israel did not (Israel was commanded by Moses in Deuteronomy 17 not to multiply horses to themselves). These answers are thrilling in that in their seeming insignificance they speak so powerfully against Scriptural error.

Most importantly, the doubter will inevitably become an unbeliever because he cannot recognize throughout Scripture the absolute love and lordship of Jesus Christ. He must fail in this endeavor because he lacks the wisdom to do so. Scripture is clear that the beginning of wisdom is the fear of the Lord. The doubter, in rejecting truth as much as the full-blown unbeliever but lacking even the courage to acknowledge his rejection, lacks the Holy Spirit, the embodiment of wisdom and knowledge, and is lost in his blindness of sight and deafness of hearing. He is destined himself eventually to fully accept his unbelief. Not trusting in the faithfulness of Scripture to represent the full truth, it is virtually certain that he will eventually succumb to popular secular teachings regarding the world about him.

Contrast again the unhappy state of the doubter to the blessed condition of the man of faith. The doubter, unwilling to remove himself from the world, knows full well how the Christian individual is perceived by the world at large. Faith, to the secular individual, is blind. As the man of the world openly claims in his many commentaries on the practice of reason, faith is intolerable, being antithetical to the openness of mind required for the dispassionate evaluation of the world about us. The scholar of religious orientation, to the secular world, is limited by his faith to the most trivial sort of mundane and unrealistic perception of reality. Worse, the doubter fully understands that to the secular scholar the notion of religious faith carries with it the stigma of cowardice, a lack of intellectual courage. It represents a self-imposed stifling of the imagination borne out of a weakness of the mind, a need for a crutch, an inability to face the world as it really exists with all its imperfections, pains and magnificent challenges. The closet doubter who maintains a false claim of faith is the unhappiest of all, as he perceives full well his position as the object of ridicule as a foxhole digger, a creature content to hide behind the protective blanket of a nonexistent God, never willing to venture out into the real world. The doubter will bow to the pressure of this attitude sooner than later, because he has insufficient reason or capability to withstand it.

The believing Christian, of course, sees faith in quite a different light. The fully committed believer in Scripture enjoys the benefit of having already exercised his faith through his thorough digestion of God's Word and stands equipped for the larger trials to come. Upon reflecting on the notion of faith, he is irresistibly drawn to the Book of Hebrews, where in the eleventh chapter he encounters the people before him whose God, through their faith, had fashioned lives of heroic stature. These men and women defined the meaning of real faith, the selfless kind with substance behind it that gave them character, grit, and, above all, nobility.

After he recounts the faith of individuals from Adam to Moses and what that faith had wrought, the writer of Hebrews makes a magnificent summation of the subject:

And what more shall I say? I do not have time to tell about Gideon, Barak, Samson, Jephthah, David, Samuel and the prophets, who through faith conquered kingdoms, administered justice, and gained what was promised; who shut the mouths of lions, quenched the fury of the flames, and escaped the edged of the sword; whose weakness was turned into strength; and who became powerful in battle and routed foreign armies. Women received back their dead, raised to life again. Others were tortured and refused to be released, so that they might gain a better resurrection. Some faced jeers and flogging, while still others were chained and put into prison. They were stoned; they were sawed in two; they were put to death by the sword. They went about in sheepskins and goatskins, destitute, persecuted and mistreated – the world was not worthy of them. They wandered in deserts and mountains, and in caves and holes in the ground. These were all commended for their faith, yet none of them received what had been promised. God had planned something better for us so that only together with us would they be made perfect."

Faith, to the Christian, is the beginning of courage, the wherewithal to stand fast in the battles that God inevitably brings his way. Some of these battles might be against the Christian's own lustful nature;

others may be physical, where the Christian is placed into harm's way. Or they may be of an intellectual nature. In this arena, however, faith is more than a prerequisite to courage. It is also a necessary prerequisite to a logical investigation of God. To perceive God in anything more than the most mundane, trivial way our gift of reason must be tempered with the wisdom to understand that we must do so on His terms. And His terms begin with faith, the kind of faith that demands that we accept the Word of God as inerrant and accessible to our hearts and minds.

Indeed, with today's explosively expanding technology, the intellectual battle may be the most significant of all. Here, in the midst of the many intellectual cults engaged in the worship of their computers and cell phones, the Christian of faith is being called upon to exercise that faith, to demonstrate the logical viability of his God as at once more grand by far and the ultimate ruler of the secular god of scientific achievement. It rests upon persons of faith to present to the modern world the magnificent face of a God who, though ancient as time itself, yet is the ultimate Creator of the science and technology that His scoffers so lovingly embrace.

All of these pursuits, for the man of God who actually possesses selfless courage, are capable of representing the most incredibly exciting, wonderful adventures. But to the person who is drawn to the intellectual arena, the most awesome challenge awaits, and with it the most wonderful rewards. For it is here that so many citadels of science falsely so called stand on the brink of collapse. The geological sciences, having been recently embarrassed by the matter of the ubiquitous tell-tale layer of iridium ash at the sites of dinosaur bones, were forced into retreat over the unwelcome implication of that association as pointing to an extraterrestrial source of violence. They eventually acknowledged with great reluctance the encroachment of catastrophism into the domain formerly occupied exclusively by uniformity. Now geology awaits a bold Christian researcher who can re-open the breach initiated by Dr. Velikovsky over six decades ago and so profoundly expose the catastrophic events accompanying the Exodus that the breach will remain open, never to be shut again by narrow-minded and godless politicians who masquerade as scientists. The same doorway beckons the Christian biological scientist, for whom, despite the frantic proclamations of foolish liberals to the contrary, the collapse of macroevolutionary theory is already underway. Thanks to the brilliant efforts of a growing number of pioneering researchers to peer into the incredibly complex and sophisticated world of molecular biology and to write honestly about what they see, as well as the many dedicated Christians who have taken it upon themselves to disseminate these findings to the Christian Community, evolution is being brought down to its rightful place in God's amazing economy of life.

But of all the intellectual pursuits that await the Christian explorer, the theological one beckons the most warmly. We seem indeed to be at the time of the end spoken of in Daniel 12, where the book that has been sealed for so long finally is being opened. Scientific knowledge is now increasing at an exponential rate, providing Christian researchers with the tools and information to look anew at Scripture, probing deeper into favorite topics and investigating hitherto untapped areas: Bible codes, mathematical relationships, the startling relevance of Mosaic law to the life and earthly mission of Jesus Christ, archaeological confirmation of Bible stories, the fulfillment and prospects for further fulfillment of prophetic statements and, more generally, the reconciliation to a higher level of understanding those Scriptural topics that appear to the shallow observer to conflict with each other.

How ironic it is that just as these exciting opportunities for Christian research and thought have become available, so many so-called Christians have given up, having surrendered in abject cowardice to an enemy who is weaker by far than the mighty God whom we Christians claim as our own.

We shall now leave the personal aspect of our inquiry behind and move on to demonstrate that Scripture is indeed worthy of being trusted in its entirety as representing absolute truth, not requiring the device of allegory for its interpretation. In other words, rather than continue in terms of the benefit to us of faith in inerrancy and the consequence to us of a lack of such faith, we shall focus on the attributes of Scripture that speak of inerrancy.

In addition to the support which we have noted above in the 'phenomenon of Undesigned Coincidences' for the notion that for the items A and B in Scripture that we might come across there do exist reconciliatory concepts C and D, we shall demonstrate that the Holy Spirit has furnished the believer with numerous proofs of both the inspiration and the accuracy of Scripture, removing all doubt as to its divine origin.

Foremost among these proofs is the proven accuracy of the Biblical prophets. In Isaiah 53, for example, the very purpose of Jesus' mission on earth as a man is detailed in startling accuracy. But long before Isaiah, the Law in its rituals and observances not only foretold that same mission, but pointed to the day in which its fulfillment would be completed; beyond that, these feasts pointed to the formation of the Church following Jesus' resurrection. Yet even before the Law, the very clothing of Adam and Eve pointed to the cross, as did the animosity between their sons Abel and Cain over their gifts to God. The first book of the Bible, Genesis, contains so much information about Jesus, in fact, that it is often named among the Gospels. Included in this information are moving accounts of Abraham, Isaac and Joseph in which facets of their lives preenacted Jesus' sacrificial love with startling precision. This theme is also presented elsewhere in the Old Testament, as in the story of Jonah, in such depth that it is remarkable that Jesus was not immediately recognized for His Old Testament credentials by everyone who came into contact with Him either by His physical presence or by reading of Him in New Testament Scripture.

There is a good reason why believers insist on the supernatural endowment of prophets such as Isaiah with truth in the face of scholarship that suggested (prior to the discovery of the Dead Sea Scrolls) that their books were written after Jesus came to earth and therefore did not embody elements of the supernatural. Above all, they do so because they possess faith, without which it is impossible to please God. But their faith has also been rewarded with plenty of corroboration in the exposure of the doubters' suggestions as fraudulent. Among the Dead Sea Scrolls, for example, which have been dated by modern methods as preceding the life of Jesus, is the complete text of Isaiah, including that all-important Messianic Chapter 53. The same can be said of Daniel's prophecy which foretold to the day Jesus' entry into Jerusalem precisely 483 years (69 weeks) from an event that was over a century in the future to Daniel. In Chapters 44 and 45, the prophet Isaiah called Cyrus of Persia by name even farther into the future. Before Isaiah and Daniel, David accurately described Jesus' suffering on the cross in Psalm 22 a thousand years before the great event. Micah foretold the place of Jesus' birth where the manger itself was the same one used to birth the special lambs bred for the temple sacrifice. A host of other prophecies describe many other details of Jesus' life and mission. In Chapter 28 of Deuteronomy, Moses foretold the Diaspora of the Jews and gave the reason for it. Both Moses, in Chapter 30 of Deuteronomy, and Ezekiel, in Chapters 36 and 37, foretold in great detail the return of Israel to their land. The date of that return was hinted at in Hosea 4:4 and 5 and 6:2, and pinpointed to 1948, as discovered by Dr. Jeffrey, in the combination of Ezekiel 4:4-6, Leviticus 26:17, 18, 27 and 28, and Jeremiah 25:11. In the Book of Revelation, the apostle John foretold a currency system that is impossible to implement without modern electronics and computer science. In addition to the overt words of the prophets, Scripture has defined with astonishing accuracy the purpose of God in its record of the lives of Biblical characters.

Then too, Scripture involves a precision of time beyond that already noted above of which most Christians are largely ignorant today, but which occupied great minds in the nineteenth and early twentieth centuries. Men such as Sir Edward Denny and Henry Gratton Guinness, having uncovered some of these time patterns, could only describe the precision of prophetic fulfillment as supernatural. Denny, having verified that Daniel's prophecy of 69 weeks from Artaxerxes' command to Nehemiah to rebuild Jerusalem to the coming of Messiah was fulfilled to the very day, then went on to identify the ubiquity of 70-week (490 year) intervals throughout the Scriptural history of man, of which a total of twelve spanned a 5880-year time from Adam to what he expected would be the thousand-year reign of Christ. He noted in particular that if the times during which Israel had strayed from representing God's plan of redemption (e.g. the time from the birth of Ishmael to the birth of Isaac) were not counted, the time of Israel spanned the middle four 70-week intervals as follows, with each interval being marked by profound events in the history of Israel and mankind: the birth of Abram to the Exodus, 490 years; the Exodus to the dedication of Solomon's temple, 490 years; the dedication of Solomon's temple to Nehemiah's commission from Artaxerxes to rebuild Jerusalem, 490 years; and from Nehemiah's commission to Messiah's crucifixion, 490 years. He then noted that since the Jubilee years were observed in parallel with the 49th year of one Jubilee interval and the first year of the next rather than being inserted between them, these special years dedicated to God would, if they were added to each 49-year interval to make 50 years, result in transforming the 5880-year span of man's history to six thousand years. Furthermore, the placement of the Jubilee year between the 49th year of one cycle and the first year of the next in overlapping fashion leads to the surprising understanding that Jesus, in His crucifixion during the Passover of the Jubilee year, fulfilled the Levitical feasts of both the first month of that year and the seventh month of the first year of the next Jubilee cycle. That understanding is but one item among the multiplicity of rewards that God offers those who seek His wisdom.

Guinness approached this precision of time issue from an entirely different tack than Denny. He arrived at the conclusion, both from Scripture and astronomical data, that God has ordered time in sevens. From Scripture, for example, he observed that the creation week contained seven days as does the sabbath week, that a week of years is a sabbath year, that a week of weeks of years is a Jubilee year, that Abraham's lifetime of 175 years spanned seven 25-year time periods of which the end of each marked a major event in his life, that Daniel's prophecy of weeks contained a multiplicity of sevens, and that Jesus Himself made remarks involving sevens. Noting next that the duration of Jesus' time on earth was 33.6 years, and assuming that Abraham's lifetime was a cameo of mankind's history on earth, he substituted one 33.6-year lifetime of Jesus for each year of Abraham's 175-year life, arriving at seven periods of 840 years each. The amazing thing about it is that the total duration of 5880 years exactly matches Denny's duration for mankind. This duration can also be factored into 49 intervals of 120 years apiece. If a 50th Grand Jubilee of 120 years is added to this sum, it yields a period of six thousand years. Guinness also apprehended grand cycles of 2520 years, each of which contains three intervals of 840 years. Three such 2520-year cycles fit easily into his seven periods of 840 years by overlapping one 840-year interval of one cycle with the next, such that the middle cycle has two overlapping 840-year intervals and one non-overlapping 840-year interval. The astonishing thing about these various cycles is their harmonious relationship among each other as well as their intimate relationship with Jesus Christ.

Moreover, Michael Drosnin in writing of Bible Codes, notes that at the dawn of the modern age Sir Isaac Newton, one of the greatest mathematicians the world has produced, suspected the existence of hidden information embedded in the text of the Hebrew Scriptures. As noted by Bible Scholar Grant Jeffrey, in Proverbs 25:2, Scripture itself furnishes a tantalizing hint of that possibility:

It is the glory of God to conceal a matter, but the glory of kings is to search out a matter.

Perhaps having been spurred on by this passage, Newton, who was an avid scholar of Scripture when not engaged in inventing the calculus or developing the basics of physics, devoted many hours in a search for a code embedded in the Bible. (As a side point, his calculus, while usually considered to be a purely secular mathematical tool, displays such intrinsic beauty, majestic elegance and universal utility that one can easily attribute its invention to divine inspiration. Newton himself certainly did.) He also may have known of the work of rabbi Rabbeynu Bachayah in the fourteenth century, who discovered an encoding pattern in the Torah (our Pentateuch), as noted by Bible Scholar Grant Jeffrey in his *The Signature of God*. However, the first real progress in uncovering the code was initiated by rabbi Dov Weissmandl in the early years of the twentieth century, who discovered that he could form meaningful words by assembling sequences of characters separated by fixed intervals of skipped characters. Describing this process as the creation of 'equidistant letter sequences' (ELS), Weissmandl was forced by the lack of technology in his day to perform the work meticulously by hand. Given the difficulty of the task, he was unable to say with certainty that his results were more than coincidental. That issue was resolved nearly a half century later by Israeli mathematician Eliyahu Rips, who, along with Doron Witztum and Yoav Rosenberg, applied the emerging computer technology to the process. The results were so spectacular as to convince the researchers that they had come face-to-face with the supernatural. As the price of computers dropped while they increased in speed and capability, a host of interested parties joined the ELS search. Among the claims made for the results are those published in *Bible Code I and Bible Code II* by Michael Drosnin, which indicate that the encoded data includes a number of fulfilled prophecies, many of which relate to our own time.

One of the earlier results may well be the most spectacular. As noted by scholars Grant Jeffrey and Chuck Missler, an examination of the Torah revealed that a 50-character ELS interval yielded the word 'Torah' in the books of Genesis, Exodus, and Numbers, and that a 49-character interval yielded the same word in Deuteronomy. In Leviticus, the only book of the Torah that failed to produce that word, an 8-character sequence formed the word 'God'. Curiously, while in the books of Genesis and Exodus the word 'Torah' is spelled in the forward direction, it is spelled backwards in Numbers and Deuteronomy. Upon their noting the sequence of these five books with Leviticus in the center, they were surprised to observe that 'Torah' in each book pointed toward 'God'.

Chuck Missler notes another authentication code in the Bible that is completely separate from the ELS code. This time it is found in the New Testament Greek. This code has to do with the pattern of the text, which evokes the number seven in so many various ways that the improbability (impossibility, actually) of its being generated by the hand of a human immediately places it among the supernatural manifestations of God. The first instance of it occurs at the very beginning of the New Testament, in the geneology of Jesus Christ as presented in the Greek version of Matthew 1, verses 1 through 11. In this passage, there are a number of various text elements precisely divisible by seven: words; letters; vowels; consonants; words beginning with a vowel; words beginning with a consonant; words occurring more than once in the passage; words that occur in more than one form; words that occur in only one form; nouns; non-nouns (only 7); names; male names; and generations.

Missler attributes this discovery to Dr. Ivan Panin, who was born in Russia December 12, 1855, and emigrated first to Germany and then to the United States, where he graduated in Harvard in 1882 with a PhD. in mathematics. He discovered this structure of sevens in 1890, after which he devoted the remainder of his life to a study of the Bible. According to Missler, Panin generated 43,000 pages of discoveries before his death in October of 1942. Oddly, the disputed final twelve verses of Mark (Mark 16:9-20) are among the other texts where the number seven was found to be prominent. Most translations of the Bible carry a footnote to these verses to the effect that they were missing from important Scriptural sources, such as the Alexandria codex. However, Missler emphasizes that Irenaeus quoted from them around 150 A.D., as did Hypolatus in the second century, whereas the Alexandria codex came several hundred years later. Missler notes that this virtually proves that the verses were part of the original Gospel of Mark and later expurgated, rather than having been added later as claimed by some modern scholars. He also notes that Chapter 16 of Mark's Gospel requires these final verses to tie up what otherwise would be loose ends.

Again, in verses 9-20 of Mark 16 the following text elements are precisely divisible by seven: words; vocabulary; letters; vowels; consonants; words found elsewhere in the Gospel of Mark; words only found in these verses; and the words found in the Lord's address (verses 15-18).

As noted earlier, Scripture itself claims to have been inspired by God. Paul, in 2 Timothy 3:16 and 17 states with certainty that the text came directly from God:

> *All Scripture is given by inspiration of God, and is profitable for doctrine, for reproof, for correction, for instruction in righteousness: That the man of God may be perfect, thoroughly furnished unto all good works.*

Again, in 2 Peter 1:20 and 21, that apostle affirms Paul's assessment of Scripture:

> *Knowing this first, that no prophecy of the scripture is of any private interpretation. For the prophecy came not in old time by the will of man: but holy men of God spake as they were moved by the Holy Ghost.*

Of course, the ultimate authority on this matter is Jesus Christ. Scripture records numerous instances of His quoting directly from it. Moreover, in Matthew 5:17 and 18, and in John 10: 35 and 36, He claimed that Scripture had the authority of God behind it:

> *Think not that I am come to destroy the law, or the prophets: I am not come to destroy, but to fulfill. For verily I say unto you, Till heaven and earth pass, one jot or one tittle shall in no wise pass from the law, till all be fulfilled.*

> *If he called them gods, unto whom the word of God came, and the Scripture cannot be broken; Say ye of him, whom the Father hath sanctified, and sent into the world, Thou blasphemest ; because I said, I am the Son of God?*

The Greek word *theopneustia*, meaning 'inspiration from God', describes this movement of the Holy Spirit upon the souls and minds of men, directing their thoughts, actions and words. It is key to note that divine inspiration has impacted the lives and actions of the people of God as well as what they wrote in Scripture, for much of its instruction comes from its recalling of historical events and deeds of people other than the writers. Nevertheless, these lives and actions had the ultimate purpose of furnishing the information that went into Scripture. A good part of Joseph's life, when recalled in the Bible, was a defining forecast of Jesus, as were those of many of the characters of the Bible, which obviously include the

Patriarchs and the prophets. A casual glance at the Book of Acts is sufficient to perceive the grand movement of the Holy Spirit upon the actions of the Apostles. After Paul's conversion from a vehement Christian-hater to a dedicated Christian, his very life was directed continuously and fully by the Holy Spirit. The point of this is that if one is inclined to doubt the inspiration of Scripture, he must apply that same reservation to the actions of all the Biblical heroes, including those of Paul and the other Apostles, to the extent of questioning their motivation, ability to heal or perform other inspired works and even their general conduct. At best they would be terribly conflicted in their denial of the indwelling Holy Spirit on persons of faith, for who could deny the inspiration behind the willing, self-sacrificial martyrdom of Christians throughout history and the radically changed lives of dedicated Christians to this very day?

Why then, if so many proofs exist of Scripture's inerrancy, are there so many doubters? One would think that in the interest of eternal self-preservation these people would be inclined to give God the benefit of the doubt. Why isn't that the case?

In our world of technological sophistication and moral degeneration, there are two very powerful obstacles to the man on the street's acceptance of Scripture as infallible. The first obstacle is a matter of character and has been noted in Scripture as the ultimate reason for the rejection of God: scoffers of God and the Bible do so not on the basis of intellect but for the sole reason of their selfish lusts. They just don't want God telling them what to do (or, more to the point, what not to do). Appreciating subliminally if not overtly that Christianity implies selfless nobility, they want none of that. They want instead to maintain the right to put self above others— to get what they claim as their due, regardless of the implications regarding those who also want the same. They wish to continue rooting around in the filth of pornography, or to pursue those sexual deviations which so deliciously capture their imaginations. They want to get high whenever they like. They'd hire lawyers to sue their wealthier family members if they could get away with it. They live in the world of "To Thine Own Self be True" which amounts to

"Me first." Understand what Paul in 2 Timothy 3:1-9 and Peter in 2 Peter 3:3-10 have to say about that sort of person:

> *This know also, that in the last days perilous times shall come. For men shall be lovers of their own selves, covetous, boasters, proud, blasphemers, disobedient to parents, unthankful, unholy, without natural affection, truce-breakers, false accusers, incontinent, fierce, despisers of those that are good, traitors, heady, high-minded, lovers of pleasures more than lovers of God; having a form of godliness, but denying the power thereof: from such turn away. For of this sort are they which creep into houses, and lead captive silly women laden with sins, led away with diverse lusts, ever learning, and never able to come to the knowledge of the truth. Now as Jannes and Jambres withstood Moses, so do these also resist the truth: men of corrupt minds, reprobate concerning the faith. But they shall proceed no further: for their folly shall be manifest unto all men, as theirs also was.*
>
> *Knowing this first, that there shall come in the last days scoffers, walking after their own lusts, and saying, Where is the promise of his coming? For since the fathers fell asleep, all things continue as they were from the beginning of the creation. For this they willingly are ignorant of, that by the word of God the heavens were of old, and the earth standing out of the water and in the water: whereby the world that then was, being overflowed with water, perished. But the heavens and the earth, which are now, by the same word are kept in store, reserved unto fire against the day of judgment and perdition of ungodly men. But, beloved, be not ignorant of this one thing, that one day is with the Lord as a thousand years, and a thousand years as one day. The Lord is not slack concerning his promise, as some men count slackness; but is long-suffering to us-ward, not willing that any should perish, but that all should come to repentance. But the day of the Lord will come as a thief in the night; in the which the heavens shall pass away with a great noise, and the elements shall melt with fervent heat, the earth also and the works that*

are therein shall be burned up.

The other obstacle to the acceptance of Scripture as inerrant appears to be an intellectual one, but it is not—it is rooted in materialism and the placement of the world and its things and delights over God, thereby putting it into the same category as the first obstacle. This obstacle is the belief, as most of us have been taught in school, that modern science clashes with Scripture with Scripture as the loser. It is not. Informed Christians, if not the public at large, are well aware of the many frauds that have been perpetrated in the name of science, particularly over the past century or so. Examples include the numerous fossil 'discoveries' of missing links between ape and man that turn out to be fakes (including the highly-touted Lucy), the circular reasoning behind the dating of strata, the glaring lack of a complete geological column, dating hanky-panky (and the constant revisions thereto), the intrusion of catastrophism on uniformitarian turf (an unwelcome turn of events that modern scientists have been forced to accept with great reluctance after realizing, from the ubiquitous presence of iridium ash wherever dinosaur bones were found, iridium being rare on earth but a common component of asteroids, that the dinosaurs died *en masse* and quite violently), the disturbing features of Venus and Mars that corroborate our recently-acquired picture of the dinosaur extinction event, and the development of devastatingly logical scenarios for the world as described by Scripture prior to the Flood, and for the Flood itself (which, as many have demonstrated, had to be universal). The driver behind many of these false beliefs is itself the greatest of the frauds, the theory of evolution. Before specifically addressing that item, it is worth noting that a Biblically-based reconstruction of the Flood naturally accommodates several apparent anomalies that mainstream science has been incapable of explaining and has therefore largely ignored. These include: the findings of mammoths flash-frozen in place, still edible, at least in the early 1900s, having well-preserved buttercups between their teeth, in regions where buttercups cannot grow and where insufficient food is available to maintain a mammoth population; the discovery of coal and oil in polar regions; the discovery of human artifacts embedded in coal;

and the finding of fossilized trees in the upright position extending through multiple layers of strata that are supposedly separated in time by millions of years.

Unfortunately, we believe what we want to believe, and we believe who we want to believe. Given a set of false beliefs to begin with, we have an uncanny ability to construct logical proofs of their validity. Here is what Scripture, in 1 Timothy 6:20 and 21, and has to say about the matter:

> *O Timothy, keep that which is committed to thy trust, avoiding profane and vain babblings, and oppositions of science falsely so called: which some professing have erred concerning the faith.*

By what right does the arrogant skeptic think that science, metaphysics, and religion must be mutually exclusive domains? The truly exciting thing about the Word of God is that, if it is indeed given to us by Divine Inspiration by the Lord of creation, it will necessarily contain knowledge and wisdom about that creation. It will teach of things that we usually allocate to science and metaphysics rather than to the presently-assigned domain of the purely theological. We have noted a number of items presented in Scripture that serve not only to demonstrate its divine origin, but to give us understanding of the world about us that we usually attribute to the domain of science. Impressive as these numerous factors are, they represent but a tiny fraction of the information with which God has provided man to substantiate the truth of His Book. Furthermore, the accumulated knowledge of mankind over the millenia since our history began has opened but a tiny foothold in our ability to understand the depth of wisdom and knowledge contained in that Book, for even to our best and most devoted, godliest minds the unsearchable riches of Scripture remain largely untapped. Is it not the ultimate objective of the scientist and the metaphysician to comprehend the universe that God created? Does this universe not include even the mind that was made to comprehend it and its interaction with the world that it sees? And does it not also include the tools, both mathematical and physical, that man develops to facilitate that comprehension?

Yet, as we have said, we believe what we want to believe.

We have attempted in this summary presentation to establish through a diverse assortment of perspectives the inherent truth of Scripture and its corresponding infallibility as to its basic message, the presentation of God to man. These various corroborating factors have included: the teaching of Scripture itself regarding its inspiration and truth; its influence on the lives of those who have believed in its truth and, conversely, the inability of the nonbeliever by his lack of the indwelling Holy Spirit to comprehend it; the gold mine of information embedded in Scriptural minutiae and apparent inconsistencies; the precision and detail with which prophecies have been fulfilled; the precision of timing in the events of Israel and the nations at large throughout history; the Bible Codes; and the recent overthrow of major tenets of science falsely so called which have contradicted Scripture, including uniformitarianism and the theory of evolution with its inability to create life from non-life or any kind of being from a lesser kind.

With so much ahead of us remaining yet to be understood, it is a tragic thought that so many of our best minds might fall short of the attempt to acquire that wisdom, and for no reason except that they willingly believe a lie. Knowing that Scripture represents absolute truth, and knowing further that true believers in Christ must have the ability to understand Scripture sufficiently to love Him and obey His commandments, we find that this same Scripture fully and without equivocation identifies those who are unable to comprehend the truth which it contains.

In John 14:17, for example, Jesus associated the Holy Spirit with truth. In the process of making that association, Jesus also identified those who, in their inability to receive the Spirit, could not comprehend truth. Of the Holy Spirit He said

". . .whom the world cannot receive, because it seeth him not, neither knoweth him: but ye knoweth him; for he dwelleth with you, and shall be in you."

Here Jesus was speaking to His disciples who, as He noted, were indwelt with the Spirit as believers in Him. The world at large stood in opposition to them as unbelievers who were unable to receive the Holy Spirit.

Scripture often declares understanding to follow belief. Conversely, faithlessness is presented in Scripture as bereft of understanding. To declare, then, that one cannot understand Scripture is fully equivalent to declaring one's unbelief. An inability to understand the Word of God does not proclaim meekness and humility. It is, instead, a declaration of a skepticism so profound as to cause dullness of hearing and sightless eyes. In Chapter 6, verses 9 and 10, Isaiah spoke of this situation:

> *And he said, Go, and tell this people, Hear ye indeed, but understand not; and see ye indeed, but perceive not. Make the heart of this people fat, and make their ears heavy, and shut their eyes; lest they see with their eyes, and hear with their ears, and understand with their heart, and convert, and be healed.*

In Matthew 22, verses 10 through 16, Jesus repeated these words, acknowledging that Isaiah was speaking on His behalf. According to Matthew,

> *And the disciples came, and said unto him, Why speakest thou unto them in parables? He answered and said unto them, Because it is given unto you to know the mysteries of the kingdom of heaven, but to them it is not given. For whosoever hath, to him shall be given, and he shall have more abundance: but whosoever hath not, from him shall be taken away that which he hath. Therefore speak I to them in parables: because they seeing see not; and hearing they hear not, neither do they understand. And in them is fulfilled the prophecy of Esaias, which saith, By hearing ye shall hear, and shall not understand; and seeing ye shall see, and shall not perceive: For this people's heart is waxed gross, and their ears are dull of hearing, and their eyes have closed; lest at any time they should see with their eyes, and hear with their ears, and should understand with their hearts, and should be converted, and I should heal them.*

The apostle John just as boldly associated through this statement of Isaiah a lack of understanding due to a fatal unbelief. Later, Luke attributed that statement to Paul in Acts chapter 28, associating it again with unbelief. In John 12, verses 35 through 41, he records what Jesus had to say on that subject:

> *Then Jesus said unto them, Yet a little while is the light with you. Walk while ye have the light, lest darkness come upon you: for he that walketh in darkness knoweth not whither he goeth. While ye have light, believe in the light, that ye may be the children of the light. These things spake Jesus, and departed, and did hide himself from them. But though he had done so many miracles before them, yet they believed not on him: That the saying of Esaias the prophet might be fulfilled, which he spake, Lord, who hath believed our report? and to whom hath the arm of the Lord been revealed? Therefore they could not believe, because that Esaias said again, He hath blinded their eyes, and hardened their heart; that they should not see with their eyes, nor understand with their heart, and be converted, and I should heal them. These things said Esaias, when he saw his glory, and spake of him.*

This same association between unbelief and an inability to understand Scripture may be found elsewhere and often throughout its pages.

In Psalm 14:1-4, for an example from the Old Testament, David speaks about unbelief and its implications:

> *The fool hath said in his heart, There is no God. They are corrupt, they have done abominable works, there is none that doeth good. The Lord looked down from heaven upon the children of men, to see if there were any that did understand, and seek God. They are all gone aside, they are all together become filthy: there is none that doeth good, no, not one. Have all the workers of iniquity no knowledge? who eat up my people as they eat bread, and call not upon the Lord.*

Proverb 1:1-7, for another example, states the issue in a positive sense, directly equating understanding with wisdom, and wisdom with belief:

> *The Proverbs of Solomon the son of David, king of Israel; To know wisdom and instruction; to perceive the words of understanding; To receive the instruction of wisdom, justice, and judgment, and equity; To give subtilty to the simple, to the young man knowledge and discretion. A wise man will hear, and will increase learning; and a man of understanding will attain unto wise counsels: To understand a proverb, and the interpretation; the words of the wise, and their dark sayings. The fear of the Lord is the beginning of knowledge: but fools despise wisdom and instruction.*

Returning to the New Testament, Paul describes in a particularly damning manner the character of those who persistently fail to apprehend the truth. In 2 Tim 3:1-9, he as this to say about such people:

> *This know also, that in the last days perilous times shall come, For men shall be lovers of their own selves, covetous, boasters, proud, blasphemers, disobedient to parents, unthankful, unholy, Without natural affection, trucebreakers, false accusers, incontinent, fierce, despisers of those that are good, Traitors, heady high-minded, lovers of pleasures more than lovers of God; Having a form of godliness, but denying the power thereof: from such turn away. For of this sort are they which creep into houses, and lead captive silly women laden with sins, led away with divers lusts, Ever learning and never able to come to the knowledge of the truth. Now as Jannes and Jambres withstood Moses, so do these also resist the truth: men of corrupt minds, reprobate concerning the faith. But they shall proceed no further: for their folly shall be manifest unto all men, as theirs also was.*

In this same letter, Paul exhorts Timothy to present Scripture to others as understandable to salvation before a time to come when many who will claim to be Christians will be unable to receive the truth. In 2 Tim 3:15-17; 4:1-4, Paul specifically claims that:

And that from a child thou hast known the holy Scriptures, which are able to make thee wise unto salvation through faith which is in Christ Jesus. All Scripture is given by inspiration of God, and is profitable for doctrine, for reproof, for correction, for instruction in righteousness: That the man of God may be perfect, thoroughly furnished unto all good works. I charge thee therefore before God, and the Lord Jesus Christ, who shall judge the quick and the dead at his appearing and his kingdom; Preach the word; be instant in season, out of season; reprove, rebuke, exhort with all long-suffering and doctrine. For the time will come when they will not endure sound doctrine; but after their own lusts shall they heap to themselves teachers, having itching ears; And they shall turn away their ears from the truth, and shall be turned unto fables.

In a nutshell, our incapability of understanding truth equates to an incapability to know God, which itself is equivalent to lacking the Holy Spirit Who indwells believers. Throughout Scripture there is a consistent theme as to why that is, but Paul, in Romans 1 and throughout his letters makes it very clear what causes that lack: it is a moral issue. Intellect has little or nothing to do with the unbeliever's decision to harden his heart, reject Jesus and remain in unbelief. Here again, the truth is presented with such clarity that it is accessible to all but those who may be burdened with the most profound mental disorder.

If you would give Scripture the credit it deserves for representing truth, listen to Paul in this matter:

For I am not ashamed of the gospel of Christ: for it is the power of God unto salvation to every one that believeth; to the Jew first, and also to the Greek. For therein is the righteousness of God revealed from faith to faith: as it is written, The just shall live by faith.

For the wrath of God is revealed from heaven against all

ungodliness and unrighteousness of men, who hold the truth in unrighteousness; Because that which may be known of God is manifest in them; for God hath showed it unto them. For the invisible things of him from the creation of the world are clearly seen, being understood by the things that are made, even his eternal power and Godhead; so that they are without excuse: Because that, when they knew God, they glorified him not as God, neither were thankful; but became vain in their imaginations, and their foolish heart was darkened.

Professing themselves to be wise, they became fools, And changed the glory of the uncorruptible God into an image made like to corruptible man, and to birds, and four-footed beasts, and creeping things.

Appendix Five

A COMMENTARY ON THE INCOMPATIBILITY OF MACROEVOLUTION WITH BOTH JUDEO-CHRISTIAN SCRIPTURE AND PHYSICAL REALITY

Introduction

We are in a war, and as Christians we are in the front lines. The war is a spiritual one, in which we are fighting for human souls. Our opposition is the humanist camp, which already has achieved a position of dominance over our media, our schools, and our government.

One of the main battles in this warfare is over the general acceptance of evolution as the factual paradigm of the origin of life. In this battle, our opposition has largely succeeded. Despite the claims of some Christians that Christianity and evolution are compatible, they are not. Committed Christianity, as noted by both Peter and Paul, demands the acceptance of Scripture as inerrant as to substance and as divinely inspired. Evolution directly undercuts Scripture and ultimately disposes of the necessity for God.

This appendix addresses the theory and scientific/intellectual shortcomings of naturalistic evolution. In its broadest sense, this theory embraces Darwin's theory of evolution, Neo-Darwinian evolution and in general all theories of the origin of life that propose that life originated without the necessity of a Designer.

Claims for evolution of the magnitude sufficient to create life or even a new kind of creature are generally associated with what is called *macroevolution*, which is distinct from *microevolution*.

Dr. Michael Behe has demonstrated that microevolution actually works, but only for the tiniest, most insignificant of changes, at the cost of huge amounts of time, and always at the cost of information loss.

The adaptive ability of living creatures, or the very small-scale evolutionary process by which living things undergo superficial changes in response to changes in their environments, is within the ability and scope of microevolution. An example of such changes are the modifications of coloring in some moths as a result of changes in environment, or the mutational changes to viruses and bacteria by which they evade measures taken by the immune systems of animals to ward off diseases. Books dealing with the topic of evolution, particularly those offered to the public and students, often deceptively resort to microevolutionary changes to demonstrate the viability of macroevolution.

It is a fact, as noted above, that evolution as proposed by Charles Darwin in his book *The Origin of the Species,* first published in 1859, does indeed work under some very limiting constraints. It has been demonstrated recently to work at the micro-evolutionary level by Dr. Michael Behe[1], the science professor who wrote the controversial book *The Edge of Evolution.* In that work he also demonstrated, on the basis of a detailed study of the interactive evolution of both malaria and the human body's response to it, that micro-evolutionary changes occur at the cost of information loss. He further demonstrated the complete failure of Darwin's theory and its more modern expressions to account for changes beyond one or at most two tiny steps. As we shall show herein, his demonstration of evolution's failure is intellectually convincing. Indeed, it is more convincing than the so-called "proofs" cited by evolution's supporters of its supposed basis in fact. Moreover, Dr. Behe's work is not a singular effort, but is supported by the works of a growing number of professionals in the fields of molecular biology, mathematics, and philosophy.

The material in this appendix focuses in general on the non-viability of macroevolution, or the inability of evolution to accomplish functionally beneficial large-scale changes in living beings, and particularly its failure to account for the generation of life from nonliving matter. A side discussion will speak to the demonstrable futility of attempting to reconcile evolution with Christianity. For the sake of brevity in the following work, the term *evolution* shall be used with the understanding that the term refers to naturalistic macroevolution.

The theory of evolution is precisely what this descriptor suggests: evolution is a theory. It is not a natural law like gravity, but merely a proposition. It is merely a proposition because it is unproven and unverified in accordance with the standard that science itself has erected for differentiating a law from a mere theory[2].

Informational literature in some quasi-official publications, including National Geographic Magazine, school textbooks, governmental placards located in National Parks and other popular tourist attractions, do indeed present evolution as fact. They do so in violation of that scientific standard. Every so-called "proof" of evolution to date, including the numerous "missing links" has subsequently been exposed as either an intentional fraud or a misapplication of scientific tools or knowledge[3].

In 2 Thessalonians 2, Paul talks about the mystery of iniquity as the world approaches the end of the Church age. In verses 8 through 12, he describes a grave indifference to the truth represented by the

Word of God. Paul then indicates that because of this indifference, God will allow those who are infected with this attitude to be deluded even more:

> *And then shall that wicked one be revealed, whom the Lord shall consume with the spirit of his mouth, and shall destroy with the brightness of his coming. Even him whose coming is after the working of Satan with all power and signs and lying wonders, and with all deceivableness of unrighteousness in them that perish, because they received not the love of the truth, that they may be saved. And for this cause God shall send them strong delusion, that they should believe a lie, that they all might be damned who believed not the truth, but had pleasure in unrighteousness.*

Evolution is just such a falsehood that is generally accepted as truth in today's sophisticated, technology-embracing world, and it is glaringly overt in nature. God tells us in First Timothy Chapter 6:20 and 21 that such a condition will prevail in the last days. Moreover, the falsehood will be distinctly scientific in character, and it will even be accepted among some ill-informed Christians:

> *O Timothy, keep that which is committed to thy trust, avoiding profane and vain babblings, and oppositions of science falsely so called. Which some, professing, have erred concerning the faith. Grace be with thee. Amen.*

Peter sheds further light on the nature of this falsehood. According to Second Peter 3:3 and 4, the lie will involve a deep sense of the unpunctuated continuity of the earth and life within it, such as is embodied in the principle of uniformity. This principle embraces the notion of the great age of the earth, wherein all geological changes are of extremely modest proportions that produce measurable results only over vast intervals of time:

> *Knowing this first, that there shall come in the last days scoffers, walking after their own lusts, and saying, Where is the promise of his coming? For since the fathers fell asleep, all things continue as they were from the beginning of the creation.*

Interestingly, the principle of uniformity as expressed here by Peter represents such a necessity to the viability of Darwin's theory of evolution that uniformity and evolution may be considered to be two halves of a common philosophy.

The reason why uniformity is so key to the viability of evolution is that evolution is an intrinsically weak process. The theory, in its vehement rejection of design of any sort, demands change unguided by thought, either human or otherwise. It relies on chance as the prime mover: the random process of tiny mutationally-driven changes, collectively summing to large-scale functional variations in living creatures, and even to the production of living creatures from nonliving matter. Given the readily-acknowledged extreme unlikelihood of even one ultimately beneficial mutation, the process demands for viability truly enormous quantities of time. This necessity, in turn, demands a uniformitarian view of the processes that have shaped the world we live in.

The problem with this is that, aside from its support of evolution, there is no logical justification whatever for the claim that uniformitarian processes governed the earth's history. Demanding its validity is equivalent to demanding that the earth be flat, or that something is true merely because we wish it to be so. The 'standard geologic column' as developed out of uniformitarian presuppositions, does in fact exist in its entirety nowhere on earth. The fossil basis for its construction shows circular reasoning, proving nothing.

The theory of uniformity, as a matter of fact, has already been overtaken by the acceptance within the scientific community of facts that contradict it. These facts include the well-known discovery by the Alvarez team of the extinction of the dinosaurs by an asteroid impact event. The theory of uniformity had led the scientific community to categorically deny the possibility of a catastrophic event of that magnitude to have occurred. After being confronted with uncontestable proof that the event did indeed occur and was indeed of enormous proportions, the scientific community quite reluctantly backed off from its rigid stance in opposition to the reality of catastrophism. They made no effort to convey this radical change in position to the schools or to the public at large, nor did they consider or wish to address the implications of this change on evolutionary theory.

The Christian doesn't have to accommodate his understanding of the world to the theory of evolution, because despite the extensive hype about evolution put out by the superficial popular media, an increasing number of experts in the field of microbiology have themselves rejected the theory as an unworkable folly. In other words, to be blunt about it, science itself is backtracking away from the evolutionary notion, leaving the general public holding the bag of science falsely so called.

The intellectual retreat from evolution has been slow and quite reluctant, to be sure. Many scientists who privately reject the theory continue to espouse it publicly for the simple reason that they fear for their careers if they don't go with the flow. Eminent professors, despite the presumed safety net of tenure, have lost their positions by politically being on the wrong side of this issue, as have competent scientists.

But more courageous souls are becoming involved in the issue, and their works quite thoroughly explain why the theory of macroevolution cannot work. Among these works are what are becoming classics in the genre: *Darwin's Black Box* and *The Edge of Evolution* by Michael Behe; *Intelligent Design* by William Dembski; *Reason in the Balance* and *Objections Sustained* by Phillip Johnson; *What Darwin Didn't Know* by Geoffrey Simmons; *Creation* by Grant Jeffrey; *Dismantling Evolution* by Ralph Muncaster; and the seminal work *Signature in the Cell*, by Stephen Meyer.

The discussion to follow briefly examines key demonstrations of the failure of evolutionary theory to perform the functional changes attributed to it by its proponents.

Evolution lacks the ability to anticipate

Naturalistic processes are, by intrinsic definition, non-intelligent.[4] A fundamental feature of non-intelligent processes is that they are unable to anticipate. They can't form *a priori* an objective or goal for a system. If a system function or feature doesn't yet exist, a non-intelligent process cannot envision it, for to do so demands intelligence.

Take the following example, among a very large number in which evolution has claimed the ability of sweeping functional changes, as a simple demonstration of the implication of this inability to anticipate: that of a land animal that walks with the aid of legs which is eventually going to achieve the ability to fly. To accomplish this, its bones need to become hollow and highly efficient with respect to weight; it has to develop the keen eyesight unique to birds that is appropriate to its mode of hunting from the air; its bone structure, particularly in its chest, needs to be arranged to be a proper scaffold for its ligaments and muscles; its arms need to assume the shape of airfoils; it needs the lightness, shape, and variability of shape of feathers for fine control over flight; its respiratory system must become suitable for the demands of flight, which involve hefty changes from the comparable functions of a land animal; its balance mechanism must be revamped to handle flight attitudes; its entire nervous system must be altered to furnish the ability to control its airfoil surfaces; and, perhaps not least, it must acquire some pretty disgusting eating habits. Each of these functional modifications involves very large numbers of changes that have to be coordinated in the proper sequence. This requirement for a large number of sequentially-supportive steps, highly-coordinated such that all are mutually compatible over a variety of different subordinate functions to the end of achieving flight, virtually demands the quality of anticipation or goal-setting which is the hallmark of a designer. As if that isn't contradictory enough of evolution, consider the implication of the large time scale evoked by most evolutionists to accomplish these changes. During the time frame over which these changes are supposedly accomplished, there will be of necessity several periods in which the unfortunate beast will be struggling with intermediate forms, such as arms that are developing into wings. In these transitional stages, the creature must continue to survive within its environment and to eat and mate. It must do so while suffering the disadvantage of a limb that functions less well as an arm than it used to, and is not yet functional as a wing. At this stage, it is suited far more as a food source for some other less-advanced animal. At the other extreme, some supporters of evolution who have come to understand and appreciate just these implications of large functional changes have proposed that such changes must have occurred quite suddenly. The *punctuated equilibrium* offshoot of Darwinian evolution, first proposed by evolutionist Stephen J. Gould[5] attempts to avoid the consequences of prolonged transition periods. The problem with this notion's supporters is that in the process of forming their opinions, they also have avoided doing the math: the odds against all these coordinated modifications occurring all at once are so astronomically huge and the numbers against even one instance of such an event having taken place are so vast that they outweigh by an enormous margin all the time available even by the most far-fetched uniformitarian assumptions of the age of the universe.

Dr. William Dembski did the math that evolutionists refrain from performing. In his book *Intelligent Design,*[6] he picked a real-life example of a well-investigated biological subsystem, the bacterial flagellum that Dr. Behe had made famous, and calculated the probability of its various components having been formed and assembled together by chance to implement the function of motation. The numbers are greater by a huge ratio than what outspoken evolutionist Richard Dawkins' admitted was an upper limit for the operation of chance. As quoted by Dembski, Dawkins had written:

> We can accept a certain amount of luck in our explanations, but not too much. . .In our theory of how we came to exist, we are allowed to postulate a certain ration of luck. This ration has, as its upper limit, the number of eligible planets in the universe... We [therefore] have at our disposal, if we want to use it, odds of 1 in 100 billion billion as an upper limit (or 1 in however many planets we think there are) to spend in our theory of the origin of life. This is the maximum amount of luck we are allowed to postulate in our theory. Suppose we want to suggest, for instance, that life began when both DNA and its protein-based replication machinery spontaneously

chanced to come into existence. We can allow ourselves the luxury of such an extravagant theory, provided that the odds against this coincidence occurring on a planet do not exceed 100 billion billion to one.[7]

The number 100 billion billion amounts to 10^{20}. Dembski imposes a far more generous upper limit for chance, 500 bits or 10^{150}, which, as he notes, represents the number of *particles* (not planets) in the observable universe. Yet, he claims that the mere flagellum, a relatively simple subsystem within the scheme of life, is far more complex than can be embraced within 500 bits of information.[8] Furthermore, just the DNA within the cell of that simple bacterium of which the flagellum is a component contains far more than 100 thousand base pairs[9], that number representing the minimum size of DNA in the first living cell, according to evolutionists. Since each base pair position within the DNA chain can accommodate one of four base/positional states, each position is equivalent to two bits of information. All together, then, the DNA itself represents at least two hundred thousand bits of information, or four hundred times the upper limit for chance.

Dr. Michael Behe[10], in his earlier work *Darwin's Black Box*, captured the essence of this need to anticipate that is so prevalent in living systems through the term he coined "irreducible complexity." A system that requires several parts all present, correctly configured for interaction, and working together to produce a specific well-defined function, to paraphrase Dr. Behe, is "irreducibly complex." If any of its necessary components is absent or improperly configured to make its contribution to the function, the function itself cannot be performed; all of the parts must be present and working together for the system to work at all. An irreducibly complex system, to continue to paraphrase Dr. Behe, requires so many mutually-supportive subsystems that the very existence of the top-level system without the input of anticipation is out of the question; yet the existence of such systems is so ubiquitous in living entities that such input must be acknowledged as having been present.

Dr. Behe's development of the notion of irreducible complexity is now several years old. A few years back, one of the more liberal bookstores (no longer in existence) carried more than one book that claimed, in a pro-evolution stance, to rebut Dr. Behe's notion. They did so by noting that in one of Dr. Behe's irreducibly complex systems, the flagellum that serves as the motive device of a bacterium utilizes a microbiological component that is virtually identical to the corresponding component of a completely different functional entity. "Foul!" the books cried at the perceived offense. The similarity of these components, to paraphrase the books, meant that they weren't unique to one specific function.

All but the most superficial of thought processes can see through the flaw in this line of reasoning. Dr. Behe never claimed uniqueness for the components of his irreducibly complex systems. That simply wasn't the thrust of his argument, which was to claim that all the components had to be present and working together for the system itself to work. Whether or not a component was borrowed from another system is irrelevant and misses the point; it's a shabby, logically sloppy red-herring argument that serves simply to throw the reader off-track from the real issue. We'll try to refrain from commenting further on how this kind of reasoning typifies the pro-evolutionist mindset, or the mindset of those who are taken in by their polemics.

All life possesses a non-material element: an extremely complex software code

The focus of discussion shall turn next to an example taken from molecular biology to demonstrate the failure of evolution to account for the development of life from non-life. This example considers the structure of the deoxyribonucleic acid (DNA) molecule[11], the story of mankind's understanding of its structure and function which is of itself a real scientific thriller. Only recently has man acquired an understanding of the advantages of having a generalized multipurpose machine, the computer, whose functional qualities are defined not by its physical characteristics, its hardware, but rather by the instructions that are applied to it in software code. This code may assume a number of different possible forms. There is the 8-bit ASCII code (an acronym for American Standard Code for Information Interchange), for example, wherein each group of 8-bit binary characters represents an alphanumeric symbol, such as the letter "G" or the numeral "5". This binary-encoded alphabet is useful for communicating among humans, but machines have a language of their own. At the lowest level of machine language, the data is encoded in a form compatible with the computer hardware, wherein groups of binary characters (0 or 1) represents specific instructions, like telling the computer memory to accept data immediately following the code and store it in a particular location. The medium by which the code was input to the computer started out as a sequence of stiff paper cards where the information was embodied in a pattern of punched holes. The preferred medium then transitioned to tape, and after that data was stored on laser-readable discs. Beyond the disc technology, RAM (random-access memory) circuitry became so spectacularly dense that cost-effective, ultra-large capacity flash drives (memory sticks) became available .

In its most straightforward functional context, the DNA molecule represents the purest, most compact and efficient structural embodiment imaginable of a chemically-implemented storage medium for software code. It reeks of anticipation, the creation of exquisitely complex order out of chaos. Its very existence inspires the awe of someone monitoring a SETI screen, like Jodie Foster in the movie "Contact", and suddenly viewing an intelligent signal from outer space.

DNA has a skeletal backbone structure consisting of alternate sugar and phosphate molecules interconnected to form a chain of arbitrary length. The size of this chain for most animals is quite huge. Functionally it is similar to the magnetic tape medium for the storage of computer software. Embedded within two such chains is the actual software, in which each sugar-phosphate pair forms a nest for any one of four different hydrocarbon molecular pairs/positions from the following repertoire: adenine (labeled "A"), guanine ("G"), cytosine ("C") and thymine ("T"). An essential feature of these four chemicals is that they are always coded in pairs: A to T and C to G. On the surface, these pairs seem to represent just two possibilities, but in fact their physical reversal within the sugar-phosphate matrix adds another two possibilities. The four possibilities are: A-T, T-A, C-G, and G-C. An interesting feature of these pairs is that while A is of a different size than T, and C is of a different size than G, the two pairs are virtually identical in size, so that when one end of a pair nests on one sugar-phosphate chain and the other nests into the other sugar-phosphate chain, there is no distortion of the two-chain system due to size differences. Another interesting feature of the matrix is that the system has no preferential affinity for any one pair over another and no pair has an affinity for any other pair, rendering the system completely contingent, meaning that there is no bonding preference for any particular code pattern, a necessary feature of any true software encoding medium. Another key feature of the system is that it expresses chirality,[12] which means that while there are two equally-probable directions in which the sugar and phosphate molecules bond together, the life-supporting nucleotides may only be of the right-handed form. This requirement alone virtually eliminates the possibility that the first DNA string was formed by chance.

The dual-nucleotide chain, together with the specific arrangement of embedded pairs within it, form what can only be characterized as a highly-organized structure of software code. But it does more than make a machine perform a function, because first it contains the instructions to build the machine itself. As software code, theoretically one could arrange the embedded pairs to form an ASCII code, which would then be able to represent anything in the English language through this DNA string, including a complete work of Shakespeare or, better yet, the Bible. The major difference between this chemical ASCII code and its binary equivalent would be the greater transmission efficiency of the DNA over the binary code. In fact, a revised equivalent ASCII code could be formed out of just four characters instead of eight.

Scientists haven't yet decoded a single DNA string. They haven't even come close. What they have done so far, impressive as that is, is to define the entire character sequence of human DNA, in all 46 chromosomes. But they have decoded the function of only a small portion of that sequence. What they have decoded is those portions of human DNA that are gene-specific, which represent but a tiny fraction of the entire string. Genes are sections of DNA code (subroutines, if you will) that specify and direct the manufacture of proteins. Even that portion of the overall decoding task is a major accomplishment, because the process by which a cell replicates a gene-specific portion in DNA into an RNA copy (RNA stands for ribonucleic acid), and then 'reads' the RNA code into the process that assembles the corresponding amino acids into another sequence representing a specific protein, is so startlingly high-tech that if one can instantly recognize a designer behind an intricate wristwatch or an automobile, the designer recognition for the process of protein manufacture is so over-the-top that only a person blinded by a God-denying agenda can possibly fail to perceive it.

As added complicating factors, the amino acids, which also express chirality in their natural states, must all be of the left-handed variety, and only twenty out of a possible eighty amino acids are useful components of proteins.

Then there's the "chicken-egg" problem: proteins are manufactured from software instructions, but the software reader itself is a complex assembly of proteins. This situation implies that both the first software and the first hardware had to exist simultaneously. Given the enormous complexity of both, the odds against their simultaneous creation by chance alone are beyond astronomical.

Complexity on top of complexity

On top of the enormous complexity of DNA and its interaction with RNA and the Ribosome protein to manufacture other proteins, and the chirality situation, there is another cellular mechanism beyond DNA, newly-discovered and possibly even more complex than DNA. This system, labeled the "epigenome", has been found so far to consist of three major subsystems.[13] One subsystem consists of the information embedded within the three-dimensional pattern of the microtubule structural girders that support the cell. Another subsystem is the tagging, or labeling, of various proteins, the histone spindles upon which DNA is wrapped, and selected cytosine characters within the DNA itself. The cytosine labeling is so important to the operation of the associated gene that it is sometimes referred to as "the fifth DNA letter." A third subsystem consists of the various amazing little protein machines that go around adding labels, removing labels, and reading them. It is thought that the process of adding and removing labels may be directed by segments of DNA that were once considered to be "junk," an erroneous concept that arose from evolutionary suppositions.

In the early days of developing an understanding of the protein manufacture process, some of the scientists involved were rather arrogant about the role of those portions of DNA that weren't specifically associated with proteins. Being of the evolutionary persuasion for the most part (for many of them, their grant money and even their jobs depended on their loyalty to evolution), they considered the portions of DNA for which they could find no specific use to be "junk DNA,"[14] DNA that represented earlier stages of evolution and was no longer useful to and was ignored by the living system. Those who possessed this attitude were pruned back a bit by subsequent discoveries of uses that included error-correcting codes like checksum values, and sequence-control commands like punctuation marks. Further developments in the decoding of DNA await minds of sufficient genius to see more of the mechanisms in certain sections of DNA that God may have had specific uses for, like the processes associated with embryology and growth. We've often wondered whether God has put His own verbal imprint in a secluded section of code that some arrogant scientist has relegated to "junk DNA." A delightful example might be a segment in direct, in-your-face ASCII code that says "In the beginning was the Word, and..."

The discovery of what DNA is and does gave us an understanding of life that simply wasn't accessible to Sir Charles Darwin or his contemporaries. Actually, this one insight has only been available to us for a few short decades, and it changes everything, particularly as we can only now view its implications in the context of some other very recent technological developments, including the structure of the computer and the development of information science, the understanding of which occurred simultaneously with our understanding of DNA.

A string of DNA is nothing more nor less than software code. If we had the ability to create our own string of DNA and manipulate the coding pairs to insert them in the sugar-phosphate matrix in the sequence that we ourselves specified, we could create an ASCII-encoded version of any book we wished to. If we could then develop a machine that could accept this chemical information and read its contents, we could insert our encoded string of DNA and the machine would then print the book we had chemically encoded, or, better yet, display it on a screen like a Kindle reader. As an information storage medium, our encoded strand of DNA would be the most compact device available.

The essence of life is information

In speculating how we ourselves might employ this basic element of life, we have naturally extracted the essence of what DNA represents: pure information. Philosopher/Mathematician William Dembski came to that same conclusion several years ago, and successfully applied the principles of information science to life itself and from that synthesis developed the first principles of an exciting new mathematical discipline centered on the information-richness of life. In his book *Intelligent Design,*[15] Dr. Dembski develops a theoretical model for naturalistic evolution in terms of the operation of chance on natural laws. He then develops a means of scrutinizing a living system to distinguish a naturalistic process from the input of design. He does so by means of a flowchart that he labels an explanatory filter. If, in this flowchart, a system is observed to be 'contingent', which means that it is capable of forming a variety of equally probable patterns, then its examination passes down to the next criterion; otherwise, the pattern is taken to be a predetermined necessity, like the formation of crystals, and the design hypothesis is rejected for this system. The next criterion is complexity. If the system is sufficiently complex, then its examination passes down to the third criterion; otherwise, its existence may be ascribed to chance and the design hypothesis is again rejected. The third criterion is specification. If the system exhibits the quality of specification, meaning that it serves to fulfill an identifiable and useful function, then it may be considered to have been brought into existence through design; otherwise the design hypothesis is again rejected. In all cases where the design hypothesis is rejected, the existence of the object is ascribed to a naturalistic process, either necessity or chance.

Dembski then continues to flesh out the practicality of this model by placing the complexity criterion on the firm footing of mathematical probability theory. In doing so, he transforms the expressions dealing with probabilities into information-theoretical terminology, in effect equating odds to bits of information. Having performed that translation, Dr. Dembski offers a quite generous cutoff point, as we had noted earlier, of 500 bits of information which, he assumes with considerable justification, would be acceptable to all reasonable people. A system so complex as to represent over 500 bits of information, he claims, can exist only by the aid of design. He inserts the value of 500 bits of information into his complexity criterion, thus reducing its evaluation to a straightforward and repeatable computation.

Dembski pursues the issue of complex specificity by noting that naturalistic evolution can be expressed as the operation of chance on natural laws, Dembski applies his contributions to information theory to the development of an information-theoretical proof of the inability of chance acting on laws of nature to create complex specified information. He formally states it as his Law of Conservation of Information as follows: "Natural laws are incapable of generating complex specified information."[16] He states three corollaries as immediate consequences of this law:

1) The complex specified information (CSI) in a closed system of natural causes remains constant or decreases. 2) CSI cannot be generated spontaneously, originate endogenously

or organize itself... 3) The CSI in a closed system of natural causes either has been in the system eternally or was at some point added exogenously... 4) In particular any closed system of natural causes that is also of finite duration received whatever CSI it contains before it became a closed system.

While Dembski's Law of the Conservation of Information appears more akin to a version of the First Law of Thermodynamics (conservation of matter and energy) than the Second Law, its corollaries are actually closer to the Second Law. One controversial argument between design advocates (formerly labeled as creationists) and evolutionists was the use of the Second Law of Thermodynamics, which stated in one version that all natural processes tended to disorder. The design advocates (including us) would periodically trot out this energy-based law as a proof that the order intrinsic to life represented a reversal (and violation) of the Second Law. The evolutionists would consistently respond to this charge by declaring that the Second Law applied only to closed systems. Open systems, they claimed, permitted the input of energy (such as radiation from the sun), which negated the effect of the Second Law. While we recognized this as somewhat of a red-herring argument, we didn't come up with a refutation that clearly addressed the open system issue. The beauty of Dembski's expression of the Law of Conservation of Information is that for any attempt to evoke the possibility of an open system, the immediate implication of the external input of information is the presence of a Designer.

Dr. Dembski performs the evaluation as directed by his explanatory flowchart on actual living systems by observing whether it exhibits contingency, and if it does, then mathematically evaluating the information complexity of the system and by observing whether the quality of specificity is present. If the system passes these hoops, then he concludes that a designer was involved in its existence. He has applied this procedure to several living systems, concluding that some of them exhibit unmistakable evidence of design.

Summarizing Evolution's Basic Problems

This very brief overview of DNA represents the tip of the iceberg regarding what scientists have discovered about the intricacy of living creatures at multiple levels from top level functions on down to machine operations at the molecular level. The references cited earlier provide much more detail, some of it of a spectacular nature. They, too, cite further references that the interested person may wish to pursue.

Many of the amazing processes associated with living systems also can be viewed via the Internet, simply by Googling on an appropriate topic, such as "DNA", "DNA replication", "cell replication", "prokaryotic cell structure", "eukaryotic cell structure", "RNA", "ribosomes", "gene transcription", and "protein manufacture" to give just a few examples. One cannot view this information without obtaining a sense of awe at the complexity of life's most basic processes.

This appendix has addressed just a few problems out of the very many difficulties with evolution that any objective pursuit of the truth of the matter must consider. Among the ones that have been touched on here are Dr. Behe's notion of irreducible complexity, Dr. Dembski's notion of the conservation of information, the chirality obstacle, and DNA's immense complexity as well as its feature of embedded software code.

There is a rather substantial political element to the issue of the viability of evolution. This element confirms the role that "believing what we want to" plays in the acceptance or rejection of the idea of evolution. It also has led to outright deception.

Evolution's glaring frauds

Although he preferred the since-discredited Lamarckian mechanism of the inheritance of acquired characteristics over Darwin's natural selection, one of Darwin's contemporaries, the German zoologist and biologist Ernst Haeckel (1834-1919),[17] not only helped to popularize Darwin's theory in Germany, but had furnished a notion of his own that both strengthened Darwin's position and increased its popularity. This concept borrowed from Etienne Serre's earlier proposals and from Darwin's concept of homology, which, according to Darwin, was "that relation between [body] parts that results from their development from corresponding embryonic [body] parts."[17] The point here is that in seeing the same similarities between embryonic and adult body parts among various life forms, Darwin perceived embryonic development as representing a history of speciation. Haeckel picked up on this notion, formalizing it in his famous Biogenetic Law that "ontogeny recapitulates phylogeny". Stated in layman's terms, the law expresses the notion that the various stages of embryonic development (ontogeny) revisit the history of evolutionary change (phylogeny). He went so far as to create a number of drawings that expressed his law in pictorial form. Generations of students throughout the world have been exposed to these pictures, which include a stage of human development marked by what are supposedly gill slits.

The pictures themselves long ago have been exposed as frauds, Haeckel having doctored the transcription from source object to painting to emphasize features that promoted his "law". Furthermore, his "law" has since been rejected in its entirety, modern science having exposed his "gill slits" as something else altogether and his ideas in general as oversimplifications of more complicated patterns in embryology. In Chapter 5 of *Darwin on Trial,*[17] Phillip Johnson succinctly states the problem:

> Describing the facts of embryology to be 'second to none' in importance for his theory, he remarked that the early embryo is 'a picture, more or less obscured, of the progenitor, either in its adult or larval state, of all members of the same great class.' Any exceptions to this rule of early embryonic resemblance, Darwin believed, could be explained as adaptations of larval stages to differing environments. Since a larva must compete for food and survive predators, it might be modified by natural selection, even though later stages would be unaffected.

This statement is tied to the basic logic of the Darwinian understanding of homology. If similarities inherited from an ancestral form are traceable to common developmental processes and common genes, it is logical to expect these ancestral features to be generated early in the process of embryonic development. The differing organisms in a single group (like vertebrates) should start out in life as relatively similar organisms and then form their differing features later. As with Haeckel's law, the picture is so pleasing that generations of biology students have been taught it as fact.

Unfortunately for the theory, however, the facts do not fit so neatly into the theoretical preconception. Far from providing the simple confirmation that [modern evolutionist Dr. Douglas J.] Futuyma suggests, the embryonic patterns generate a monumental puzzle for the theory. Although it is true that vertebrates all pass through an embryonic stage at which they resemble each other, in fact they develop *to* this stage very differently (italics in the original). After a vertebrate egg is fertilized, it undergoes cell divisions and cell movements characteristic of its class: fishes follow one pattern, amphibians another, birds yet another, and mammals still another. The differences cannot be explained as larval adaptations, since these early stages occur before larvae form and thus are apparently not exposed to natural selection. Only by ignoring the early stages of development can one fit Darwin's theory to the facts of embryology, but it was precisely the early stages that Darwin claimed were the most significant! [Exclamation in the original.]

The same fraudulent picture emerges from the evolutionary presentation of the so-called "fossil record." "Evolutionary science" continues to teach our children and the public that the fossil record demonstrates the viability of evolution by confirming: first, that the "tree" of life branches out from a single base ancestor to the many varieties that are observed today, producing many intermediate and transitional forms along the way; second, that the fossil record "proves" the existence of many transitional forms. It does not; instead, the actual observations and facts disprove those very same claims.

The tree of life that is supposed to branch outward from a simple beginning has never been found. Nor will it ever, as what has been found instead throughout the earth is a phenomenon that is called the Cambrian Explosion,[18] wherein multiple fully-formed species emerged from one stratum to the next, the previous stratum being almost entirely void of life.

The glaring discrepancy between the fossil record as Darwin envisioned it and its actual state was touched on earlier. But Darwinists have been so misleading about this issue that it deserves more of our attention. The public at large has been and continues to be subjected to periodic announcements by the pro-evolution media that a new and exciting 'find' has confirmed the existence of a transitional form, just as Darwin had predicted all along. Then, when the latest of such "finds" has been discredited as fraudulent, a period of grace ensues wherein nothing is said either way about it. Eventually after the passage of sufficient time for the public to forget about the issue entirely, some popular magazine will scream out that a new and conclusive 'find' has proven Darwin right. Time-Life and the National Geographic Magazines are major offenders in this regard, but there are many others who are willing to follow suit.

The late Dr. Grant Jeffrey supports Phillip Johnson and others who have assessed the claims of Darwinists about the fossil record and have concluded that they are not only in error, but intentionally so. According to Dr. Jeffrey,[19]

> There is no fossil evidence to support evolution. Many Christians and Jews who have been troubled by the claims of evolution will be astonished to discover that the evolutionists knew all along that there was *no* fossil evidence in support of evolution. Yet, many textbooks and teachers boldly declared that the fossils proved evolution to be true.
>
> After a century and a half of claims by evolutionists that just a little more time would produce the necessary fossil evidence of the missing links between species that would confirm the theory of evolution, we find there is an astonishing and *total lack of fossil evidence* to confirm any indisputable transitional forms, or 'missing links,' that must exist if the theory of

evolution were actually scientifically true. However, in over one hundred and fifty years of a massive global search by scientists that has catalogued over one hundred million fossil specimens in museums and laboratories, they have failed to discover a single "missing link" fossil. If the evolutionists were intellectually honest, they would have abandoned evolution long ago.

In 1859, Charles Darwin acknowledged that the utter lack of fossil evidence for these missing links between one species and another provided "an unanswerable objection" to the theory of evolution. However, Darwin assumed that the search for fossils that would establish the truth of evolution was just beginning and that, given sufficient time and effort, scientists would soon discover the millions of transitional fossils required to prove that one species gradually transformed itself by natural selection into a new species. [Italics in the original]

Jeffrey goes on to say that "To date, though, every species discovered in the fossil record appears perfectly formed. Paleontologists have never discovered a fossil showing a partially formed species or a partially formed organ."[20]

He furnishes detailed accounts of a number of supposed "missing links" between ape and man, all of which were subsequently exposed as outright frauds. They are listed below.

With the help of untrained convicts, fossilized bone fragments of what came to be called Java Man were dug up in 1891 on the Indonesian island of Java. On the basis of nothing more than a fragment of a skull cap, three molar teeth and a bone fragment of a thighbone, the director of the find, Dr. Eugene Dubois, identified the fossils as belonging to *Homo erectus,* a humanoid three quarters of a million years old. Attempts to confirm his claims uncovered the following facts: the thighbone fragment was identical to that of a modern human; the skull cap was found forty-six feet away from the other fragments; there was no logical reason to associate the skull cap with the thighbone.

Piltdown Man I and II were supposedly discovered in 1912

and 1917 at the Piltdown quarry in England by amateur geologist Charles Dawson. In 1953, after over forty years of unquestioning acceptance of these findings as genuine, the skulls, after being examined by more modern techniques, were found to be intentional frauds. The skull described by Jeffrey was a composite of skull fragments of modern man and orangutan jaw. Worse, the bones had been dyed with bichromate of potash to make them appear ancient. Although evolutionists generally agree that Piltdown man was an outright fraud, they don't speak much about this incident.

Nebraska Man was found in 1922 in western Nebraska by Professor Harold Cook. His find was supported by Dr. Henry F. Osborn, head of the American Museum of History, who touted the find as finally representing the evidence linking chimpanzees, Java Man and modern man. The Java man, as noted above, was since exposed as fictitious. So was Nebraska Man, whose supposed existence was used as evidence in the famous 1925 Scopes evolution trial. The problem was that the "evidence" amounted to a single tooth, around which very imaginative evolution-minded artists created a picture of how they wished a missing link to look. It gets worse: the tooth was later found to have belonged to an extinct pig. The same fiction applies to the Southwest Colorado Man, another 'evolutionary discovery' that also turned out to have been based on a mere tooth, this one belonging to an ancient horse.

In 1932 another supposed missing link, Ramapithecus, was found in Africa. This "discovery" amounted to nothing more than some fossilized teeth, which were later found to belong to the modern orangutan. Here again, evolutionists generally acknowledge this "discovery" to be false.

Dr. Jeffrey also notes that the same kind of problems attend the discovery of "Lucy" in 1974. In this case, Professor Richard Leakey claimed that Lucy was an ape-like creature who walked upright. However, the lengths of the forearm fossils found in the vicinity strongly suggest that Lucy walked on all fours like any other ape-like creature. Even Dr. Leakey admitted to exercising a large amount of imagination to create a picture from a few bone fragments. What puts the lie to these excursions of the imagination is that in many, if not all, cases there is actually no logical reason to assume that the fragments belong to a single creature.

Even with such a shady history of attempting to create missing links where missing links didn't exist, the evolutionists continued to pull the wool over their own eyes as well of those of their associates and an all too-trusting public by trotting out Peking Man, Neanderthal Man, and Cro-Magnon man in a dismal and apparently desperate attempt to justify their system of belief. All three of these, it turns out, were nothing more nor less than fully human, a fact quite reluctantly admitted by the community of evolutionists.

If the history of evolutionists' attempt to find the missing link between ape and man has yielded nothing more than a sordid collection of frauds, perhaps they can fall back on the find in Australia of an archaeopteryx fossil,[8] this creature supposedly representing a link between reptiles and birds.

Perhaps not. At least not in honesty. The notion that this bird represents a transitional form came from its teeth, which are unusual in a bird and more usual to a reptile. Everything else about this fossil shows absolutely nothing contradictory to what constitutes a bird. The unusual feature of teeth is not so unusual after all, considering that some reptiles have no teeth while other fossils of birds do, and other strange creatures, like the duck-billed platypus, exist that are not considered to be missing links.

But what about the dinosaur-bird so highly publicized by the National Geographic magazine, who artistically (and fictionally) portrayed a baby dinosaur with feathers and claimed that birds belong to the family of bipedal dinosaurs.

Even the community of evolutionists was taken aback by this hasty conclusion. Jeffrey quotes Professor Storrs Olson, curator of birds at the Smithsonian in the following condemnation:

> National Geographic has reached an all-time low for engaging in sensationalistic, unsubstantiated, tabloid journalism... It eventually became clear to me that National Geographic was

not interested in anything other than the prevailing dogma that birds evolved from dinosaurs.[21]

Irreconcilable differences between evolution and Christianity

A disagreeable problem with the theory of evolution is that it undercuts Scripture. Scripture itself, being the Word of God, is one very substantial pillar of the Christian faith. Paul (2 Timothy 3:16) and Peter (2 Peter 1:20, 21) both declared Scripture to have come from God, so a Christian takes the written Word lightly at the peril of his own soul. Nobody can deny that in claiming evolution to be compatible with Scripture, the person who does so must necessarily lose something vital to the reverence of the God who is defined by that Scripture. The creation epic and the fall of man are seen in a more distant, indirect light. *Did God really say that?* the evolutionist questions. The timing of creation is met with skepticism. *Did God really say that?* The introduction of death into God's creation with the fall of man—*well, maybe what God really meant was...* Man may have fallen at one time, but since then he's been evolving into something better (on his own, with the helping hand of chance).

Quite apart from a consideration of God, the dating scheme currently accepted within the secular world suffers from some profound intellectual and suppositional errors. Yet while there are glaring logical difficulties with the dating scheme, there is a possibility that even in the face of the falsehoods the assumption of a very great age of the earth and life upon it may be reconciled with Scripture by interpreting the first few verses of Genesis 1 as permitting a large time gap between a previous era in earth's history and a reconstruction into its present form. Other interpretations involving large time periods assume that each "day" of creation was considerably longer than twenty four hours, furnishing another convenient path for reconciling Scripture with the secular paradigm of the earth's age.

On the other hand, there is no possible way that the theory of evolution can be reconciled to Christianity. Where, precisely, do evolution and Christianity clash? The specific issues presented below are but a partial listing of the most obvious areas.

As was noted above, evolution undercuts the notion that Scripture is inspired by God and inerrant. Evolution places the development of man as progressing upward, rather than downward as Scripture strongly implies, and makes light of the Genesis account of creation.

Evolution fosters a fully materialistic mindset. The theory and its numerous naturalistic offshoots place a premium on materialism, refusing to countenance the introduction of anything beyond chance and atoms in the development of life. This emphasis on the material world so intrinsic to evolution has thoroughly permeated our society, promoting hedonism and selfishness, whereas it represents the exact opposite of a major theme of Christianity, the rejection of the material world in favor of the spiritual realm. Jesus Himself said (John 18:36)

My kingdom is not of this world; if my kingdom were of this world, then would my servants fight, that I should not be delivered to the Jews; but now my kingdom is not from here.

Paul continually emphasized the greater importance of the spiritual realm over the material world. A representative passage is 1 Corinthians 2:9-14:

But as it is written, Eye hath not seen, nor ear heart, neither have entered into the heart of man, the things which God hath prepared for them that love him. But God hath revealed them unto us by his Spirit; for the Spirit searcheth all things, yea, the deep things of God. For what man knoweth the things of a man, except that spirit of man which is in him? Even so the things of God knoweth no man, but the Spirit of God. Now we have received, no the spirit of the world, but the Spirit who is of God; that we might know the things that are freely given to us of God. Which things also we speak, not in the words which man's wisdom teacheth, but which the Holy Spirit teacheth, comparing spiritual things with spiritual. But the natural man receiveth not the things of the Spirit of God; for they are foolishness unto him, neither can he know them, because they are spirituall discerned.

Evolution requires more faith in the secular paradigm than in God and Scripture. The enormous complexities and interdependencies of life recently uncovered by science are so contradictory to the causal explanations of evolution that those who embrace evolution must do so on faith alone, ignoring their own intellects and common sense. Moreover, they have suspended normal standards of proof, which for evolution are nonexistent, and have disregarded the numerous outright frauds associated with the futile search for the proof of evolution. Such individuals must place more stock in current 'science' than in God, believing without reservation that if eminent people say something must be true, that it must be true. Regarding this issue of secular faith, William Dembski says it well in reminding his readers that the Intelligent Design approach to the origin of life is not only more compatible by far with Scriptural theology, but is of itself a more up-to-date and intellectually satisfying alternative to evolution:

> Unlike full-blooded Darwinists, however, the design theorists' objection to theistic evolution rests not with what the term *theistic* is doing in the phrase *theistic evolution* but rather with what the term *evolution* is doing there. The design theorists' objection to theistic evolution is not in the end that theistic evolution retains God as an unnecessary rider in an otherwise perfectly acceptable scientific theory of life's origin and development. Rather their objection is that the scientific theory which is supposed to undergird theistic evolution, often called the neo-Darwinian synthesis, is itself problematic.
>
> The design theorists' critique of Darwinism begins with Darwinism's failure as an empirically adequate scientific theory, not with its supposed incompatibility with some system of religious belief. This point is vital to keep in mind in assessing intelligent design's contribution to the creation-evolution controversy. Critiques of Darwinism by creationists have tended to conflate science and theology, making it unclear whether Darwinism fails strictly as a scientific theory

or whether it must be rejected because it is theologically unacceptable. Design theorists refuse to make this a Bible-science controversy. Their critique of Darwinism is not based on any supposed incompatibility between Christian revelation and Darwinism. Instead they begin their critique by arguing that Darwinism is *on its own terms* a failed scientific research program – that it does not constitute a well-supported scientific theory, that its explanatory power is severely limited and that it fails abysmally when it tries to account for the grand sweep of natural history."[22]

Perhaps the most devastating problem of all in attempting to accommodate evolution into Christianity is a rather subtle one that doesn't outright deny the existence of God. The clash between evolution and Scripture, however, need not be in-your-face obvious; after all, satan is known to be subtle. This very real and pervasive problem is the unavoidable perception in the minds of evolutionists that the distance between God and His creation renders Him irrelevant to our daily lives. Evolution does not require the existence of God, particularly the God of Scripture. Beyond that, at best it removes God from the forefront of creation to a remote location in the very background and slaps His hands away from creative details, whereas Scripture as a whole presents God as in much more intimate connection with His creation. The kind of remoteness between God and man implicit in a belief in evolution demands an indifference of God toward us and of us toward God. Moreover, it trivializes the conscious disobedience of man that led to the entrance of sin and death into the world. Yet more, it renders insignificant the major theme of Scripture, both Old and New Testaments, that Jesus came in the flesh and died on the cross to reconcile mankind to God.

Most of the Christian world, as a matter of fact, assumes that an hour spent on Sunday getting preached to fulfills all the obligations that one might owe his God. Devoting the remainder of the week (including Sunday afternoons) to self is perfectly acceptable to those who choose to include evolution in their world view, for in doing so they aren't distancing themselves from their "God" any more than He has distanced Himself from them. How far indeed is that attitude from the commandment of Jesus in Matthew 22:37 and 38 to love the Lord our God with all our hearts, souls and minds! How tragically remote is that attitude from even considering Jesus to be our Lord!

Notes:

1. Dr. Michael J. Behe, *The Edge of Evolution,* Free Press Division of Simon and Schuster, 2007pp. 188-190, 233, 234

2. Dr. Phillip E. Johnson, *Darwin on Trial,* InterVarsity Press, 1993, pp. 71-100

3. Dr. Michael J. Behe, *The Edge of Evolution*, Free Press Division of Simon and Schuster, 2007 pp. 188-190, 233, 234; Dr. Grant R. Jeffrey, *Creation*, Frontier Research Publications, 2003, pp. 191-212

4. Dr.Phillip Johnson, *Defeating Darwinism by Opening Minds*, InterVarsity Press, 1997, p. 15

5. Stephen Jay Gould, *Time's Arrow, Time's Cycle*, Harvard University Press, 1987

6. Dr. William A. Dembski, *Intelligent Design*, InterVarsity Press (IVP Academic), 1999

7. *ibid.,* p. 167 (quoting from Richard Dawkins, *The Blind Watchmaker,* Norton, 1987, pp. 139, 145, 146)

8. ibid., pp. 166, 178

9. Ralph O. Muncaster, *Dismantling Evolution* Harvest House Publishers, 2003, p. 131

10.Michael Behe, *Darwin's Black Box*, Free Press, 1996

11. Stephen C. Meyer, *Signature in the Cell*, HarperOne imprint of Harper Collins, 2009, pp. 240-252; Ralph O. Muncaster,

Dismantling Evolution Harvest House Publishers, 2003, pp. 124-129

12. Meyer, *Signature in the Cell*, pp. 206, 207; Muncaster, *Dismantling Evolution*, pp. 131-136

13. Thomas E. Woodward and James P. Gills, *The Mysterious Epigenome,* Kregel Publications, 2012, p. 68

14. Meyer, *Signature in the* Cell, p. 367

15. Dembski, *Intelligent Design*

16. *ibid.*, pp. 170-174

17. Phillip Johnson, *Darwin on Trial*, pp. 71-74

18. Vance Ferrell, *The Evolution Cruncher*, Evolution Facts, Inc., 2001 pp. 420-425

19. Dr. Grant R. Jeffrey, *Creation*, Frontier Research Publications, 2003, pp. 191-212

20. *ibid.,* pp. 193

21. *ibid.,* pp. 197, 198

22. Dembski, *Intelligent Design,* pp. 109-112

ABOUT THE AUTHOR

Arthur Perkins is an electrical engineer by training and a Christian at heart who takes seriously the commandment of Moses, repeated by Jesus, to "Love our God with all our hearts, souls and might." In honor of that love, Art and his wife Carolyn have devoted time to sharing Scripture with others in nursing and assisted-living homes. Art and Carolyn live in the foothills of Mount Rainier in rural Western Washington.

In the course of the nursing home activity, Art met the key figure in *Buddy*, whose cheerful outlook in the face of the painful and seriously limiting affliction of cerebral palsy inspired him to write of their shared adventure of flight in that novel. *Buddy* was followed by two other novels, *Cathy* and *Jacob*, involving the fictional character Earl Cook and his wife Joyce. A unifying theme of this trilogy is Christian service, first toward the handicapped and, expanding outward, toward the unsaved and to the faithful adherents of Christianity's beloved mother religion, Judaism. Along with the adventures that Earl and Joyce encounter, they share with the reader topics of the Bible and the nature of God that are not commonly presented to the average Churchgoer, enriching the readers' understanding of the faith they have embraced and which are of significance in today's chaotic world.

Art and his wife Carolyn have shared together many of the experiences described in these novels. Since their retirement, they continue to build a repertoire of treasured memories out of their mutual interests and incredible adventures.

Residing above the unifying themes of Christian service and the understanding of Scripture dwells the all-important subject of love: the love of God toward us and the possibility of its return to Him by us. On top of that love between God and the human race is the amazing love that exists within the Godhead Itself.

It is the profound love that exists within the Godhead between its Divine Members that drives this nonfiction work, motivating the author to share in its appreciation with readers who wish to experience the love of God in the fullness that He intended.

We hope you enjoyed reading *Marching to a Worthy Drummer*
by Arthur Perkins.
For further reading including novels and non-fiction titles by this
author and others, please go to our online catalog at
http://www.signalmanpublishing.com

www.ingramcontent.com/pod-product-compliance
Lightning Source LLC
Chambersburg PA
CBHW071405090426
42737CB00011B/1362